Peacekeeping and the Asia-Pacific

Peacekeeping and the Asia-Pacific

Edited by

Brendan Howe
Boris Kondoch

BRILL
NIJHOFF

LEIDEN | BOSTON

The chapters in this paperback were originally published in Volumes 18:3–4 and 19:3–4 of Brill's *Journal of International Peacekeeping*.

Cover illustration: Thai peacekeepers. Courtesy of UN Photo/Albert González Farran.

The Library of Congress Cataloging-in-Publication Data is available online at http://catalog.loc.gov
LC record available at http://lccn.loc.gov/2016035540

Typeface for the Latin, Greek, and Cyrillic scripts: "Brill". See and download: brill.com/brill-typeface.

ISBN 978-90-04-32204-2 (paperback)
ISBN 978-90-04-32205-9 (e-book)

This book is printed on acid-free paper and produced in a sustainable manner.

Contents

About the Contributors

Xenia Avezov

is a researcher at the Stockholm International Peace Research Institute where she works on peace operations and conflict management issues. Her research interests include peace operations in Africa, the future of the international conflict management architecture, and the role of peace operation with regards to non-traditional threats such as terrorism, climate change and migration. Since 2012 she has been working on a project titled 'the new geopolitics of peace operations' now in its second phase, which aims to foster international dialogue on how to best prepare peace operations for the future while creating a better understanding on the role that emerging actors and troop-contributing regions will play. Her recent publications include: 'The Consensus on Mali and International Conflict management in a Multipolar World,' SIPRI Policy Brief, Sept. 2014, 'The New Geopolitics of Peace Operations: A Dialogue with Emerging Powers. Europe and North America Regional Dialogue,' April, 2014.

Niloy Ranjan Biswas

teaches International Relations at the University of Dhaka. Currently, he is pursuing a PhD in International Politics at City University London, UK. He is also a Visiting Lecturer (2015–16) in the same department. His work examines the implication of the roles of international actors and local civil society organizations on civilian security governance in Bangladesh and other South Asian nations. His research also focuses on civil society and security governance, and South Asian contributions in UN peacekeeping missions.

Alistair D.B. Cook

is Coordinator of the Humanitarian Assistance and Disaster Relief [HADR] Programme and a Research Fellow at the Centre for Non-Traditional Security (NTS) Studies, S. Rajaratnam School of International Studies, Nanyang Technological University, Singapore. His research interests include non-traditional security in the Asia-Pacific including peace and conflict studies, humanitarianism, foreign policy and regional cooperation, and domestic politics in Myanmar. His work focuses in particular on humanitarian assistance and disaster relief in the Asia-Pacific. He most recently co-edited *Civilian Protection in the Twenty-first Century: Governance and Responsibility in a Fragmented World* (Oxford, 2016). In 2012–2013, he was a visiting research fellow at the East Asian Institute of the National University of Singapore.

Sinclair Dinnen
is an academic researcher and policy adviser with interests in conflict, peacebuilding, policing, legal pluralism and state & nation-building in the Melanesian countries of the SW Pacific. His most recent publication (with Matthew Allen) is 'State Absence and State Formation in Solomon Islands: Reflections on Agency, Scale and Hybridity', *Development and Change*, vol. 47, no. 1, 2016, pp. 76–97.

Brendan Howe
is a tenured Professor and Associate Dean at the Graduate School of International Studies, Ewha Womans University in Seoul, South Korea. He is the Editor of the *Asian International Studies Review* and Series Editor for Palgrave Macmillan of the Pivot series on *Security, Development and Human Rights in East Asia*. He has held visiting research fellowships at Freie Universität Berlin (2014–2015), De La Salle University, Manila (2010), the University of Sydney (2008), Korea National Defense University (2007), the East–West Center, Hawaii (2003), and Georgetown University (1999–2000).

Boris Kondoch
is currently Professor at the Far East University/South Korea and Editor of the *Journal of International Peacekeeping* published by Brill Nijhoff. He worked at different universities in South Korea, among others as a guest professor/lecturer at the graduate school of law and the political science department of Korea University where he taught international law and ethics in international relations. From 1998 to 2002 he worked as a research fellow for the President of the German Society of International Law, Prof. Dr. Michael Bothe at the Institute of Public Law, Johann Wolfgang Goethe University, Frankfurt am Main, Germany.

Keokam Kraisoraphong
is an Associate Professor at the Faculty of Political Science, Chulalongkorn University, Thailand. She is a member of the executive board and a Senior Fellow at the Institute of Security and International Studies (ISIS), Thailand, through which she is a member of the Association for Security Sector Education and Training (ASSET). She is also a member of the National Research Council of Thailand (NRCT). Her latest publications include *inter alia*, 'Crossing the Threshold: Thailand's Path to Rethink Security Sector Governance', in *Peacebuilding and Security Sector Governance in Asia*. (Zürich: LIT Verlag GmbH, 2014), *Conflict in Southern Thailand: Seed for Security Sector Reform* (Asia Security Initiative Policy Series no. 21, Singapore: RSIS Center for

Non-Traditional Security (NTS) Studies, 2013); and 'Thailand and the Responsibility to Protect', *The Pacific Review*, vol. 20, issue 1, 2012.

Peter Londey

worked as a historian at the Australian War Memorial from 1991 to 2007. During that time he wrote the only complete narrative of Australian peacekeeping, *Other People's Wars* (Sydney, 2004). He is now a member of the project writing the Official History of Australian Peacekeeping, Humanitarian and Post-Cold War Operations. Since 2008 he has returned to his original field, and teaches ancient Greek history, and is now Head of the Centre for Classical Studies at the Australian National University.

Yuji Uesugi

is a Professor at the School of International Liberal Studies, Waseda University, Japan. He holds a Master of Science in Conflict Analysis and Resolution from George Mason University, USA, and a PhD in International Conflict Analysis from the University of Kent, UK. His latest publications in English include *Peacebuilding and Security Sector Governance in Asia* (Zürich: LIT Verlag, 2014), 'Building a Foundation for Regional Security Architecture in the Asia-Pacific: Human Resource Development for Peacebuilding', in William T. Tow and Rikki Kersten (eds.), *Bilateral Perspectives on Regional Security: Australia, Japan and the Asia-Pacific Region* (London: Palgrave Macmillan, 2012), and others.

Rashed Uz Zaman

teaches in the Department of International Relations, University of Dhaka, Bangladesh. He was educated at Dhaka, Hull and Reading. In 2009 he was awarded an Alexander von Humboldt Postdoctoral Research Fellowship and was at the University of Erfurt, Germany. He was also a Fulbright Visiting Lecturer in the Department of Political Science, Vanderbilt University, USA. His most recent publication is 'UN Peacekeeping Mission' in Ali Riaz and Mohammad Sajjadur Rahman (eds.), *Routledge Handbook of Contemporary Bangladesh* (London and New York: Routledge, 2016).

CHAPTER 1

Introduction to the Developments, Trends and Challenges to UN Peacekeeping Operations

Boris Kondoch and Brendan Howe

I Introduction

Peacekeeping is the flagship operation of the United Nations (UN), and its major contribution to global governance and the protection of vulnerable groups. Uniquely universal and legitimate, it is seen as a "strong and effective tool that is protecting people, saving lives and helping countries to emerge from conflict."[1] Between 1948 and March 2016, the UN conducted 71 peacekeeping operations (PKOs). As of 31 March 2016, there are currently 16 UN peacekeeping operations and 123,053 personnel deployed from 123 countries.[2] The budget for UN PKOs for the fiscal year 1 July 2015–30 June 2016 is about $8.27 billion, and the main financial contributors to UN peacekeeping operations from 2013–2015 were the United States (28.38%), Japan (10.83%), France (7.22%), Germany (7.14%), United Kingdom (6.68%), China (6.64%), Italy (4.45%), Russian Federation (3.15%), Canada (2.98%) and Spain (2.97%).[3] By the end of 2012, however, 85% of all UN peacekeepers came from Asia and Africa. Indeed, in July 2014 the top 15 military and police contributors were Bangladesh, India, Ethiopia, Pakistan, Rwanda, Nepal, Senegal, Ghana, China, Nigeria, Burkina Faso, Indonesia, Egypt, Tanzania, Morocco – all from these two continents.[4]

The majority of current UN peacekeeping operations take place in the Africa and the Middle-East. Thus the participation of regional African powers with their local self-interest and responsibilities is perhaps not surprising. Asia is the home to some of the greatest challenges and triumphs of the UN. These have included peacekeeping and state-building operations in Cambodia – the

1 UN Secretary General Ban Ki-moon, *Remarks at Security Council Open Debate on Trends in United Nations Peacekeeping* 11 June 2014, http://www.un.org/sg/statements/index.asp?nid=7769 (accessed on 12 May 2016).

2 United Nations, *UN Peacekeeping Operations Fact Sheet*, http://www.un.org/en/peacekeeping/resources/statistics/factsheet.shtml (accessed on 12 May 2016).

3 United Nations, *Financing Peacekeeping*, http://www.un.org/en/peacekeeping/operations/financing.shtml (accessed on 12 May 2016).

4 Ranking of Military and Police Contributions to UN Operations, http://www.un.org/en/peacekeeping/resources/statistics/contributors.shtml (accessed on 12 May 2016).

 | DOI 10.1163/9789004322059_002

UN Transitional Authority in Cambodia (UNTAC), and Timor-Leste – the UN Transitional Administration in East Timor (UNTAET), and the UN Integrated Mission in Timor-Leste (UNMIT). Asia is also home to the second oldest UN peacekeeping operation, the UN Military Observer Group in India and Pakistan (UNMOGIP), which was established in 1948, and is still ongoing. Other landmarks include the Korean War, the largest enforcement action ever undertaken; and the United Nations Assistance Mission in Afghanistan (UNAMA) – the only political mission under UNPKO auspices. Non-UN peacekeeping operations were deployed among others to Papua New Guinea and the Solomon Islands. In 1999, the Security Council authorized the International Force in East Timor (INTERFET) led by Australia. INTERFET was another non-UN operation mandated to provide security and peace on East Timor. Yet given that states and international organizations within the region (such as the Association of Southeast Asian Nations (ASEAN) and the Shanghai Cooperation Organization (SCO)) have a reputation for resistance to multilateral security operations, and advocacy of the principles of state sovereignty and non-intervention, Asian enthusiasm for participation in UN PKOs represents something of a conundrum. Thus this volume explores the motivations for the contemporary, and growing participation of Asian states as a central conceptual theme.

II Developments and Trends

Since the end of the Cold War most of the conflicts the UN has had to face have been domestic rather than international. During the 1990s, after a preceding decade which saw no new missions, UN peace operations mushroomed around the world. The sudden upsurge was not limited to the number of missions, but also involved a dramatic increase in scope. Increasingly the UN has become engaged in more complex missions including tasks like state-building, the protection of human rights, and election monitoring. Another development has been the authorization of UN peacekeeping operations under Chapter 7 of the UN Charter; wherein one can find the enforcement activities of the United Nations Security Council (UNSC). This has come about because the UNSC adopted a more co-operative approach towards peacekeeping.[5]

Many missions established in the last decade have, in fact, had a significant military component and a strong mandate to protect civilians. In 2013, the

5 For further discussion, how peacekeeping operations have changed over time James Cockayne, David M. Malone, 'The Ralph Bunch Centennial: Peace Operations Then and Now', *Global Governance*, vol. 11, pp. 331–350.

Security Council established the United Nations Force Intervention Brigade within the existing United Nations Organization Stabilization Mission in the Democratic Republic of the Congo (MONUSCO) which is the largest current UN peacekeeping operation.[6] The Intervention Brigade is unique because the force has a mandate to carry out offensive operations in order to neutralize and disarm rebel groups in the DRC. Another robust stabilization mandate was given to the UN Multidimensional Integrated Stabilisation Mission in Mali (MINUSMA) established by Security Council Resolution 2100 in 2013.[7] These type of operations raises not only legal issues[8] but also whether peace enforcement and robust peacekeeping can be reconciled with traditional peacekeeping principles of consent, impartiality and the use of force.[9]

Since the end of the Cold War new elements have been added to UN peacekeeping operations. Contemporary missions include human rights components, gender units, child advisors, rule of law specialists. Mandates of current peacekeeping operations include many of the following tasks: (a) monitoring the implementation of peace agreements; (b) policing and other law and order functions; (c) re-establishing national authority; (c) providing security; (d) demobilization, disarmament and reintegration of former combatants; (e) security sector reform; (f) human rights monitoring and training and (g) protection of civilians. Despite these changes, some of the core elements of UN PKOs will remain with us for the foreseeable future, whereas other elements will see a consolidation of long-term trends.

Arguably, UN peacekeeping will remain a unique tool of conflict resolution. For Richard Gowan and Meagan Gleason, there will be a steady overall demand in the Middle East and there will be at least two or more large scale operations in Africa[10] These regions then will continue to be the main focus of UN PKOs.

---

6 See UN doc. SC Resolution 2098 of 28 March 2013.

7 See UN doc. SC Resolution 2100 of 25 April 2013.

8 See in detail, Patrick Cammaert, Fiona Blyth, 'The UN Intervention Brigade in the Democratic Republic of the Congo', *International Peace Institute, Issue Brief*, July 2013, https://www.ipinst.org/wp-content/uploads/publications/ipi_e_pub_un_intervention_brigade_rev.pdf (accessed on 12 May 2016); Bruce Oswald, 'The Security Council and the Intervention Brigade: Some Legal Issues', *ASIL Insights*, 2013, vol. 17, issue 5, http://www.asil.org/insights/volume/17/issue/15/security-council-and-intervention-brigade-some-legal-issues (accessed on 12 May 2016).

9 Ian Johnstone, 'Dilemmas of Robust Peace Operations' in *Annual Review of Global Peace Operations* 2006 (Boulder, London: Lynne Rienner, 2006), pp. 1–17.

10 Richard Gowan and Megan Gleason, 'UN Peacekeeping: The Next Five Years', NYU Center on International Cooperation, http://cic.es.its.nyu.edu/sites/default/files/cic_un_fiveyears.pdf (accessed on 12 May 2016).

The growing importance of civilian actors and the expanding roles of private military and security companies constitute additional long-term trends. In addition, for many commentators, the trend of an increasing role for regional organizations and regional and rising powers such as Brazil, China, India, Russia, and South Africa, in peacekeeping operations will continue, whereas Western states will become less involved in peace operations.[11] Although other international organizations, including NATO, the European Union and African Union, may play an increasing role in global peace operations, as pointed out by the former UN Under-Secretary-General for Peacekeeping, Alain Le Roy "it is probably inevitable that the UN will be the organization of last resort, when others either cannot gain the necessary consensus, or maintain the staying power over a the long term, or indeed where no one major actor has enough abiding interest but the world must nevertheless act".[12]

III Challenges

There are many political, strategic, operational, legal and normative challenges to current UN peace operations. UN Secretary General Ban Ki-moon has highlighted four aspects of peacekeeping that are particularly important for discussion at this time: "First, UN peacekeeping operations are increasingly mandated to operate where there is no peace to keep"; second, some UN peacekeeping operations are being authorized in the absence of clearly identifiable parties to the conflict, a viable political process, or when there is no clear path towards peace; "third, UN peacekeeping operations are increasingly operating in more complex environments that feature asymmetric and unconventional threats"; and fourth, the need to build on the renewed commitment of the Security Council to respond to our changing world.[13] Secretary

11 For further analysis, see Xenia Avezov, 'The New Geoplitics of Peace Operations: A Dialogue with Emerging Powers. North East Asia Regional Dialogue', *SIPRI Workshop Report*, Ulan Bator, 11–12 April 2013, p. 6, http://www.sipri.org/research/conflict/pko/other_publ/ngp-workshop-report-april-2013 (accessed on 12 May 2016); Jane Dundon, 'Global Trends in Peace Operations' in *SIPRI Yearbook* (Oxford: OUP, 2013), pp. 62–66, http://www.sipri.org/yearbook/2013/files/sipri-yearbook-2013-chapter-2-section-1 (accessed on 12 May 2016), Sharon Wiharta, Neil Melvin, and Xenia Avezov, 'The New Geopolitics of Peace Operations', *SIPRI*, September 2012, http://www.sipri.org/research/conflict/pko/other_publ/NGP-Policy-Report.pdf (accessed on 12 May 2016).

12 Speech to the UN Security Council, 26 August 2011.

13 Ban Ki-moon, *Remarks* 11 June 2014, http://www.un.org/sg/statements/index.asp?nid=7769 (accessed on 12 May 2016).

General Ban further notes that Resolution 2098 on the Democratic Republic of the Congo was a milestone which signaled the resolve of the Security Council to address the changing nature of conflict and the operating environment of UN peacekeeping.[14]

Meanwhile the extensive contemporary literature on the subject[15] overall identifies the following challenges:[16]

- How to manage the current level of UN operations;
- How to make UN peacekeeping operations more efficient and effective;
- How to achieve close co-ordination between the UN Security Council, the Secretariat and Troop Contributing Countries (TCCs);
- How to broaden the base of troop- and police-contributing countries;
- What is the right moment and timing to start a peacekeeping operation?
- When is it the right moment to leave and what kind of exit strategy should be in place?
- What should be the rights and roles of troop contributing countries?
- How to share the burden of peacekeeping responsibilities regarding funding and staffing between developing and developed countries;
- How to integrate the different components in a UN peacekeeping mission;
- How to improve the command and control structures;
- How to co-ordinate peacekeeping operations with already existing activities on the ground

14 *Ibid.*

15 Chiyuki Aoi, Cedric de Coning, Ramesh Thakur (eds.), *Unintented Consequences of Peacekeeping Operations* (Tokyo: UNU Press, 2007); Alex J. Bellamy, and Paul D. Williams (eds.), *Providing Peacekeepers. The Politics, Challenges, and Future of United Nations Peacekeeping Contributions* (Oxford: OUP, 2013), pp. 299–396; Charles T. Hunt, Alex Bellamy, 'Mainstreaming the Responsibility to Protect in Peace Operations', *Civil Wars*, vol. 13, 2011, pp. 1–20.

16 See also the reports published by the International Forum for the Challenges of Peace Operations, http://www.challengesforum.org/en/Reports--Publications/ (accessed on 12 May 2016), and the articles published in the Journal of International Peacekeeping, http://www.brill.com/journal-international-peacekeeping and International Peacekeeping, http://www.tandfonline.com/toc/finp20/current. For specific issues, see Peacekeeping Working Report Meeting on Safety and Security of Peacekeepers, What's in Blue, 31 May 2013, http://www.whatsinblue.org/2013/05/meeting-of-the-working-group-on-peacekeeping.php (accessed on 12 May 2016); Peacekeeping Working Group Meeting on the Use of Technology, What's in Blue, http://www.whatsinblue.org/2013/07/working-group-on-peacekeeping-operations-meeting.php (accessed on 12 May 2016).

- How to develop a conceptual framework for the protection of civilians (PoC) in high risk environments and implement it in practice;
- How to mainstream the responsibility to protect in peace operations;
- How to ensure effective peacebuilding measures;
- How to establish security and the rule of law after the end of conflicts;
- How to operate in an environment where consent is only partial or limited;
- How to provide essential field intelligence;
- How to deal with unconventional threats in the peacekeeping environment including terrorism and transnational crimes;
- How to integrate gender perspectives into UN peacekeeping operations;
- How to develop capability standards for all military contributors;
- How to prevent and deal with unintended consequences of UN peacekeeping operations;
- How to improve accountability in case of human rights violations committed by UN peacekeepers;
- How to ensure the safety and security of UN peacekeepers;
- How to conduct successful joint operations between the UN, regional organizations, NATO, the OSCE, and UN mandated forces;
- How to provide for local ownership;
- How to provide high standard education and training to UN peacekeepers;
- How to define the role of and the impact of large peacekeeping operations in environments already affected by climate change;
- How to use modern technology including drones;
- How the Security Council can provide clear and achievable mandates;
- What is the proper relationship between preventive diplomacy and peacekeeping?
- What is the proper extent of the use of force in peacekeeping operations?
- Whether the focus should move more to preventive diplomacy and to mediation;
- Whether political missions are an alternative to the traditional model of peacekeeping;
- And last but not least how to set priorities when addressing the different challenges.

For these reasons, Secretary General Ban has asked the Secretariat to initiate work on a review of UN peacekeeping including but not limited to mandates, political leverage, logistical support, training, accountability, rules of engagement, technological innovation, and clarity on caveats of troop- and police-contributing countries.[17] In the year 2015, reports by the High-Level Independent Panel on Peace Operations and the Secretary-General put forward sets of recommendations for reforming how operations are carried out. Many of these recommendations required a change of approach by the major actors, including the United Nations Security Council, which has prime responsibility in the organization for matters pertaining to international peace and security. In May 2016, the Council responded by publishing a report, *The Security Council and UN Peace Operations: Reform and Deliver* addressing what the peace operations review requires of the Council, and acknowledging that the "Council's usual conduct of business often undermines the objectives it sets for itself, whether in preventing conflict or in designing realistic mandates."[18] The report argues that the Council should shift its focus to actual delivery on the ground, highlights the importance of exercising the Council's collective political leverage throughout the life span of peace operations, not only when their mandate cycles come up for renewal and advocates that the Council become strategic and realistic in deciding mandates, and more timely and effective in supporting the peace operations for which it is responsible.[19]

Arguably, the most important issue concerns the protection of civilians (PoC) which has been also identified as one of the core tasks of current peace operations. Since 1999, the UN Security Council has expressly mandated UN peacekeepers to protect civilians.[20] The United Nations Mission in Sierra Leone (UNAMSIL) was the first UN peacekeeping mission which was explicitly authorized "to afford protection to civilians under imminent threat of physical violence."[21] So-called PoC mandates have been assigned to twelve different

17 Ban Ki-moon, *Remarks* 11 June 2014 (accessed on 12 May 2016).

18 United Nations Security Council, *The Security Council and UN Peace Operations: Reform and Deliver*, http://www.securitycouncilreport.org/atf/cf/%7B65BFCF9B-6D27-4E9C-8CD3-CF6E4FF96FF9%7D/research_report_peace_operations_may_2016.pdf (accessed on 12 May 2016).

19 *Ibid.*

20 For further discussion, see William J. Durch, and Alison C. Giffen, *Challenges of Strengthening the Protection of Civilians in Multidimensional Peace Operations*, (Background Paper prepared for the 3rd International Forum for the Challenges of Peace Operations, 27–29 April 2010); Victoria Holt, Glyn Taylor, with Max Kelly, *Protecting Civilians in the Context of UN Peacekeeping Operations: Successes, Setbacks and Remaining Challenges* (United Nations, New York, 2009); Siobhán Wills, *Protecting Civilians* (Oxford: Oxford University Press, 2009).

21 See Security Council Resolution 1270, UN Doc. S/RES/1270 (1999), 22 October 1999. See also Security Council Resolution 1291, UN Doc. S/RES/1291 (2000), 24 February 2000; Security

missions. Currently nine UN missions have a protection mandate. There are a number of important questions to be raised in this context. Key among them are: what does protection of civilians mean in practice, what kind of training is required, and which role should be played by the different components in peacekeeping operations? Again, as pointed out by Secretary General Ban Ki-moon, speed is also critical:

> When civilians are under imminent threat, every minute counts. While there have been improvements in the mechanisms and speed with which the United Nations deploys uniformed personnel, it does not have a standing reserve force that it can deploy on short notice once a Council decision is taken.... It is important that we all work together to ensure we are able to deploy or reinforce our missions, when necessary, as quickly as possible. We need to have a clear-sighted view of what capabilities peacekeeping will need to the meet the challenges ahead. Peacekeeping will need to be more mobile, more flexible and adaptable.[22]

IV Chapter Overview

The remaining chapters of the book explore these themes from the perspectives of different sub-regions of the Asia-Pacific, different country perspectives, and

---

Council Resolution 1493, UN Doc. S/RES/1493 (2003), 28 July 2003, regarding the United Nations Mission in the Democratic Republic of Congo (MONUC); Security Council Resolution 1528, UN Doc. S/RES/1528 (2004), 27 February 2004; Security Council Resolution 1609, UN Doc. S/RES/1609 (2005), 24 June 2005; Security Council Resolution 1793, UN Doc. S/RES/1793 (2007), 21 December 2007, regarding the United Nations Operation in Côte d'Ivoire (UNOCI); Security Council Resolutions 1590, UN Doc S/RES/1590 (2005), 24 March 2005; Security Council Resolution 1870, UN Doc. S/RES/1870 (2009), 20 May 2009, regarding the United Nations Mission in Sudan (UNMIS); Security Council Resolution 1990, UN Doc. S/RES/1990 (2011), 27 June 2011, regarding the United Nations Interim Security Force for Abyei (UNIFSA); Security Council Resolution 1925, UN Doc. S/RES/1925, 28 May 2010, regarding United Nations Organization Stabilization Mission in the Democratic Republic of the Congo (MONUSCO); Security Council Resolution 1996, UN Doc. S/RES/1996, 8 July 2011, regarding the United Nations Mission in the Republic of South Sudan (UNMISS) and Security Council Resolution 2100, UN Doc. S/RES/2100, 25 April 2013, regarding the United Nations Multidimensional Integrated Stabilization Mission in Mali (MINUSMA).

22 Ban Ki-moon, *Remarks*, 11 June 2014, http://www.un.org/sg/statements/index.asp?nid=7769 (accessed on 12 May 2016).

in regional case studies. The first section looks at contributions from the sub-regions: Northeast Asia, Southeast Asia, and South Asia. The second section of the book looks at individual country case studies including: Australia, Solomon Islands, Japan, and Thailand. The third, and concluding, section consists of a theoretical summary on the central conceptual theme of Asian motivations for PKO contributions.

In Chapter 2, Brendan Howe and Boris Kondoch focus on contributions from Northeast Asia. They note that although for historical, cultural, and political reasons states from Northeast Asia have been hesitant in their support, and limited in their contributions, regional actors are no longer as resistant to collective security and international governance initiatives as they have historically been portrayed. With the exception of the Democratic People's Republic of Korea (DPRK), a rogue regime often at loggerheads with the UN, and the Republic of China (ROC) in Taiwan, a province currently denied independent UN membership, the three remaining regional powers, the People's Republic of China (PRC), Japan, and the Republic of Korea (ROK), have become increasingly engaged in regional and global peace operations, particularly since the end of the Cold War in 1991. This chapter, therefore, examines the contributions to UN PKOs by these three Northeast Asian powers. It further explores the motivational impetuses for policy changes and increasing contributions. Finally the authors assess both the obstacles to, and the potential for future peacekeeping contributions emanating from the region.

Since the 1950s both Indonesia and Malaysia have contributed to United Nations peace operations across the world to varying degrees. Both states have contributed to regional peace initiatives as well; again to varying degrees and levels of success. In Chapter 3, therefore, Alistair Cook examines these Southeast Asian regional initiatives through the prism of greater regionalism, which reflects a shift in focus to regional organizations in the pursuit of peace. Furthermore, he contends, understanding the motivations and decisions to contribute to peace operations requires a multifocal lens that recognizes the various manifestations of this commitment and identifies the salient motivations behind these decisions. This lens illustrates that both competition and cooperation co-exist in the Indonesian and Malaysian decisions to contribute to peace operations in pursuit of increased political legitimacy in the global system.

Rashed Uz Zaman and Niloy Ranjan Biswas address South Asian regionalism and PKOs in Chapter 4. They note that in the face of new challenges, the UN has often highlighted the importance of regional organizations getting more involved in undertaking and sustaining PKOs. South Asian countries provide a large number of troops to UN missions and yet, a regional collaboration has not been accorded much importance by countries of the region. This chapter argues, therefore, that given the emerging challenges, South Asian countries may have to resort to a regional approach with regard to peacekeeping missions.

In Chapter 5, Peter Londey traces the history of Australian peacekeeping since its beginnings in September 1947. He shows that, while there have always been Australian peacekeepers in the field since 1947, the level of commitment in different periods has varied greatly. The chapter sets out to explain this phenomenon, chiefly in political terms. It argues that Australia's early involvement in the invention of peacekeeping owed much to External Affairs Minister H.V. Evatt's interest in multilateralism, but that under the subsequent conservative Menzies government a new focus on alliance politics produced mixed results in terms of peacekeeping commitments. By contrast, in the 1970s and early 1980s, for different reasons Prime Ministers Whitlam and Fraser pursued policies which raised Australia's peacekeeping profile. After a lull in the early years of the Hawke Labor government, the arrival of internationalist Gareth Evans as Foreign Minister signaled a period of intense peacekeeping activity by Australia. For different, regionally-focused reasons, Australia was again active in peacekeeping in the late 1990s and early 2000s. In recent years, however, Australia's heavy commitment to Middle East wars has reduced its peacekeeping contribution once again to a low level.

Sinclair Dinnan revisits the Solomon Islands in Chapter 6. The archipelagic nation in the Southwestern Pacific became the site of a major regional assistance mission following a debilitating internal conflict between 1998 and 2003. What began as an ethnic conflict evolved into a wider breakdown of law and order that led to the progressive collapse of government, closure of commercial enterprises and threat of national bankruptcy. In mid-2003 the Regional Assistance Mission to Solomon Islands (RAMSI) was mobilized and deployed under the auspices of the Pacific Islands Forum. Led and largely funded by the Australian government, RAMSI sought to restore security and stability to the troubled nation through a combination of policing and law enforcement, institutional strengthening with central government agencies and measures aimed at reviving and growing the national economy. Ten years later the mission underwent drawdown and the transition of its development programs into regular bilateral and multilateral aid programs. While RAMSI made a substantial contribution to the restoration of security and stability in the aftermath of conflict, Dinnan claims that many outstanding challenges remain.

These include issues of political economy and how these are impacting on the quality of governance, service delivery and nation-building, as well as long-standing structural issues with the formal economy, set against prevailing patterns of population growth and internal migration. This chapter examines the challenges in the context of Solomon Islands socio-economic characteristics and recent history with a view to assessing the country's prospects for enduring stability in the post-RAMSI era.

Chapter 7 discusses the development and features of the All-Japan approach that can be restated as integrated inter-agency/civil-military coordination, which has been placed in Japan's policy for international peace cooperation (IPC), and has a potential to constitute Japan's unique contribution to international peace operations. Yuji Uesugi provides an overview of Japan's recent involvement in international peace operations such as in Timor-Leste, Iraq, Haiti and South Sudan, paying special attention to inter-agency/civil-military nexus in each operation both at the strategic/policy level and the operational/field level. He argues that the All-Japan approach can offer a framework for better coordination among Japanese actors on the ground, and thus it can make Japan's contribution more "visible" to the local community and populations concerned. At the same time, this chapter presents a warning that such an approach may infringe on the unity of the mission, especially if it is a UN peacekeeping operation, and disturb the coherence of multilateral efforts on the ground. Furthermore, the All-Japan approach can jeopardize genuine decision-making of Japanese actors on the ground because of the unspoken pressure from their government to formulate All-Japan activities. In short, the All-Japan approach may become an end in itself rather than a means.

In Chapter 8 Keokam Kraisoraphong and Brendan Howe discuss the participation of the Royal Thai Armed Forces in UN PKOs. A relatively small troop contributor at first, Thailand later took a high-profile role in the UN operations in East Timor during 1999–2005, and has continued since then to support several UN peacekeeping forces. The chapter first addresses the rationales, development, and current status of Thailand's contributions. It then goes on to explore how, and to what extent, tasks and duties assigned under the UN peacekeeping framework to the dispatched forces, as well as experiences and lessons the Thai armed forces gained from their participation in missions, contribute to the diffusion of norms and the development of functional competencies relating to peacekeeping and human security protection within the Thai military. The authors find that while the dispatched forces received invaluable benefits in terms of prestige, economic rewards and learning experiences from the peacekeeping operations under the UN command, including approaches to humanitarian assistance during the time of acute conflict and monitoring human rights violations, the human security norm underlying these functional competencies has yet to be fully internalized by the military as an institution. Yet, there are some areas, especially in civil-military affairs where competencies developed from the internal security operations and international peacekeeping operations can be mutually reinforcing.

In the final substantive chapter, Xenia Avezov provides an overview of South and Northeast Asian motivations for contributing troops to United Nations peace operations. She identifies five groups of countries based on their motivations and characteristics: (1) Bangladesh, Sri Lanka, and Nepal, (2) India and China, (3) Japan and South Korea, and two individual cases, (4) Mongolia and (5) Pakistan. Chapter 9 argues that the size and level of development of a troop-contributing country are important determinants for the pattern a country follows and for the size of its contribution. In addition, the chapter suggests that countries with both political and military motivations for contribution tend to provide the most troops, with either economic or geostrategic motivations reinforcing the commitment for contribution. In every case, normative considerations and the perception of a positive international image serve as motivations for contribution, but these do not explain the size of a country's contributions.

V Conclusion

United Nations peacekeeping operations are more relevant and needed in the contemporary international operating environment than perhaps at any other time in their history. At the same time, however, that we are asking more of UN PKOs, in terms of both number and scope of operations, the United Nations is faced with a growing list of challenges in terms of bringing them to successful conclusions. Although Western nations continue to foot well over half of the total cost of missions, non-Western financial contributions are growing steadily. Furthermore, the overwhelming majority of uniformed personnel taking part in UN PKOs come from Asia and Africa. Thus not only must we address the new challenges to UN peacekeeping, we must also explore the new resources, and perhaps solutions to these challenges, which are becoming available to planners and implementers of operations.

CHAPTER 2

Northeast Asian Perspectives on UN Peacekeeping: China, Japan, Korea

Brendan Howe and Boris Kondoch

> Peacekeeping is fraught with risk, but it is also filled with promise. Our blue helmets bring hope to millions of people in some of the most troubled parts of our world.[1]
>
> SG BAN KI-MOON (2013)

•••

> The United Nations was not created to bring us to heaven but to save us from hell.[2]
>
> SG DAG HAMMARSKJÖLD (1954)

1 Introduction

Northeast Asia is a region deeply affected by conflict. Colonial, ideological, and national wars have left their scars and legacies.[3] At the level of international governance, practitioners have looked to minimize the worst manifestations of interstate conflict through emphasizing non-intervention in the internal affairs of neighboring states, and domestic governance has emphasized

1 Secretary-General's Remarks at Dag Hammarskjöld Medal Awards Ceremony to Honour Fallen Peacekeepers, New York, 29 May 2013, http://www.un.org/en/events/peacekeepersday/2013/sgmedals.shtml (accessed on 17 August 2014).

2 Dag Hammarskjöld: 'A Man of the Next Generation,' http://www.unesco.org/new/en/media-services/single-view/news/dag_hammarskjoeld_a_man_of_the_next_generation/ (accessed on 17 August 2014).

3 For the purposes of this chapter, Northeast Asia is considered to include China, Japan, the Korean Peninsula, and Taiwan.

 | DOI 10.1163/9789004322059_003

national interest and strength in terms of security and economic growth.[4] Hence Northeast Asia remains a decidedly state-centric operating environment, resistant to Western concepts of universalism, solidarism, and collective security, and to external intervention in domestic affairs.[5] Nevertheless, regional actors are not consistently resistant to international and global governance initiatives, and are, in fact, increasingly active in the field. With the exception of the Democratic People's Republic of Korea (DPRK), a rogue regime often at loggerheads with the United Nations (UN), and the Republic of China (ROC) in Taiwan, a province currently denied independent UN membership, the three remaining regional powers, the People's Republic of China (PRC), Japan, and the Republic of Korea (ROK), have become increasingly engaged in regional and global governance and security operations. This has been particularly apparent since the end of the Cold War in 1991. This chapter, therefore, examines the contributions to UN peacekeeping operations by these three Northeast Asian powers, the motivations behind the provision of these contributions, and the potential future contributions emanating from the region.

As a permanent member of the Security Council, the People's Republic of China plays the most important role within the UN security apparatus. In the UN, China has generally taken the view that disputes should be solved through peaceful negotiation and has traditionally taken a stance of strict non-interference in the affairs of other states. Although certainly not an ardent supporter of potential intervention, China is not, however, the steadfast opponent of related principles, like peacekeeping operations and the Responsibility to Protect (R2P), that it is often portrayed. Even with regard to Darfur, where the PRC has blocked UN Resolutions targeting the Sudanese regime, China supported the deployment of African Union peacekeepers, and its diplomacy was seen as key to getting Sudanese consent for their deployment. Likewise, with regard to Myanmar, it has provided diplomatic support for the use of the Secretary-General's good offices, securing a visa for the Special Representative, Ibrahim Gambari, and remains open to the idea of ASEAN playing a leading role in addressing Myanmar.[6] At the United Nations Security Council (UNSC), China refrained from vetoing the 2011 R2P action against Libya, and has supported international measures against the DPRK.

4 There is no regional international security organization in Northeast Asia, itself something of an anomaly, but organizations to which regional states have signed up, the Shanghai Cooperation Organization (SCO), and cooperative arrangements with the Association of Southeast Asian Nations (ASEAN) place a premium on non-interference (the Shanghai Spirit and ASEAN Way respectively).

5 Shulong Chu, 'China, Asia and Issues of Sovereignty and Intervention', *Pugwash Occasional Papers*, vol. 2, Jan. 2001, pp. 39–51 .

6 *Ibid.*, p. 557.

Japan which joined the world organization in 1956 considers international co-operation within the United Nations as a basic foreign policy tool. Japan is the second major contributor to the UN budget and an advocate of human security within the United Nations. While human security was introduced to the mainstream of Japanese foreign policy by Prime Minister Keizo Obuchi in 1998 in response to the Asian financial crisis,[7] a similar concept was first outlined as a key foreign policy perspective and main objective of Japanese ODA disbursement in 1995.[8] Obuchi advanced a vision of human security as 'a comprehensive view of all threats to human survival, life and dignity' and as one of the three areas on which Asia should focus for a 'century of peace and prosperity', stressing the need to 'implement measures for the socially vulnerable who are affected by the Asian economic crisis'. The other two areas were Asia's recovery from economic crisis, and the further promotion of intellectual dialogue to tackle numerous other challenges after overcoming the Asian economic crisis.[9] Obuchi also contributed 500 million yen (US$4.2 million) for the establishment of the human security fund under the UN, (later renamed the United Nations Trust Fund for Human Security, UNTFHS), as an expression of Japan's commitment to promoting the paradigm and supporting related projects by UN agencies. Together, these speeches laid the foundation for the rise to prominence of human security as the main pillar of Japan's foreign policy agenda. With the fusion of human security and ODA, Japanese aid policy has been transformed into a vehicle for transporting the human security idea.[10]

South Korea, which acceded to membership of the UN in 1991, is widely regarded as a role model for developing countries. Through the 'Miracle on the Han River', South Korea grew from a devastated shell of a state, one of the poorest in the world, let alone the region, and itself heavily dependent on Official Development Assistance (ODA) for 50 years (1945–95), to become the 13th largest economy, the newest member of the Organisation for Economic

7 Keizo Obuchi, 'Opening Remarks by Prime Minister Obuchi at An Intellectual Dialogue on Building Asia's Tomorrow', http://www.mofa.go.jp/announce/pm/obuchi/index.html (accessed on 17 August 2014).

8 Akiko Fukushima, 'Human Security and Japanese Foreign Policy', paper presented at UNESCO/Korea Conference on Human Security, Seoul, Korea, 16–17 June 2003, pp. 132, http://unesdoc.unesco.org/images/0013/001365/136506e.pdf (accessed on 17 August 2014).

9 Keizo Obuchi, Policy Speech, Toward the Creation of A Bright Future for Asia, 16 December 1998, http://www.mofa.go.jp/region/asia-paci/asean/pmv9812/policyspeech.html (accessed on 17 August 2014).

10 Corinna Konrad, 'The Japanese Approach: Tracks of Human Security Implementation', *Human Security Perspectives*, vol. 1, issue 3, 2006, pp. 22–38.

Co-operation and Development (OECD) Development Assistance Committee (DAC), and host of both the G20 and the High Level Forum (HLF-4) on Aid Effectiveness. A second, political, miracle on the Han has seen the ROK successfully transition to, and then consolidate as, a representative liberal democracy. This has been achieved in the context of ongoing security challenges. Korea has also grown from being the host of the largest UN enforcement operation to date, to being a major contributor to international peacekeeping operations. Thus South Korean politicians and the wider public see a duty to pay back to the international community through public service for the help previously received. Several South Koreans currently serve in high ranking positions at the United Nations including UN Secretary-General Ban Ki-moon, and South Korea was elected as a non-permanent member to the Security Council for a second time in 2012.

UN peacekeeping operations are the most visible activity of the United Nations and widely considered an important tool for conflict resolution. The following sections provide an overview on China's, Japan's and South Korea's participation in UN peacekeeping operations and explain the different rationales why states from Northeast Asia are contributing to the UN. Finally, areas where states from Northeast Asia could potentially increase their participation are identified.

II China's Participation in UN Peacekeeping Operations

The People's Republic of China could not join the United Nations until 1971. From 1950 to 1971 it actively opposed UN peacekeeping operations because it considered peacekeeping as a tool of Western imperialism and an instrument of US hegemony. When the UN established the United Nations Operation in the Congo (ONUC) in 1960, the PRC viewed the operation as an attempt by the United States to suppress the national liberation movement in the Congo. China's attitude towards peacekeeping has, however, changed over time. By the end of 1970s, the PRC had adopted a new foreign policy opening Beijing to international co-operation. In 1988, China joined the UN Special Committee on Peacekeeping Operations. For the first time, China dispatched military observers to the United Nations Disengagement Observer Force (UNDOF) and non-military personnel to the UN Transitional Assistance Group in Namibia (UNTAG) in 1989.

In the last ten years, China has become the major troop contributor among the permanent members of the Security Council to UN peacekeeping operations and there has been a twenty-fold increase since the early 2000s. The People's Republic of China has in general not participated in robust operations. In 2013, however, Beijing decided to send combat forces to the

United Nations Multidimensional Integrated Stabilization Mission in Mali (MINUSMA).[11] China had already deployed an infantry unit to the United Nations Mission to South Sudan (UNMISS) in 2012. Chinese peacekeepers have been sent among others to the UN Truce Supervision Organization (UNTSO); UN Iraq-Kuwait Observer Mission (UNIKOM); UN Mission for Referendum in Western Sahara (MINURSO); UN Transitional Authority in Cambodia (UNTAC); UN Operation in Mozambique (ONUMOZ); UN Observer Mission in Liberia (UNOMIL); UN Mission in Afghanistan (UNSMA); UN Mission in Sierra Leone (UNAMSIL); UN Support Mission in East Timor (UNMISET); UN Mission in Ethiopia and Eritrea (UNMEE); UN Mission in Bosnia and Herzegovina (UNMIBH); UN Mission in Congo (MONUC); UN Mission in Liberia (UNMIL); UN Operation in Cote d'Ivoire (UNOCI); UN Mission in Kosovo (UNMIK); UN Stabilization Mission in Haiti (MINUSTAH); UN Action in Burundi (ONUB); UN Mission in Sudan (UNMIS); UN Interim Force in Lebanon (UNIFIL); UN Integrated Mission in Timor-Leste (UNMIT); UN Integrated Office in Sierra Leone (UNIOSIL); AU-UN Hybrid Operation in Darfur, Sudan (UNAMID); United Nations Multidimensional Integrated Stabilization Mission in Mali (MINUSMA).[12]

In the past, most of the Chinese peacekeepers have been transport staff, engineers and medical workers. The first platoon of Chinese infantry was dispatched to South Sudan in 2012.[13] As of July 2014, the PRC ranks 14 among

---

11 Kathrin Hille, 'China Commits Combat Troops to Mali', *Financial Times*, 27 June 2013, http://www.ft.com/cms/s/0/e46f3e42-defe-11e2-881f-00144feab7de.html#axzz3AyxCRECW (accessed on 20 August 2014.); 'Over there. China Ponders Sending More Combat Troops on UN Peacekeeping Missions', *The Economist*, 15 July 2013, http://www.economist.com/news/china/21579495-china-ponders-sending-more-combat-troops-un-peacekeeping-missions-over-there (accessed on 20 August 2014). For further discussion on China's participation in UN peacekeeping operations, see Bates Gill and Chin-Hao Huang, China's Expanding Role in Peacekeeping, Prospects and Policy Implications. *sipri Policy Paper*, 25 November 2009, http://books.sipri.org/files/PP/SIPRIPP25.pdf. (accessed on 17 August 2014); Chin-Hao Huang, *Contributor Profile: The People's Republic of China*, http://www.ipinst.org/images/pdfs/china-hao130208.pdf (accessed on 20 August 2014); Sarah Teitt, 'The Responsibility to Protect and China's Peacekeeping Policy', *International Peacekeeping*, vol. 18, no. 3, 2011, pp. 298–312 and Liu Tiewa, 'Marching for a More Open, Confident and Responsible Great Power: Explaining China's Involvement in UN Peacekeeping Operations', *Journal of International Peacekeeping*, vol. 13, issue 1–2, 2009, pp. 101–130.

12 China's Participation in UN Peacekeeping Operations (1990–2008), http://www.china-un.org/eng/zt/wh/t534321.htm (accessed on 17 August 2014).

13 'Over There. China Ponders Sending More Combat Troops on UN Peacekeeping Mission', *Economist*, 15 June 2013, http://www.economist.com/news/china/21579495-china-ponders-sending-more-combat-troops-un-peacekeeping-missions-over-there (accessed on 17 August 2014).

the troop contributors to UN peacekeeping operations and is providing 21,387 military and police personnel to UN missions.[14] In the Security Council, China has been reluctant to authorize the use of force in peace operations. It has taken the view that UN peacekeeping operations should not infringe the principle of sovereignty and require the consent of the host state. This position has been for example reiterated by Ambassador Wang Min in 2013:

> We must adhere to Dag Hammarskjöld's three principles for the smooth conduct of peacekeeping operations. Deviation from or dilution of the basic peacekeeping principles will jeopardize the presumed objectivity and impartiality of peacekeeping operations and may even create a situation where the United Nations becomes a party to a conflict, hence hampering international efforts to resolve it. Peacekeeping operations, in the discharge of their mandate, should fully respect the sovereignty of the host countries, strengthen coordination with the parties concerned and work to win the trust, understanding and support of host countries.[15]

There have, however, also been exceptions when China did not insist on the requirement of consent, for example in case of UNPROFOR in Bosnia and in case of UNOSOM in Somalia which lacked an effective government at the time. In the past, Beijing has also supported the adoption of Chapter VII mandates providing for the protection of civilians but emphasized that national authorities should assume primary protection responsibilities. In 2013, China voted in favor on the establishment of the United Nations Force Intervention Brigade within the existing United Nations Organization Stabilization Mission in the Democratic Republic of the Congo (MONUSCO).[16] The Force Intervention Brigade is unique because the force has a mandate to carry out offensive operations in order to neutralize and disarm rebel groups in the Democratic Republic of Congo (DRC). China voted in favor because of the worsening humanitarian situation in the DRC, and because the resolution stated clearly that "the creation of the specialized intervention brigade would not create a precedent or undercut traditional peacekeeping principles."[17] In the same year, China also supported the establishment of

14 Statement by Ambassador Wang Min at the Security Council Open Debate on United Nations Peacekeeping Operations, http://www.china-un.org/eng/hyyfy/t1063862.htm (accessed on 17 August 2014).

15 *Ibid.*

16 See UN doc. SC Resolution 2098 of 28 March 2013.

17 'Intervention Brigade' Authorized as Security Council Grants Mandate Renewal for United Nations Mission in Democratic Republic of Congo', SC 10964 of 28 March 2013, http://www.un.org/News/Press/docs/2013/sc10964.doc.htm (accessed on 20 August 2014).

another robust stabilization operation under Chapter VII of the UN Charter, the UN Multidimensional Integrated Stabilization Mission in Mali (MINUSMA).[18] MINUSMA's mandate is, however, more defensive in nature. Peacekeepers are authorized to use all necessary means to address threats to the implementation of its mandate, which would include protection of civilians under imminent threat of physical violence, and protection of United Nations personnel from residual threats, within its capabilities and its areas of deployment.[19]

In general, China wants to strengthen the effectiveness of peacekeeping operations and to increase the coordination and cooperation with regional organizations including the African Union.[20] Another element of China's policy in the Security Council was that Beijing vetoed in general the authorization or extension of UN peacekeeping operations in countries that recognized Taiwan. An exception was the deployment of MINUSTAH, even though the Haitian government recognized Taiwan. China has, in fact, twice endorsed R2P at the UN, first at the World Summit in 2005 and later in Security Council Resolution 1674, since which time, the PRC has "clearly and consistently affirmed the R2P principle and issued corresponding statements in favor of bolstering the UN's capacity to avert mass atrocity".[21] As further noted in an International Crisis Group (ICG) report in 2009:

> [China] supported the resolutions authorizing IFOR and KFOR in Bosnia and peace enforcement operations in Somalia in the early 1990s. Although it opposed the first Gulf War, China abstained and allowed Resolution 678, authorising member states to use all necessary means to restore international peace and security after Iraq's invasion of Kuwait, to pass. Despite its opposition to intervention in Kosovo and damage to its embassy in Belgrade, China has supported every operation in Kosovo since, including peace enforcement operations.[22]

As pointed out by Sarah Teitt's detailed report on the subject, insofar as China's interpretation of R2P is representative of the views of similarly cautious, yet

---

18 See UN doc. SC Resolution 2100 of 25 April 2013.

19 See UN doc. SC Resolutions 2100 of 25 April 2013 and 2164 of 25 June 2014.

20 Statement by Ambassador Wang Min at the Security Council Open Debate on United Nations Peacekeeping Operations, 11.6.2014, http://www.china-un.org/eng/hyyfy/t1168830.htm (accessed on 20 August 2014).

21 Teitt, p. 2.

22 International Crisis Group (ICG), 'China's Growing Role in UN Peacekeeping', Asia Report N°166 – 17 April 2009, http://www.unhcr.org/refworld/pdfid/49ec24ca2.pdf (accessed on 18 August 2014), p. 3.

engaged states, these developments hold out hope for deepening the consensus on R2P and for translating the Responsibility to Protect from words to deeds.[23] In terms of peacekeeping China's attitudinal change is nothing short of revolutionary. In the last decade and a half, China has deployed over 10,000 peacekeepers serving in more than 20 UN peacekeeping operations worldwide, including Asia, balancing new motivations against its traditional adherence to nonintervention.[24] It regularly has more than 2,000 peacekeepers in the field at any one time, and is currently the top contributor among the five permanent members (P-5) of the Security Council.[25] China belongs to the top ten providers of assessed contributions to the UN peacekeeping budget as of 2013. The PRC is ranking 6th and is listed as providing 6.64% to the peacekeeping budget.[26] While China's support for regimes seen by some as unsavory has fed suspicions that Chinese peacekeeping is primarily motivated by economic interests, in fact China's economic and peacekeeping decision-making tracks operate separately. Furthermore, China's relationships with difficult regimes may well benefit UN peacekeeping efforts, as the PRC "can bring to the table valuable political capital and economic leverage, in some cases even encouraging host countries to consent to peacekeeping operations".[27]

III Japan's Participation in UN Peacekeeping Operations

Japan's active involvement in UN peacekeeping operations is of recent history. As early as 1961, Secretary-General Dag Hammarskjöld asked the Japanese government to contribute to UN peacekeeping missions, but Tokyo rejected the proposal. The first civilian peacekeepers were sent to the UN Transition Assistance Group in Namibia (UNTAG) in 1989 but no military personnel were dispatched until the early 1990s. Bert Edström has argued that Japanese foreign policy initiatives are concerned almost exclusively with economic development and humanitarianism rather than national security policy.[28] Yet, in fact, it is the combination of international and domestic constraints that gives Japanese

23 Teitt, p. 2.

24 International Crisis Group (ICG), p. 1.

25 http://www.un.org/en/peacekeeping/contributors/2014/jul14_2.pdf (accessed on 22 August 2014).

26 Financing Peacekeeping, http://www.un.org/en/peacekeeping/operations/financing.shtml (accessed on 2 September 2014).

27 International Crisis Group (ICG), p. i.

28 Bert Edström, 'Japan's Foreign Policy and Human Security', *Japan Forum*, vol. 15, issue 2, 2003, pp. 209–225, 220.

national security and strategic policy-making in general, and its human security prioritization in particular, its distinctive characteristics.[29] Japanese foreign policy-making is fundamentally non-military as a result of internal constraints, but it is certainly still concerned with security, both national and human. Constrained by its pacifist constitution and lingering animosity in the region over Japan's historic role, planners have looked to non-traditional security policies to further Japanese interests. These conditions have provided added impetus for successive Japanese governments to develop non-military concepts of security and to practice them in order to play a leadership role in the global politico-strategic sphere. In particular, the emergence of the human security concept within security discourse allowed the country to combine its traditional regional aid operations with an initiative with global reach.

Kent Calder, the originator of the 'reactive state' hypothesis sees Japan as occupying the unique position of having the power potential of a mid-range European state, yet the political leverage of much smaller and weaker reactive states.[30] Perhaps most importantly, Calder claims that the fragmented character of state authority in Japan makes decisive action more difficult than in countries with strong chief executives, such as the United States thereby explaining Japanese passivity in international affairs when activism would have been both possible and beneficial for Japan.[31] Such has been the impact of Calder's hypothesis that the dominant view of Japan's international behaviour is one where Japan is portrayed as passive, risk-avoiding, and ineffective in conducting foreign policy.[32] Japan is essentially seen as a power that inevitably bandwagons on the policy initiatives of the global hegemonic leader. Indeed, partly for this reason – i.e. as a result of exogenous pressures, Japan has become increasingly involved in UN PKOs at the operational level.

The Yoshida Doctrine, which involved placing the highest national priority on economic development, while simultaneously keeping a low diplomatic profile worked well until the end of the Cold War and the Gulf War that followed, when despite 'check-book diplomacy' that underwrote much of the allied campaign, Japan was nevertheless severely criticized for not putting the

29 See Brendan Howe, 'Between Normality & Uniqueness: Unwrapping the Enigma of Japanese Security Policy Decision-Making', *Modern Asian Studies*, vol. 44, no. 6, 2010, pp. 1313–1336.

30 Kent E. Calder, 'Japanese Foreign Economic Policy Formation: Explaining the Reactive State', *World Politics*, vol. 40, no. 4, 1988, pp. 517–541.

31 *Ibid.*, 518–28.

32 Keiko Hirata, 'Japan as a Reactive State? Analyzing Japan's Relations with the Socialist Republic of Vietnam', *Japanese Studies*, vol. 18, no. 2, 1988, pp. 1–31.

Self Defense Force in harm's way.[33] As a result of the external pressures brought on by the Gulf War and its aftermath, on June 15, 1992, the Japanese Diet passed the Law Concerning Cooperation in U.N. Peacekeeping and Other Operations (otherwise known as the PKO Law or IPC Law), which went in to effect on August 10 of that same year. This meant that for the first time since World War II, Japanese soldiers could be sent on missions outside Japan.[34] According to the IPC Law, certain conditions need to be met before Japanese peacekeepers can be dispatched. A cease-fire must be in place; the parties to the conflict must have given their consent; the peacekeeping force must be impartial; the Japanese may withdraw their troops if one of the criteria is no longer being met; and force can only be used in self-defence.[35]

Japan's humanitarian assistance (including peacekeeping) can, however, also be seen not only as an area of autonomous Japanese foreign policy formation that defies the reactivist hypothesis, but even as an alternative form of security policy formation. While Japanese statesmen and institutions may be backing away from the express use of human security terminology, they are still following policies guided by related principles. In part this is because there is no alternative. The Japanese public is deeply wedded to the idea of non-militarism in their nation's foreign policy. There is no political constituency for transforming the Japanese Self Defense Forces into a force capable of force projection. Opinion polls in 2007 and 2008 found only 39% supported the renewal of the Anti-Terrorism Special Measures Law (which initially expired on 1 November 2007) permitting the dispatch of the Maritime Self Defense Forces to the Indian Ocean in support of antiterrorism measures in Afghanistan, and only 35% were in favour of allowing the Self Defense Forces to be dispatched overseas.[36] There is, however, continued domestic support for the Japanese government to play a more active role in non-traditional and multilateral areas of foreign and security policy such as global climate change and humanitarian assistance.[37] As long as Japanese missions have a clear humanitarian or support focus rather than robust or combat-orientated roles, public support in Japan for involvement in UN PKOs is likely to grow.

---

33 Christopher W. Hughes, *Japan's Re-emergence as a ‚Normal' Military Power* (London: Oxford University Press for the International Institute for Strategic Studies), p. 42.

34 Kevin Cooney, *Japan's Foreign Policy since 1945* (New York: M.E. Sharpe, 2007), pp. 6–7.

35 Available at http://www.pko.go.jp/pko_j/data/law/pdf/law_e.pdf (accessed on 17 August 2014).

36 Nikkei Shimbun Opinion Polls, December 2007 and January 2008.

37 Yomiuri Shimbun Opinion Polls, 19 and 20 May 2007.

Since 1992 Japan has participated in fifteen peacekeeping operations. The first Japanese peacekeepers were sent to the UN Transitional Authority to Cambodia (UNTAC). Japanese Self-Defence Force (JSDF) and police officers participated among others in the missions in Cambodia (UNTAC); Mozambique (ONUMOZ); the Golan Heights; Haiti; East Timor/Timor-Leste (UNTAET and UNMISET); Nepal (UNMIN) and South Sudan (UNMIIS).[38] Activities ranged among others from engineering, cease-fire monitoring, humanitarian assistance, and medical care to transportation. As of July 2014, Japan is providing 269 peacekeepers to the UN and ranking 47 among troop contributing countries.[39] In addition to the dispatch of peacekeepers, Japan is the 2nd largest financial contributor to the UN peacekeeping budget. It has also played an active role in the SC Working Group on Peacekeeping Operations. Furthermore, Japan launched the Human Resource Development Program to develop Japanese and Asian civilian experts in the area of peace-building.

In general, the deployment of the Japanese Self-Defence Force has remained a controversial issue because of constitutional constraints, domestic politics, public opinion and Japan's history as an aggressor state during WWII. According to Article 9 of the National Constitution of Japan, "the Japanese people forever renounce war as a sovereign right of the nation and the threat or use of force as means of settling international disputes." Japan has therefore never contributed combat troops to UN peacekeeping operations. In June 2014, however, the Japanese cabinet approved a reinterpretation of the constitution.[40] This

38 Permanent Mission of Japan to the United Nations, *Peace and Security*, accessible at http://www.un.emb-japan.go.jp/topics.en/peace_and_security.html (accessed on 17 August 2014).

39 See Ranking of Military and Police Contributions to UN Operations, 31 July 2014, http://www.un.org/en/peacekeeping/contributors/2014/jul14_2.pdf (accessed on 17 August 2014). In detail on Japan's contribution to UN peacekeeping operations, Chiyuki Aoi, 'Beyond Activism-Lite"?: Issues in Japanese Participation in Peace Operations', *Journal of International Peacekeeping*, vol. 13, nos. 1–2, 2009, pp. 72–100; Nik Hynek, 'Japan's Return to Chequebook? From Military Peace Support to Human Security Appropriations', *International Peacekeeping*, vol. 19, no. 1, pp. 62–76; Katsumi, Ishizuka, 'Japan' in Alex J. Bellamy and Paul D. Williams (eds.), *Providing Peacekeepers. The Politics, Challenges, and Future of United Nations Peacekeeping Contributions* (Oxford: OUP, 2014), pp. 396–414; Frank A. Stengel, 'Zögerlicher Friedensstifter: Japans ambivalente Haltung zu den Friedensmissionen der Vereinten Nationen / The Reluctant Peacekeeper: Japan's Ambivalent Stance on UN Peace Operations', *Japan aktuell*, 1, 2008, pp. 37–55.

40 On the constitutional debate, Craig Martin, "Reinterpreting' Article 9 Endangers Japan's Rule of Law', *The Japan Times*, 27 June 2014, http://www.japantimes.co.jp/opinion/2014/06/27/commentary/japan-commentary/reinterpreting-article-9-endan

change would permit Japan's Self-Defence Force to participate in "collective self-defence" but also in more robust UN peacekeeping operations. Japanese UN peacekeepers will be allowed to use force for the protection of civilians and to rescue peacekeepers from other countries if they are under attack.[41]

IV South Korea's Participation in UN Peacekeeping Operations

The Republic of Korea (ROK) was a relative latecomer to the United Nations. After several failed attempts to become a member of the UN, it finally succeeded in joining the world organization in 1991.[42] The UN, however, has played an important role in the history of South Korea.[43] The UN was instrumental in establishing the Republic of Korea. The United Nations Temporary Commission on Korea observed free and fair election after World War II and the UN General Assembly recognized the ROK as the solely legitimate government on the Korean peninsula in 1948.[44] The UN also provided crucial military help to repel the aggression from North Korea during the Korean War.

South Korea actively supports and participates in collective international efforts to promote human security and protect the entitlement rights of those in crises caused by hunger, diseases, or natural and man-made disasters. The ROK supports all internationally agreed-upon humanitarian principles such as impartiality, neutrality and independence, and applies them to foreign, security, and assistance policies. As part of its efforts, South Korea has made good progress towards ensuring better humanitarian donorship through a legislative framework

gers-japans-rule-of-law/#.VAiTpUog-M8 (accessed on 4 September 2014); Izumi Sakurai, 'Major Security Shift: Scholars Blast Constitutional Reinterpretation as Attack on Democracy', *The Asahi Shimbun*, 4 July 2014, http://ajw.asahi.com/article/behind_news/politics/AJ201407040078 (accessed on 4 September 2014).

41 'Japan's Security. Clear and Present Dangers', *The Economist*, 5 July 2014; Lisa Sharland, 'Reinterpreting Article 9: Enhancing Japan's Engagement in UN Peacekeeping', *The Strategist*, 10 July 2014, http://www.aspistrategist.org.au/reinterpreting-article-9-enhancing-japans-engagement-in-un-peacekeeping/ (accessed on 20 August 2014); 'SDF May Get Green Light to Rescue U.N. Peacekkepers under Attack', *The Japan Times*, 31 May, 2014, http://www.japantimes.co.jp/news/2014/05/31/national/sdf-may-get-green-light-to-rescue-u-n-peacekeepers-under-attack/ (accessed on 20 August 2014).

42 During the Cold War, neither China nor the Soviet Union supported the admission of South Korea to the United Nations.

43 Chi Young Pak, *Korea and the United Nations* (The Hague: Kluwer Law International, 2000).

44 UN Doc. GA Resolution 195 (III) of 12 December 1948.

for its humanitarian action, and a commitment to increase its humanitarian aid. In March 2007, Korea enacted the Overseas Emergency Relief Act designed to allow the Korean government to provide more effective and prompt overseas emergency relief in order to play a greater role in the concerted efforts of the global community towards disaster management. Korea has been part of the UN Disaster Assessment and Coordination (UNDAC) teams since 2003 and the International Search and Rescue Advisory Group (INSARAG) since 1999. Since Korea specializes in search and rescue efforts, it has participated in the OCHA-administered Asia-Pacific Humanitarian Partnership (APHP) since its establishment in 2004.

Specifically, on the issue of Korea's participation in UN PKOs, for Eun-Sook Chung, Seoul's support "conveys the message of reciprocating international assistance it received after 1945, and it also demonstrates the nation's will and capabilities to contribute to the maintenance of peace in the international community".[45] This is symptomatic of the "paying back syndrome" prevalent among the majority of South Korean citizens who believe that it is their "moral duty to help those who are caught in armed conflict" in return for the international assistance the country received during the Korean War.[46] Furthermore, for Sangtu Ko peacekeeping operations (PKOs) represent the one field where South Korea aspires to middle power activism.[47]

Upon assessing South Korea's role in UN peacekeeping operations from a strictly numerical perspective, one must come to the conclusion that its contribution is relatively modest, bearing in mind the Republic of Korea has the world's sixth largest army. The major reason why there has not been a stronger commitment to UN peacekeeping operations appears to be the unstable situation on the Korean peninsula which is the major security concern for the South Korean government. That being said, Korea's troop contributions are already substantial when compared with other medium-size country members of the Organisation for Economic Co-operation and Development (OECD) such as Japan, the UK, or Germany. Furthermore, the 2010 Defense White Paper announced a plan steadily to expand Korea's participation in international peacekeeping operations. This ambition has, in fact, repeatedly been reiterated by senior military and political leaders.

---

45 Eun-sook, Chung, 'Korea's Law on UNPKO and Its Role in International Peacekeeping Missions', *Korea Focus*, vol. 18, issue 2, 2010, pp. 98–102, 101.

46 Kyudok Hong, 'South Korean Approaches to Peacekeeping and Peacebuilding: Lessons Learned and Challenges Ahead', *The Journal of East Asian Affairs*, vol. 23, no. 1, 2009, pp. 23–46, 24.

47 Sangtu Ko, 'Korea's Middle Power Activism and Peacekeeping Operations', *Asia Europe Journal*, vol. 10, 2012, pp. 287–299, 288.

Lee Myung Bak (President of the Republic of Korea 2008–2013) sought to strengthen Korean dedication to international peacekeeping, pursuing an active PKO policy under the name of "Global Korea" diplomacy which in turn aimed to reflect the international responsibility, of which Korea is increasingly aware, commensurate with its rising international status. "The president stated in 2009, at an event commemorating national independence, that he would raise the value of the national brand through optimal use of two instruments, namely ODA and PKO".[48] In July 2013, the Joint Chiefs of Staff (JCS) talked of further beefing up Korea's presence in international PKOs.[49] Also in 2013, in order to improve functioning of Korean peacekeeping operations, the government increased the staff of the Peacekeeping Operations (PKO) Center, and relocated it from the ROK Joint Staff College to the National Defense University. The PKO center provides pre-deployment education and training to military and police personnel, writes up the 'after action' reports to assess the effectiveness of the unit, and gathers any lessons learned for future missions, while also participating in exchange programs with PKO military from other countries to improve training and coordination.[50]

These aspirations have started to be reflected in practice. Following the invasion of Iraq, from 2003 to mid-2007 the number of Korean peacekeepers dropped from over 450 to an average of around 42 per annum, as a result of several thousand Korean service personnel being dispatched in support of the US-led coalition's operations in Kazakhstan, Kyrgyzstan, and Northern Iraq. "From July 2007, however, Korea not only recovered its previous level of commitment to UN peacekeeping it expanded the number of troops committed, the scope of their work, and areas of operation".[51] In recent years in particular, the Republic of Korea has increased the numbers of peacekeepers sent to UN missions. While in July 2004, the Republic of Korea sent only 39 peacekeepers to UN missions ranking 60 among Military and Civilian Police contributing countries, South Korea is currently providing 616

48 *Ibid.*, p. 296.

49 Seung-woo Kang, 'Korea Beefing up Presence in PKO', *The Korea Times*, July 11, 2013, https://www.koreatimes.co.kr/www/news/nation/2013/07/116_139642.html (accessed on 17 August 2014).

50 Terence Roehrig, 'South Korea, Foreign Aid, and UN Peacekeeping: Contributing to International Peace and Security as a Middle Power', *Korea Observer*, vol. 44, no. 4, 2013, pp. 623–645, 639.

51 Shin-wha Lee and Joon Sung Park, *Contributor Profile: South Korea* (Seoul: Korea University) http://www.providingforpeacekeeping.org/wp-content/uploads/2013/02/Korea-Lee-16-June-2014.pdf (accessed on 24 August 2014) pp. 1–8, 1.

peacekeepers to the UN and ranking 35 among troop contributing countries.[52] In addition to the deployment of troops, South Korea has actively participated in the debate on peacekeeping in the Security Council and for example, suggested that development co-operation mechanisms should be included into multiple dimensions of peace operations. Due to the nature of the Korean role in the Iraq-related missions as well as in similar activities in Afghanistan, the Ministry of Defense considers these also to be peacekeeping operations.

Since the dispatch of its first peacekeepers, the Ever Green Unit, which constituted part of the 1993 UNOSOM II UN peacekeeping mission in Somalia, the ROK has deployed some 40,000 globally. 2014 marked the 20th anniversary of South Korea's participation in UN peacekeeping operations.[53] The full list of South Korea's contributions to PKOs is as follows: Two years after becoming a member of the United Nations in 1991, South Korea sent an engineering battalion to the United Nations Operations in Somalia II (UNOSOM II). The Republic of Korea also dispatched personnel to the United Nations Mission for the Referendum in Western Sahara (MINURSO); to the United Nations Angola Verification Mission III (UNAVEM III); to the United Nations Military Observer Group in India and Pakistan (UNMOGIP); to the United Nations Observer Mission (UNOMIG); to the United Nations Mission in Liberia (UNMIL); to the United Nations Assistance Mission in Afghanistan (UNAMA); to United Nations Integrated Mission in Timor-Leste (UNMIT); to the United Nations Mission in Nepal (UNMIN); the United Nations Interim Force in Lebanon (UNIFIL); to United Nations Stabilization Mission in Haiti (MINUSTAH), to the United Nations Operation in Côte d'Ivoire (UNOCI), to the United Nations Mission in Darfur (UNAMID) and the United Nations Mission in South Sudan (UNMISS).[54]

52 Ranking of Military and Police Contributions to UN Operations, http://www.un.org/en/peacekeeping/contributors/2014/jul14_2.pdf (accessed on 2 September 2014).

53 For further discussion, see Key-young Son, 'From a Garrison State to a Humanitarian Power?: Security Identities, Constitutive Norms and South Korea's Overseas Troop Dispatches', *The Korean Journal of Defence Analysis*, vol. 23, no. 4, 2011, pp. 557–573 and Tae-hyun Park, 'South Korea's Overseas Troop Dispatch', *Asian Politics & Policy*, vol. 5, issue 2, 2013, pp. 167–182.

54 In addition to the participation in UN peacekeeping operations, the Republic of Korea has also taken part in a number of military operations abroad. South Korea supported South Vietnam during the Vietnam War by sending the second largest contingent of foreign troops (312,853 troops) after the United States. South Korea sent non-combatant troops to the Gulf War in 1991, provided troops to Multi National Force Operations in Iraq and Afghanistan and is currently sending the Cheonghae Unit to combat piracy near the coast of Somalia. In 2010, South Korea also dispatched Special Forces to the United Arab Emirates.

Again, the ROK has enacted a sound legal framework for these activities. "Korea at first lacked clear and specific guidelines for contributing and there were lengthy bureaucratic and parliamentary deliberations that resulted in troop deployment delays".[55] Several years of discussions and preparations among members of the Ministry of Foreign Affairs and Trade (MOFAT), the Ministry of National Defense (MND) and the National Assembly led, however, to the implementation of key legislation.[56] The National Assembly passed the "Law on Participation in United Nations Peacekeeping Operations" in December 2010 (supplemented by a related presidential decree), and it took effect in April the following year. Korea's UNPKO law includes a definition of the UN peacekeeping operations, principles of mission performance, the legal basis for establishing standing forces, parliamentary approval procedures for dispatching forces, and authorizes the administration to make "provisional" agreements with the UN on the scale of forces for dispatch (up to 1,000 personnel each time), subject to and in anticipation of National Assembly approval.[57]

It needs to be stressed that the law only regulates the participation in certain types of UN peacekeeping operations; for example missions mandated to supervise ceasefires, to provide humanitarian assistance, or to monitor elections but not robust operations. The law also does not provide for participation in military operations by other international organizations such as NATO or coalitions of the willing.[58] In the past, various Korean governments considered the safety of their own soldiers the first priority. With few exceptions, medical and engineering units were the main forces sent to UN missions. The focus was on non-military assignments such as civil reconstruction or medical support.[59] For example, South Korean peacekeepers provided medical support, computer training and even Taekwondo and Hangul lessons to the local population in South Lebanon.

In general, South Korea receives high marks for its performance in UN peacekeeping operations and it is well suited for peacekeeping as a middle

55 Lee and Park, p. 2.

56 Eun-sook Chung, 'Korea's Law on UNPKO and Its Role in International Peacekeeping Missions', *Korea Focus*, vol. 18, issue 2, 2010, pp. 98–102, 98.

57 *Ibid.*, 98.

58 See Ministry of Foreign Affairs, Republic of Korea, Policy Issues, PKO, http://www.mofat.go.kr/ENG/policy/pko/overview/index.jsp (accessed on 17 August 2014).

59 Jung-ho Nam, 'Korea's Duty in Peacekeeping. Participation in International Peacekeeping Activities Can Be a Precious Experience for a Divided Nation like Korea', *JoongAng Daily*, 24th April 2008, http://koreajoongangdaily.joins.com/news/article/article.aspx?aid=2888998 (accessed on 17 August 2014).

power because of its geographical and political distance to many conflicts in the world.

V Conclusion: Rationales for Providing Peacekeepers and Areas for Potential Increased Participation

There are many different factors why states participate in peacekeeping operations. In a recent study, Alex Bellamy and Paul Williams indentified five rationales for the participation in peacekeeping operations: political, economic, institutional, security and normative concerns.[60] Political reasons may include "pressure or persuasion by allies, great powers, or the UN Secretary-General or Secretariat, and perceptions that peacekeeping contributions enhance the country's 'national prestige' or might strengthen its bid to acquire a non-permanent seat on the UN Security Council (or for some states, their bid for a permanent seat on a reformed Council)".[61] While economic rationales refer to economic incentives, security rationales serve broader national security interests.[62] As Bellamy and Williams explain, institutional rationales may 'stem from motives related to the country's armed forces, security sector, and bureaucratic dynamics'.[63] Normative reasons, for example, play a role when states want to promote the greater good as "good Samaritans", or when they want to show a principled commitment to the world organization as "good international citizens".[64] Furthermore, peacekeeping provides a valuable practical experience for all states in Northeast Asia.

From a country-specific perspective, China views peacekeeping as a means to enhance its international standing. Another motivation is to demonstrate China's peaceful development and commitment to a harmonious world. For Japan, international peace and stability are indispensable foundations for achieving the country's own stability and prosperity.[65] In addition to humanitarian motives, the overseas deployment of the Japanese Self Defence Forces is motivated by the quest for international status and the pursuit of a permanent

60 Alex J. Bellamy and Paul D. Williams (eds.), *Providing Peacekeepers. The Politics, Challenges, and Future of United Nations Peacekeeping Contributions* (Oxford: OUP, 2013), pp. 17–21.

61 *Ibid.*, p. 18.

62 *Ibid.*, p. 19.

63 *Ibid.*, p. 20.

64 *Ibid.*, p. 20.

65 Permanent Mission of Japan, *Peace and Security*, http://www.un.emb-japan.go.jp/topics/peace_and_security.html (accessed 17 August 2014).

seat in the UN Security Council. Several rationales play a role for Korea's participation in peacekeeping operations. One the one hand, South Korea views "UN Peace-keeping Operation as integral to maintaining international peace and security" and wants to contribute to this facet of global governance. On the other hand, South Korea benefited greatly from the support by the United Nations and would like to reciprocate.[66] When South Korea joined the UN in 1991, Seoul's motivation for participation in peacekeeping operations was also linked to a quest for a non-permanent seat in the Security Council at that time. Peacekeeping also helps to improve South Korea's image as a responsible middle power in international relations and it allows South Korea "to differentiate itself in a proactive manner from its Northeast Asian neighbors China and Japan."[67] Further Korean motivations include securing international support vis-à-vis North Korea; keeping up with the neighbors, China and Japan; supporting the Korean-born Secretary General of the UN.[68]

A regional meeting of the project "New Geopolitics of Peace Operations: A Dialogue with Emerging Powers" organized by SIPRI and the Friedrich-Ebert-Stiftung (FES) in spring 2013 identified a number of areas where states from Northeast Asia could increase their participation in UN peacekeeping operations: involvement in the policy-development and reforms process within the UNDPKO; technological capabilities; medical support; financial contributions; police training; and regional assistance with maritime security.[69] An important aspect is that co-ordination and co-operation in the areas of training and education need to be enhanced on the regional level. As stated elsewhere, "participants in peace operations shouldn't meet for the first time in the maelstrom of a peace operation."[70]

Japan and South Korea may also consider providing more police and skilled civilians to UN missions. There seems to be no official reason why both countries have provided so few police personnel and civilians in the past. One of the

66 See Ministry of National Defense, Republic of Korea http://www.mnd.go.kr/mbshome/mbs/mnd_eng/subview.jsp?id=mnd_eng_020300000000 (accessed on 25 April 2014).

67 Balbina Hwang, 'Peacekeeping' in Scott Snyder (ed.), *The US-South Korea Alliance: Meeting New Security Challenges* (Boulder: Lynne Rienner, 2012), pp. 173–194, 184.

68 Lee and Park, p. 4.

69 Xenia, Avezov, 'The New Geoplitics of Peace Operations: A Dialogue with Emerging Powers. North East Asia Regional Dialogue', *SIPRI Workshop Report*, Ulan Bator, 11–12 April 2013, p. 6, http://www.sipri.org/research/conflict/pko/other_publ/ngp-workshop-report-april-2013 (accessed on 17 August 2014).

70 Sir Roger Jacklin, Shrivenham Challenges Seminar, 3 March 2005, quoted in The Challenges Project, *Meeting the Challenges of Peace Operations: Cooperation and Coordination* (Stockholm: Elanders Gotab), p. 124.

major challenges for the UN is finding skilled police officers and civilian personnel with expertise in justice, civil administration and other specialized areas such as economic development. International policing is an area of exponential growth for the United Nations.[71] In 1995, there were only 35 UN police deployed in Cyprus. As of 2014, 12,197 police are serving in UN missions.[72] States in Northeast Asia could contribute greatly to supporting academic research and international conferences dealing with the challenges to 21st century peacekeeping operations. There might also be calls to get involved in more robust peacekeeping operations. For any government in Northeast Asia or in the world this will be a difficult decision. Critics would contend that peacekeepers are not war-fighters, and should not go to places where no peace can be kept. Additional pressure may come from the general public, opposition parties and the press pointing out that their governments should not risk the lives of their own citizens in remote places of the world.

States from Northeast Asia already make a significant contribution to UN peacekeeping operations although as pointed out above there are still areas of improvement. While there is a growing trend of the Security Council authorizing the use of force in peacekeeping operations, states from Northeast Asia have remained reluctant to participate in more robust missions. This reluctance is likely to come under pressure, however, from external normative constituencies championing a global responsibility to prevent genocide and crimes against humanity, and internal constituencies who either feel an obligation for their countries to play a greater role, or a national right to do so on the global stage.

71 See in detail, Phillip Rotmann, 'Police in 21st Century Global Peace Operations: Achievements and Challenges', *GPI Policy Brief*, October 2012; Bryn W. Hughes, Charles T. Hunt and Boris Kondoch (eds.), *Making Sense of Peace and Capacity-Building Operations. Rethinking Policing and Beyond* (Leiden, Boston: Martinus Nijhoff Publishers, 2010).

72 Peacekeeping Fact Sheet, http://www.un.org/en/peacekeeping/resources/statistics/factsheet.shtml (accessed on 17 August 2014).

CHAPTER 3

Southeast Asian Perspectives on UN Peacekeeping: Indonesia and Malaysia

Alistair D. B. Cook

Last year the United Nations ranked Indonesia as the seventeenth and Malaysia as the twenty-sixth largest contributors to UN peace operations worldwide and the two largest contributors among ASEAN member states. Indeed, at the end of January 2014, total Southeast Asian contributions to UN peace operations were 26 from Brunei Darussalam, 342 from Cambodia, 1697 from Indonesia, 909 from Malaysia, 703 from the Philippines, 22 from Singapore and 33 from Thailand.[1] Both Indonesia and Malaysia have long histories in United Nations peace operations including Sinai, Egypt in the 1950s, Congo in the 1960s, Vietnam in the 1970s, Angola, the Balkans and the Iran-Iraq conflict in the 1990s. Yet the history of independent Indonesia is full of civil-military conflict and domestic political struggles illustrating potential contradictions with its external image projection and domestic realities. The most notable internal security issues are found in Aceh, East Timor (until c.1999) and Papua. Since the end of the Cold War and a shift to democracy, Indonesia has not only contributed to United Nations peace operations but has also been the recipient of them during East Timor's transition to independence. While Indonesia as a recipient of UN peace operations is well covered in the literature for good reason, its role as a contributor has received relatively less attention. Likewise Malaysia has also hosted internal conflicts most notably between the Malayan Communist Party, Malayan National Liberation Army, and government security services from 1968 to 1989 while simultaneously contributing to UN peace operations again illustrative of a potential contradiction between external image projection and domestic realities.

First, this chapter investigates the motivations behind the decisions by Malaysia and Indonesia to contribute to UN peace operations. Second, this chapter utilises a multifocal lens to illustrate the different manifestations that these contributions to peace operations take. Through this investigation, both Indonesia and Malaysia illustrate that they seek greater political legitimacy

1 Carl Thayer, 'ASEAN and UN Peacekeeping', *The Diplomat*, 25 April 2014, thediplomat.com/2014/04/asean-and-un-peacekeeping/.

 | DOI 10.1163/9789004322059_004

and leadership through their contributions to peace operations. However, the multifocal lens uncovers that it is not only the United Nations where legitimacy and leadership is sought,[2] but also through the Association of Southeast Asian Nations (ASEAN) and the Organisation of Islamic Conference (OIC) to project themselves as middle and regional powers.

However, more recently Indonesia's frustration with more conservative ASEAN member states has led to some strategists and security scholars like Rizal Sukma to move away from regionalism and focus on global affairs and key bilateral relations if it is a better location to promote the national interest.[3] Indeed, Indonesia along with other states such as South Korea and Australia has adopted the rhetoric of middle power diplomacy and since accession to the G20 has demonstrated its reconsideration of its strategic foreign policy priorities.[4] As Beeson and Higgott (2013) argue the G20 is the "current middle power venue of choice and mark of status," which further illustrates Indonesia's self-perception and international acceptance as a middle power. In other words as a caution, groups of states in the international system come and go, and are not necessarily a stable criterion for determining middle power status. Rather more as these groups rise and fall they provide a snapshot of activity of selected states with an "active" foreign policy. In identifying middle power status with those states who demonstrate an "active" foreign policy, it makes the term "middle power" broader.[5] In this sense, with the historical commitment of both Indonesia and Malaysia to international peacekeeping, they both qualify as middle powers in the broad interpretation of the term. Indonesia has generally been recognised as first among equals within ASEAN and has demonstrated its leadership through promoting regional institution building in ASEAN most notably through the ASEAN Political Security Blueprint and contributing to conflict management through diplomacy in the region[6] like in the Thailand-Cambodia border dispute in 2011. This also reflects a broader trend,

2 Inis L. Claude, 'Collective Legitimization as a Political Function of the United Nations', *International Organisation*, vol. 20, 1966, pp. 367–379.

3 Rizal Sukma, 'A post-ASEAN Foreign Policy for a post-G8 World', *The Jakarta Post*, 5 October.

4 Mark Beeson and Richard Higgott, 'The Changing Architecture of Politics in the Asia-Pacific: Another (Lost) Middle Power Moment?' In KAIS-KF International Conference: The Role of Middle Power in the 21st Century International Relations, 19–20 April 2013, Lotte Hotel, Seoul, Korea, p. 9.

5 For debate on middle power status, see Eduard Jordaan, 2003, 'The Concept of a Middle Power in International Relations: Distinguishing between Emerging and Traditional Middle Powers', *Politikon: South African Journal of Political Studies*, vol. 30, no. 1, pp. 165–181.

6 Ralf Emmers, 'Indonesia's Role in ASEAN: A Case of Incomplete and Sectoral Leadership', *The Pacific Review*, vol. 27, no. 4, 2014, pp. 543–562.

rightly or wrongly, that regional organisations are increasingly a source of international legitimacy and location of leadership.

Since the 1990s Western states have put defence diplomacy into action to develop peacekeeping capabilities worldwide. In Southeast Asia this largely remains through bilateral arrangements between individual states and the United States, and multilateral emergent fora like the ASEAN Defence Ministers Meeting (ADMM). Prior to this investment in peacekeeping, there was a massive global increase in demand for peacekeepers since the 1980s with the UN, regional organisations and ad hoc coalitions undertaking the vast majority. There has also been a shift away from traditional interstate peacekeeping through ceasefire monitoring and towards more demanding peace enforcement and post-conflict situations involving a wide range of tasks from monitoring elections and human rights, disarming and demobilising combatants as well as social and economic reconstruction.[7] However, in contrast to Africa and Europe, regional organisations in the Asia-Pacific to date have not played a central role in peacekeeping. This role is largely seen as a threat to state sovereignty and governments in the region are apprehensive about Western agendas and there have been relatively fewer incentives to contribute forces.[8] However, while traditional sovereignty norms persist there has been a significant shift in thinking and practice of the regionalisation of peacekeeping illustrated through the development of the network of ASEAN peacekeeping centres for example. This chapter will proceed to evaluate recent regional developments to establish the current state of play, and then proceeds to investigate the emergent motivations and decision-making processes behind Malaysian and Indonesian contributions to UN peacekeeping.

Regional Developments

In Southeast Asia, there have been several developments at the national, regional, and regional-global levels for UN peace operations. The most notable developments are the establishment of logistical and training hubs in Indonesia and Malaysia illustrating their leadership roles in the region. While the regional network of peacekeeping centres is in its infancy, its coordination by Indonesia illustrates a move towards a closer working relationship between the established peacekeeping training centres in Indonesia, Malaysia,

7 Anthony Cottey and Anthony Foster, 'Enhancing Regional Peacekeeping Capabilities', *The Adelphi Papers*, vol. 44, no. 365, 2004, pp. 51–68.

8 Cottey and Foster, 'Enhancing Regional Peacekeeping Capabilities', p. 66.

Philippines and Thailand and the establishment of training programs with other ASEAN member states pushing ASEAN member states towards greater cooperation under Indonesian leadership. However, it is firstly important to recognise the nature of the ASEAN Political Security Community (APSC) as laid out in founding documents, the Bali Concord II and the APSC Blueprint amongst others to recognise the likely function and form of regional peace-keeper training and humanitarian logistical hubs in Southeast Asia.

The APSC as it stands does not address intra-state conflict but rather focuses on inter-state conflict. The current reference to the ASEAN norm of conflict prevention is meant to "mitigate tensions and prevent disputes arising between or among ASEAN member states and non-ASEAN member states."[9] With this in mind, the conducive environment towards establishing greater ASEAN involvement in peace operations at an institutional level remains stymied by the dominant traditional sovereignty norm of non-interference. Indeed the broader ASEAN Regional Forum illustrates this nature well. It was established in 1995 to develop a dialogue between participating states, promote confidence building measures (CBMs) and preventive diplomacy, share information and enhance transparency, and integrate isolated countries into the regional security system, and as such adopted a traditional form of peacekeeping, dependent on national militaries operating under the UN auspices and stipulates the principles of neutrality and non-use of force.[10] Essentially, the ARF was an attempt by ASEAN member states to transmit the organisation's norms, principles and an informal process of dialogue and consultation, but also a mode of conflict avoidance and management.[11] Indeed, informality and traditional sovereignty norms remain the default answer to regional interactions, but also highlights the dominant linear approach to regional interactions. However, there has been a noticeable shift in multilateral defence diplomacy in the region, which has evolved from a concentration on traditional sovereignty norms to a blurring of the distinction between traditional and non-traditional security issues such as peacekeeping contributions. Some argue that this blurring has provided a "building block" in the region for Southeast Asian states to move into

9 Rizal Sukma, 'The ASEAN Political and Security Community (APSC): Opportunities and Constraints for the R2P in Southeast Asia,' *The Pacific Review*, vol. 25, no. 1, 2012, p. 141.

10 Ralf Emmers, 'Regional Organisations and peacekeeping: a study of the ARF', in Lorraine Elliott and Graeme Cheeseman (eds.), *Forces for Good: Cosmopolitan Militaries in the 21st Century*, (Manchester, UK: Manchester University Press, 2004), pp. 135–136.

11 Ralf Emmers, 'Southeast Asia's New Security Institutions', in Vinod K. Aggarwal and Min Gyo Koo (eds.), *Asia's New Institutional Architecture: Evolving Structures for Managing Trade, Financial, and Security relations*, (Berlin, Heidelberg, Germany: Springer, 2008), p. 197.

the traditional security domain.[12] Whether or not the 'building block' argument holds true, it does offer an insight into regional discourse and provides a partial answer to the question of the motivation of states in the region to open up avenues of regional cooperation on peacekeeping. This chapter argues that there is an overwhelming need to refocus our understanding of the region and its contributions to peacekeeping and additionally focus on the interactions between the multiple regional and global levels, which oftentimes overlap or are the product of a negotiated compromise to a given situation.

In the ASEAN region it is more likely that a multi-level commitment will emerge to peace operations consisting of interactions bilaterally, multilaterally and different government agencies as well as with non-government actors. Indeed, the APSC Blueprint included the necessity of establishing an ASEAN arrangement for the maintenance of peace and stability through the establishment of a network of ASEAN peacekeeping centres in accordance with the ADMM Three-Year Work Programme as one such avenue. This again highlights the ASEAN level interaction with the UN as the utilisation of those trained peacekeepers in these centres would require a UN mandate. Ultimately, the development of a regional network of peacekeeping training centres is envisaged to coordinate with the United States and other global players to coordinate peacekeeping operations in the Asia-Pacific illustrating the multifaceted nature of interactions in the Asia-Pacific on peacekeeping.[13]

Further to the regional peacekeeping training centre network, a regional logistical hub was established in Malaysia to coordinate the supply of goods to complex humanitarian emergencies. While this overwhelmingly focuses on humanitarian responses to natural disasters in the region at present, the United Nations Humanitarian Response Depot (UNHRD) global network is a logistical hub for all humanitarian emergencies and identifies Malaysia as the key regional interlocutor in these affairs. As will be demonstrated later, there is a regional focus on utilising this hub on natural disaster response mechanisms. What is clear is that the Asia-Pacific region is a site of recent significant developments affecting UN peacekeeping, with Malaysia and Indonesia playing key roles in this development. It is therefore important to understand why these two countries have participated in this way as well as how these decisions were made. The following sections will address each country in turn to explain the

12 Evan A. Laksmana, 'Regional Order by Other Means? Examining the Rise of Defense Diplomacy in Southeast Asia', *Asian Security*, vol. 8, issue 3, 2012, p. 253.

13 BG Imam Edy Mulyono, 'Indonesia Viewpoints in Networking of Peacekeeping Centres', Presentation at INDF Peacekeeping Centre, 2009.

motivations behind their contributions to UN peace operations as well as the extent of their involvement.

Indonesia

Indonesia has a long history of contributing to UN peace operations, having contributed troops to the first UN Emergency Force (UNEF) which was established to oversee the removal of UK, French and Israeli troops from Sinai, Egypt mandated after the 1956 Suez Crisis. Indonesia's contribution was an Army battalion with 400 personnel including command group three gun companies, and one platoon with artillery mortar and machine gun assistance. These troops were part of the Infantry Regiment 15 of the Territorial Army IV/Diponegoro and Infantry Regiment 18 of the Territorial Army V/Brawijaya.[14] Indeed, the Indonesian constitution contains a commitment to peace and social justice and reference to this requirement in the preamble to its 1945 constitution is oftentimes sought to justify these contributions.[15] Likewise within Indonesia's constitution are the principles that underline its "free and active" foreign policy doctrine coined by Indonesian Vice-President Muhammad Hatta in 1948. The constitutional justifications are key signposts in the construction of Indonesian foreign policy more broadly as an emergent regional and global power, and as the largest ASEAN contributor to UN peace operations. As such, its contributions have played a significant part in its post-colonial identity as an independent state.[16] It is also important to consider its participation in UN peace operations as a developing state and one that has played an important role to varying degrees in international fora like the Non-Aligned Movement (NAM) and the Organisation of Islamic Conference (OIC). At present, Indonesia is participating as part of the International Monitoring Team in the Southern Philippines under the auspices of the OIC.

During the President Sukarno's period in office, Indonesia was vehemently independent as illustrated through its commitment at the 1955 Bandung Conference to the Non-Aligned Movement. Alongside this commitment, President Sukarno developed the *Pancasila* philosophy of social justice to

14 Yayan G. H. Mulyana, 'Peacekeeping Operations and Indonesian Foreign Policy', *The Jakarta Post* [Jakarta, Indonesia], 3 January 2012.

15 Susilo Bambang Yudhoyono, 'Indonesia's Role as Regional and Global Actor', Speech at The Wilton Park Annual Address, 2 November 2012, London, UK.

16 Jonathan Agensky and Joshua Barker, 'Indonesia and the Liberal Peace: Recovering Southern Agency in Global Governance', *Globalizations*, vol. 9, no. 1, 2012, p. 110.

build internal strength to project strength overseas. Indonesia's independently-minded foreign policy was further illustrated when President Sukarno withdrew Indonesia from the United Nations in 1965 in response to Malaysia taking a non-permanent seat on the UN Security Council, which it saw as a UK puppet. It also illustrated the personality-driven foreign policy-making process because after the military coup later that year, the new President Suharto re-engaged the United Nations. During his period in office, President Suharto pursued an internationalist foreign policy, seeing Indonesia contribute to multiple UN peacekeeping operations and becoming the key interlocutor with Vietnam after it invaded Cambodia. Through the facilitation of dialogue known as the Jakarta Informal Meetings, the ground was laid for the negotiations to oversee the resolution of conflict in Cambodia in 1992–1993 under the United Nations Transitional Authority in Cambodia (UNTAC).[17]

However, there were contradictions in Indonesia's policies at home and abroad. The 1962 Indonesia invasion of West New Guinea created the province of Papua in Indonesia on the one hand, which was in stark contrast to its participation in UN peace operations to alleviate suffering in the Democratic Republic of Congo in 1960 on the other. Indeed, the human rights issues in Papua that were present then, remain present today. While the Indonesian constitution has provided a framework in which its foreign policy has evolved, Indonesian foreign policy currently firmly relies on the personality of an individual president to determine their interpretation of the constitution and the direction Indonesian foreign policy takes.[18] As outlined in Indonesian law in 1999, "the deployment of troops or peacekeeping missions is appointed by the President in consultation with the Parliament."[19] Since 1999, there have been several laws governing the deployment of Indonesian peacekeepers and of particular note is Presidential Decree No 85/2011 which established the Coordinating Team for Peacekeeping Missions (TKMPP), which is a ministerial-level body responsible for coordinating Indonesia's Peacekeeping activities.[20] In 2008, President Yudhoyono issued a presidential decree on international cooperation so that Indonesia would "for the purpose of actively participating in the

17 Yayan G. H. Mulyana, 'Peacekeeping Operations and Indonesian Foreign Policy'.

18 Dewi Fortuna Anwar, 'A Journey of Change: Indonesia's Foreign Policy', *Global Asia*, vol. 4, no. 3, fall 2009.

19 Indonesian Law no. 37/1999 on Foreign Policy, Article 10.

20 Bambang Kismono Hadi and Machmud Syafrudin, Pasukan Penjaga Perdamaiandan Reformasi Sektor Keamanan (Jakarta: IDSPS, DCAF, 2009) http://www.dcaf.ch/Publications/Pasukan-Penjaga-Perdamaian-dan-Reformasi-Sektor-Keamanan [last accessed, 17 March 2014].

attainment of world peace, peacekeeping missions are *deployed only by the request and mandate of the United Nations* [emphasis added]."[21] Internally the engagement with the UN and Indonesia's overall peacekeeping role is 'directed' by the Indonesian president, and assisted by the foreign affairs and defence ministers, TNI Commander-in-chief, assistant for personnel and the Ministry of Defence, which provides the necessary assessments and feasibility requirements. This decision-making process is constructed with a 3–5 years' timeframe.[22] Increasingly, as more police are involved in peacekeeping, the role of the Indonesian Chief of National Police is increasingly part of the Peacekeeping-related decision-making process. Indeed, the establishment of the TKMPP seeks to streamline the peacekeeping decision-making process.[23]

While the ways in which Indonesia projects itself globally under different presidents is important, domestic politics is also a necessary condition to consider in assessing the motivations behind a president's decision to contribute or not to particular UN peace operations. Since the downfall of President Suharto, Islamic mobilisation has influenced key government decisions in relation to UN peace operation contributions. Most notably, Indonesia's decision to participate in Bosnia was significantly influenced by public opinion, which has become a key consideration for the government. Indeed, Indonesian civil society groups have also pushed for Indonesia to mediate in the Southern Thailand conflict;[24] a task that is currently held by Malaysia. The influence of public opinion has been seen most prominently since the beginning of the *Reformasi* period after the fall of President Suharto in May 1998 as presidents seek to win the approval of their constituents. As a result of Indonesia's decision to participate in Bosnia, Susilo Bambang Yudhoyono became Indonesia's chief military observer to the United Nations Peacekeeping Force in Bosnia 1995–6, subsequently making him the only current Head of State to have done so. This position with the United Nations peace operations provided personal experience and is one of many influences on President Yudhoyono's commitments to UN peace operations.

As one of the top 20 countries worldwide in providing peacekeepers, Indonesia announced its commitment to doubling its peacekeeping contributions from 2000 to 4000 troops under President Yudhoyono. The greatest

---

21 Presidential Decress no.7/2008 on General Policy of State Defense Point 12 on the Policy on International Cooperation.

22 Correspondence with an Indonesian defence and security scholars, May 2014.

23 Correspondence with an Indonesian official, August 2014.

24 Lina Alexander, 'Indonesia and the Responsibility to Protect', *The Pacific Review*, vol. 25, no. 1, 2012, p. 67.

challenge to achieving this increase in peacekeepers is related to budget planning.[25] Indonesia collaborates with the Global Peace Operations Initiative (GPOI) under the US State Department to develop its Peacekeeping Training Centre at Sentul, Indonesia. The GPOI is a program to build the capacity of US partners like Indonesia "to train and sustain peacekeeping proficiencies; increase the number of capable military troops and formed police units (FPUs), and facilitate the preparation, logistical support and deployments of military units and FPUs."[26] In April 2014 President Yudhoyono inaugurated seven new facilities at the Indonesia Peace and Security Centre, the largest UN peacekeeping training centre in Southeast Asia expected to be fully operational by the end of 2014. The new facilities include the Counterterrorism Training Ground, the Humanitarian and Disaster Relief Training Centre, the Standby Force Centre, the Defence University and the Military Sports Centre.[27] The GPOI assistance contributed to the construction of the military barracks and Australia established the language centre.[28] The Centre will be mainly operated by the Indonesian Military (TNI), the National Police, National Counterterrorism Agency (BNPT) as well as other agencies.

Indonesia's promotion of itself as a regional champion of democracy and human rights has become prominent in international fora since the resignation of President Suharto in 1998 and the subsequent *Reformasi* period. Its "free and active" foreign policy culminated in the establishment of the Bali Democracy Forum in 2008 to promote and strengthen democracy and the rule of law in Asia through a process of learning and sharing. Indeed, in 2011, Indonesia began its term as ASEAN Chair and continued to pursue its "free and active" foreign policy. As ASEAN Chair Indonesia made several attempts to bolster regional mechanisms with mixed results. The most notable example was Indonesian Foreign Minister Marty Natalegawa's effort to initiate dialogue and mediate with both Phnom Penh and Bangkok after skirmishes broke out between Cambodian and Thai militaries over their border dispute on 4–7 February 2011. However, this shuttle diplomacy effort did not meet expectations as by the time Thailand agreed to Indonesian monitors on behalf of

25 Correspondence with an Indonesian official, August 2014.

26 US State Department, 'Global Peace Operations Initiative (GPOI) Program Overview', available at www.state.gov/t/pm/ppa/gpoi/.

27 Bagus BT Saragih, 'SBY to Inaugurate Sentul Security Center Facilities', *The Jakarta Post* [Jakarta, Indonesia], 7 April 2014, www.thejakartapost.com/news/2014/04/07/sby-inaugurate-sentul-security-center-facilities.html.

28 Yuliasri Perdani, 'SE Asia's Biggest Peacekeeping, Anti-terror Training Camp Opens', *The Jakarta Post* [Jakarta, Indonesia], 8 April 2014. www.thejakartapost.com/news/2014/04/08/se-asia-s-biggest-peacekeeping-antiterror-training-camp-opens.html.

ASEAN to the border area, tensions had subsided as a result of bilateral negotiations.[29]

At the time, the position of ASEAN in this was bolstered by a UN Security Council judgment and seemed to be a prime example of the regional-global mechanism contained in Chapter VIII of the UN Charter,[30] with Indonesia being its greatest proponent. The idea of an "ASEAN peacekeeping force" was first floated by Indonesian Foreign Minister Hassan Wirajuda in his UN-ASEAN conference speech but it did not gain the necessary support from other ASEAN member states, and was publically rejected by Singapore and Vietnam at the March 2004 ASEAN Senior Officials Meeting.[31] Indeed, some officials say "it was an idea ahead of its time."[32] Further Indonesian efforts at bolstering the global-regional partnership included pursing the development of a network of peacekeeping centres, and pushing human rights up the ASEAN agenda. A recent example of Indonesian leadership on peacekeeping training centres in the region was the 2nd Meeting of ASEAN Peacekeeping Centres Network (ACPN), which was co-hosted by the Indonesian National Defence Forces Peacekeeping Center (PMPP TNI), Indonesia's Ministry of Defence and the Thai armed forces in Bogor, Indonesia, in September 2013.

Alongside its regional leadership role, Indonesia contributes to UN peace operations worldwide. The Indonesian national armed forces or *Tentara Nasional Indonesia* (TNI) peacekeeping unit is known as Garuda Contingent, and currently numbers 2000 troops, which serve in Lebanon, Haiti, Darfur, Liberia, South Sudan and the Democratic Republic of Congo as part of UN peacekeeping operations. Its largest current troop contribution is to the United Nations Interim Force in Lebanon (UNIFIL) where Indonesia has 1248 troops on the ground. In 2012, President Yudhuyono announced Indonesia's intention to build up a 4,000 strong peacekeeping force to contribute to UN peacekeeping operations becoming a top ten contributing country. It is through its training centre that the development of this force will be achieved as part of the larger Peace and Security Centre in Sentul, Bogor. As part of operational training, the Garuda Contingent hosts the Garuda Shield, a regularly-scheduled bilateral exercise sponsored by

29 Trevor Moss, 'ASEAN's Slow Security Evolution', *Jane's Defense Weekly*, vol. 49, no. 12, 2012.

30 Holly Haywood, 'Examining ASEAN Capacity in the Context of the Thai-Cambodian Border Dispute', NTS Alert, September (issue 1), 2011, (Singapore: RSIS Centre for Non-Traditional Security (NTS) Studies for NTS-Asia).

31 Donald Weatherbee, 'Indonesian Foreign Policy: A Wounded Phoenix', *Southeast Asian Affairs*, vol. 2005, p. 161–162.

32 Correspondence with an Indonesian official, August 2014.

the US Army-Pacific Command. In 2013, the bilateral exercise took place around Cilodong, Depok, Indonesia to strengthen military-to-military cooperation through focusing on international peace support operations. It included around 200 American and 300 Indonesian paratroopers in a joint exercise in field training, performing fundamental infantry skills and airborne operations.[33]

Indonesia's expenditure on its armed forces has historically been low with 0.7% of GDP spent in 2011.[34] It is also the lowest among ASEAN member states that average over 2% of GDP spent on their militaries.[35] In terms of comparison Malaysia spent 13.8% of the overall spending of ASEAN, while it accounted for 16.4% of overall spending despite its significantly larger population size.[36] In terms of TNI force structure, the TNI army was historically and remains the most significant branch, far more so than the navy or air force. However, under President Yudhoyono this changed both in terms of budget and distribution. That said, the contribution of the TNI navy was significant as it includes only four modern corvettes overall and one of these has been part of the UN Interim Force in Lebanon in the Eastern Mediterranean since 2009.[37] In 2010, President Yudhoyono issued a presidential decree to push the TNI towards a "Minimum Essential Force" and increased the military budget from US$5.42 billion in 2011 to US$7.53 billion in 2012 and to US$8.12 billion in 2013.[38] Furthermore, President Yudhoyono's commitment to raise peacekeeper numbers, establish the region's largest training centre was further illustrated when the UN Secretary-General Ban requested assistance in the Congo.

In response, President Yudhoyono ordered the armed forces commander and chief of army staff to prepare three transport helicopters for Congo.[39] Ultimately, Indonesian commitment to send peacekeepers to United Nations peace operations has five motivations. The first is for the continued professionalization of the TNI through experience and training as part of a UN mission;

---

33 Raymond Drumsta, 'Peacekeeping Operations Center Ribbon Cutting', *US Army* [Sentul, Indonesia], 11 June 2013. www.army.mil/article/105262/Peacekeeping_Operations_Center_Ribbon_Cutting/.

34 Fuadi Pitsuwan, 'Smart Power Strategy: Recalibrating Indonesian Foreign Policy', *Asian Politics & Policy*, vol. 6, no. 2, 2014, p. 247.

35 Stokholm International Peace Research Institute, *SIPRI Database on Military Expenditure*, 2014 available at www.sipri.org/research/armaments/milex/milex_database.

36 Pitsuwan, 'Smart Power Strategy', p. 247.

37 Pitsuwan, 'Smart Power Strategy', p. 248.

38 Pitsuwan, 'Smart Power Strategy', p. 248.

39 'Indonesia to Send 4000 Troops, Helicopters to UN Peacekeeping Missions', *The Jakarta Globe* [Jakarta, Indonesia], 20 March 2012.

the second is United Nations impartiality which is in step with its 'free and active' foreign policy; thirdly that the UN pays US$1,028 per month for each deployed peacekeeper needs to be considered;[40] fourthly the Presidential leadership shown by President Yudhoyono to contribute and actively participate in peace operations and nurturing Indonesia's position as a regional and global leader. Lastly, Indonesia produces weapons and Armoured Personnel Carriers (APCs). While these products are not as advanced as those produced in the West, deployment in peacekeeping operations gives Indonesia a chance to use and market these Indonesian goods. For example, Indonesian Formed Police Units used Indonesian-made APCs and weapons in the United Nations Mission in Darfur (UNAMID).[41]

Malaysia

Since independence in 1957, Malaysia continued with a parliamentary system based on the Westminster model. As a result, foreign policy is determined by the Prime Minister and his cabinet thus the participation in and size of UN peace operations contributions will be formally made in this way. Malaysian foreign policy making under its first post-independence Prime Minister Tunku Abdul Rahman (who was concurrently Foreign Minister), was limited to a close-knit group around the Prime Minister including three or four other ministers and the foreign office permanent secretary. Cabinet meetings were ultimately mere formalities while suggestions and questions were oftentimes informally pursued outside this setting. The influence of the foreign ministry and its permanent secretary in particular was significant as Prime Minister Tunku Abdul Rahman had limited foreign policy knowledge.[42] Subsequently under Prime Minister Abdul Razak Hussein, the process of foreign policy making remained largely unchanged with a similar sized elite dominating decision-making, which largely reflects the decision-making process today. However, Prime Minister Abdul Razak Hussein differed from his predecessor in that he had greater interest in broad foreign affairs strategy with a greater focus on regional and developing world affairs rather than a few pet projects.[43] Ultimately though, foreign policy making

40 Natalie Sambhi, 'Indonesia's Push for Peacekeeping Operations', *The Strategist* [APSI: Canberra, Australia], 17 September 2013.

41 Correspondence with an Indonesian official, August 2014.

42 Marvin C. Ott, 'Foreign Policy Formulation in Malaysia', *Asian Survey*, vol. 12, no. 3, 1972, p. 227.

43 Ott, 'Foreign Policy Formulation in Malaysia', p. 237–8.

remains an elite dominated process where personal rather than institutional relationships matter more.[44]

In the early years, Malaysia (at the time Malaya) did not have the institutional bases of prestige, so it depended on its foreign policy to boost its status in the world community. This was notably seen through its contribution to the United Nations Operation in the Congo (ONUC), established in July 1960 until June 1964.[45] Malaysia was also a strong supporter the United Nations more generally, which its leaders saw as a key security guarantee for a weak and insecure developing nation-state. Kuala Lumpur saw its participation in the UN Emergency Force in the Congolese civil war as a means to contain communist expansionism in Africa.[46] Indeed, Malaysia's most significant contribution to the United Nations was its first to ONUC where it contributed 1,413 troops at its peak.[47] Throughout the Mahathir years (1981–2003), Malaysian foreign policy underwent some significant shifts which saw it transform from a focus on military and defence to national economic development. Malaysian foreign policy further shifted towards greater engagement with developing world partners, increased regional engagement, Islamic posturing and commercial and developmental diplomacy.[48]

It was under the present Prime Minister, Najib Razak, who was then defence minister that Malaysia's contribution to the Bosnia mission was confirmed and set the precedence of avenue for future UN contributions under his leadership.[49] Malaysia's high profile policies towards Bosnia, its championing of global Muslim and developing world causes and its strong support and contribution for UN peace operations have arguably demonstrated its cool calculations as an aspirant regional and middle power under Prime Minister Mahatir Mohammad's reforms and vision for Malaysia to be a developed state by 2020.[50] Furthermore in this period, the Malaysian Peacekeeping Training Centre (MPTC) was established on 9 June 1995 following the formal cabinet agreement

44 Ott, 'Foreign Policy Formulation in Malaysia', p. 239.

45 Jayaratnam Saravanamuttu, *Malaysia's Foreign Policy: The first fifty years: Alignment, Neutralism, Islamism* (Singapore: ISEAS), 2010, p. 78.

46 Hari Singh, 'Malaysia and the Cold War', *Diplomacy & Statecraft*, vol. 6, no. 2, p. 514.

47 Saravanamuttu, *Malaysia's Foreign Policy: The First Fifty Years: Alignment, Neutralism, Islamism*, p. 61.

48 Karminder Singh Dhillon, *Malaysian foreign policy in the Mahathir era (1981–2003): dilemmas of development*, (NUS Press, Singapore), 2009.

49 Shanker Raj Ayanger, 'Dato Sri Najib Tun Razak – The Beginning of A New Era', *Malaysia Edition*, 18 March 2013 available at www.malaysiaedition.net/dato-sri-najib-tun-razak-the-beginning-of-a-new-era-part-1/.

50 Johan Sravanamuttu, 'ASEAN in Malaysian Foreign Policy Discourse and Practice, 1967–1997', *Asian Journal of Political Science*, vol. 5, no. 1, p. 49.

of Serial 4/1995, an illustration that the decision-making process regarding peacekeeping is found in the Malaysian executive at the formal cabinet level. However, the power accruing to Malaysia's Prime Ministers has been great. They have controlled the ruling party United Malays National Organisation (UMNO), the governing coalition, *Basiran Nasional* but also indirectly at the state level as well.[51] However, collective cabinet government is formally in place and under Serial 4/1995 placed the MPTC as a tri-service organisation under the training branch of the defence operation and training division of the Malaysian armed forces headquarters. The MPTC commenced the first UN military observer force on 15 January 1996 with 28 students. Malaysia also participated in the US State Department's Enhanced International Peacekeeping Capabilities (EIPC)[52] program, which was established in 1998 to support classroom and "train-the-trainer" instruction for partner militaries across the globe.

However, alongside these concrete steps as part of its strategy to become a middle or regional power, the personality traits of the outspoken Prime Minister Mahatir Mohammed played out when he blamed the west for coercing Indonesian President B. J. Habibie into approving the referendum on self-determination in East Timor in 1999 during a difficult reform and transition period. He also highlighted the West's selective approach to international human rights. However, Malaysia subsequently contributed 30 personnel (mainly interpreters) to the International Force for East Timor (INTERFET) – the smallest ASEAN member state contribution – when Indonesia invited the UN peace operation into its territory so long as there was a significant contribution from ASEAN member states. While Malaysia blamed Australia and the West, it offered a Malaysian to be the UN Transitional Administration in East Timor (UNTAET) Force Commander and contributed troops illustrating Prime Minister Mahatir Mohammed's long-standing support for and Malaysia's experience with UN peace operations.[53] However, when the post was earmarked for Thailand, Malaysia scaled down its INTERFET contribution illustrating a loss of prestige for Malaysia.[54]

Malaysia is acutely aware of the limitations to its involvement in peace operations particularly around longer term developmental issues. During the Mindanao negotiations, Malaysia jealously guarded the doors to the

51 Andrew Harding, *The Constitution of Malaysia: Contextual Analysis*, Oxford: Hart Publishing, 2012, pp. 57–58.

52 These functions are now subsumed under GPOI.

53 Alan Dupont, 'ASEAN's Response to the East Timor Crisis', *Australian Journal of International Affairs*, vol. 54, no. 2, 2000, p. 168.

54 Ian Martin and Alexander Mayer-Reickh, 'The United Nations and East Timor: from Self-Determination to State-Building', *International Peacekeeping*, vol. 12, no. 1, 2005, p. 132.

negotiations room from external involvement knowing the prestige involved in successful resolution. This was particularly the case as the mediation exercise fulfilled both its self-promotion as an influential ASEAN member state and as a leader in the OIC because of the religious dynamic to the negotiations. However, Malaysia encouraged Japanese financial involvement as this worked in both countries' interest. While Malaysia gained the kudos of successful mediation, Japan was able to fund longer term development at a distance – covering both short term and long term concerns.[55] Indeed, Malaysian Prime Minister Mahatir Mohamad argued that Japan need not be so restrictive with its self-defence force mandate limited to internal issues only. He proposed while it should not attack others, it should be prepared to contribute to UN peace-keeping operations.[56] However, that does not mean that Malaysian mediation in Mindanao has been uncontroversial. The Filipino popular press perceived Malaysia's presence as bias and in particular the involvement of chief Malaysian negotiator Osman but the press reports did not provide specific case evidence.[57] Malaysia's role in Mindanao ultimately illustrates both its ASEAN connection and OIC leadership role, and its role as a middle or regional power[58] but also as one that is reliable over the long-term as its mediation effort has spanned multiple Prime Ministers.

A further illustration of the Malaysian commitment to UN peace operations was the expansion and investment in the Malaysian Peace Training Centre. On 27 February 2006, MPTC moved to new premises and was opened by the then Deputy Prime Minister and Defence Minister of Malaysia, Najib Razak, at a cost of RM22 Million (approximately US$6.7m). In December 2012, three years into Prime Minister Najib Razak's first term the MPTC was renamed the *Pusat Pengaman Malaysia* (Malaysian Peacekeeping Centre (MPC)) and was expanded to include additional straining staff from international armed forces, police and other NGOs as well as a medical cell. By December 2012, the MPC had trained 2114 military officers, 17 police and 28 civilians from 51 countries worldwide.[59] Most reasons for participating in peacekeeping are focused more

55 Peng ER Lam, 'Japan's Peace-Building in Mindanao: Partnering Malaysia, the Philippines and the Moro Islamic Liberation Front', *Japanese Studies*, vol. 28, no. 1, 2008, p. 54.

56 Mahatir Mohamad, *Reflections on Asia*, Malaysia: Millennium Books, 2000, p. 38.

57 Joseph Raymond Silva Franco, 'Malaysia: Unsung Hero of the Philippine Peace Process', *Asian Security*, vol. 9, no. 3, p. 223–4.

58 Saravanamuttu, *Malaysia's Foreign Policy: The First Fifty Years: Alignment, Neutralism, Islamism*, p. 279.

59 Malaysian Peacekeeping Centre, *Background Overview*, Port Dickson, Malaysia available at mafhq.mil.my/mpc/index.php/en/component/content/article/23-about-us/60-back ground.

on the supply of soldiers, which are not needed at home rather than the demand for security; in other words, where they are needed. Peacekeeping therefore is like "being at the Olympics" where participating is more important than winning.[60] However, the financial benefits of contributing peacekeepers cannot be overlooked. Some argue that Malaysia indeed often sends many peacekeepers "because the flat payment per soldier from the United Nations exceeds what the government pays their soldiers, so that supplying peacekeeping troops can be a source of foreign exchange earnings".[61] However, the dominant motivations remain Malaysia's active foreign policy to promote itself as a regional or middle power and its reliance on the UN as a security guarantor for state stability.

In this latter vein, Prime Minister Najib Razak in May 2011 stated that Malaysia was ready and willing to send troops to assist Saudi Arabia and the Gulf Cooperation Council (GCC) to stabilise Bahrain after protests broke out, which had stemmed from other parts of the Middle East during the Arab Uprising. The statement was designed for the Arab world to know that Malaysia would support the GCC if invited to do so by the Bahraini leadership. Historically, Malaysia had not sent peacekeeping troops to help quell civil unrest in another country. The decision was therefore unprecedented and appeared designed to win favour from the GCC, especially Saudi Arabia, than supporting international intervention. It was also the first public indication that the Malaysian leadership was uneasy about the implications of the Arab Uprising on Malaysia.[62] Ultimately, like Indonesia, Malaysian commitment to send peacekeepers to United Nations peace operations has four motivations. The first is for the continued professionalization of the Malaysian armed forces through experience and training as part of a UN mission; the second is United Nations impartiality and security guarantor for smaller states albeit an aspiring middle power; thirdly that the UN pays US$1,028 per month for each deployed peacekeeper needs to be considered;[63] and fourthly the influence of personality politics and leadership shown by the succession of prime ministers to

60 Alrik van den Berg, 'Effective Peacekeeping and the Privatisation of Security', in Thomas Jager and Gerhard Kummel (eds.), *Private Military and Security Companies: Chances, Problem, Pitfalls and Prospects* (Wiesbaden, Germany: Springer VS Verlag für Sozialwissenschaften, 2007), p. 300.

61 Alrik van den Berg, 'Effective Peacekeeping and the Privatisation of Security', p. 299.

62 Yang Razali Kassim, *The Geopolitics of Intervention*, Singapore: Springer, 2014, pp. 57–58.

63 Natalie Sambhi, 'Indonesia's Push for Peacekeeping Operations', *The Strategist* [APSI: Canberra, Australia], 17 September 2013.

contribute and actively participate in peace operations to nurture Malaysia's position as a regional and global leader.

Conclusion

This chapter has illustrated the multifaceted nature of Indonesian and Malaysian contributions to United Nations peace operations since 1948. It has further illustrated that beyond official United Nations mandated peacekeeping forces both countries pursue a proactive foreign policy towards conflict mediation and resolution – key attributes of a middle or regional power status. Indeed, there are dominant trends which are found in both countries approaches to UN peacekeeping. In both cases the dominance of personality politics remains consistent across time in foreign policy making even though Indonesia is a presidential and Malaysia a parliamentary system. At the global level, Indonesian President Yudhoyono has committed to increasing the number of peacekeepers Indonesia contributes to 4000 troops by 2016. Indonesia will consolidate its and its partners' investment in its capacity to train peacekeepers illustrating a push to be recognised as a reliable and significant partner in the United Nations. This contrasts to Malaysia whose most significant contribution to a UN peacekeeping operation was its first in the Congo in the 1960s during the time when it wanted to reaffirm the UN role as security guarantor of its independence.

However, while the Malaysian commitment to UN peacekeeping in troop contribution terms appears to have waned, if a multifocal lens is used then the Malaysian commitment more broadly comes into view. Through this lens it becomes clear that thus far, third party mediation in regional internal conflicts has been led by Malaysia rather than Indonesia. Malaysia has been the lead facilitator between the Moro Islamic Liberation Front and the government of the Philippines. Malaysia has also facilitated negotiations between the Thai government and separatists in Southern Thailand. Both of these facilitation exercises have been at the request of the government involved namely the Philippines and Thailand. It is noteworthy that both these mediation efforts have been as a result of Malaysia's position as a Muslim-majority country mediating with Muslim minorities in neighbouring countries. In the case of Indonesia, efforts at regional mediation in the case of border clashes between Cambodia and Thailand, even with UN backing, ultimately failed. In this instance of regional leadership, Malaysia has been largely more successful in leading mediation efforts than Indonesia. What remains clear in its strategy to promote itself as a regional or middle power is that Malaysia continues to compete with Indonesia across multiple fora. This is indeed consistent with middle power status where states utilise their active foreign policy to promote themselves within the international system.

While Indonesia remains the functional point in the global-regional (UN-ASEAN) linkage for training peacekeepers, Malaysia has become the logistical hub to supply complex humanitarian emergencies through the UN Humanitarian Response Depot based in Subang, Malaysia, since its completion in March 2012. Both these positions demonstrate their regional leadership positions. With each component being a key ingredient to any peacekeeping operation, the roles of Malaysia and Indonesia in practice complement one another. This is best illustrated in April 2014, when professionals from the National Disaster Management Offices of Cambodia, Indonesia, Malaysia, Myanmar, Thailand and Vietnam took part in humanitarian logistics training in Jakarta, Indonesia, and UNHRD's depot in Subang, Malaysia. This training formed part of the AHA Centre Executive (ACE) Programme for ASEAN member states and included operational exercises such as loading ASEAN stock items into a military aircraft (C-130) at the Subang Air Base, and a visit to Port Klang to see how relief items are received at the port and dispatched via the Subang International Airport.[64] What has essentially emerged between Malaysian and Indonesian contributions to peace operations is a level of healthy competition between the two determined by the personality of their leaders, but where each state is able to carve out its contribution within a cooperative framework.

In this vein, Malaysia outlined some of the current challenges to peacekeeping at a recent UN debate and identified where it saw its emerging contribution. First, Malaysia identified the use of technology to 'increase situational awareness of peacekeepers.' Essentially, it was highlighted that there is a need to better implement peacekeeping mandates, and it was suggested the inclusion of Unmanned Aerial Vehicles (UAVs) such as 'drones' to identify groups and track their movements, as well as other technologies to enhance monitoring and surveillance peacekeeping operations.[65] However, there is caution from both Indonesia and Malaysia over their process of information gathering, as well as the need for a transparent debate over the implications and

64 UNHRD, 'Preparing the Future Leaders of Disaster Management in ASEAN', 23 April 2014 available at www.unhrd.org/index.php?s=subang.

65 Raja Reza Raja Zaib Shah, Statement at the General Debate of the 2014 Substantive Session of the Special Committee on Peacekeeping Operations, United Nations Headquarters, New York, Tuesday 25 February, 2014.

evaluation of their use.[66] Through the use of technology, Malaysia sees more effective peacekeeping, but also highlighted the need for better training for peacekeepers prior to deployment to include a substantial element on religion and cultural sensitivities of the local population as seen in the 2013 Protection of Civilians course at the Malaysian Peacekeeping Centre.[67] With an increase in availability and funding for training peacekeepers it will serve to maintain high quality personnel in its peacekeeping pool, and also ensure geographical balance on the representation of personnel and troop contributions.[68] Indeed, Malaysia sees this sensitivity training as one of its niche areas because of its long history in UN peacekeeping and its experience in successfully "winning the hearts and minds of the locals that would eventually lead to a conducive environment for socio-economic development."[69] Furthermore, Malaysia identified arrears by individual countries for peacekeeping as well as a budget in excess of $8 billion for the Department of Field Support as significant hurdles to successful implementation of peacekeeping operations.[70]

Indonesia has further added that while there has been a necessary shift from "traditional" to "non-traditional" peacekeeping, there are attendant challenges in addition to budgetary constraints and non-payment of dues. This includes the clear need to recognise the limitations to peacekeeping operations and that while there is an increase in multidimensionality, peacekeeping is primarily done by the military. By requiring the military to carry out additional tasks like public sector financial management or conducting elections can be too heavy a burden and ultimately undermine the UN's local credibility. Therefore there is a need to build local and civilian partnerships to fulfil the

---

66 Desra Percaya, Statement at the General Debate of the 2014 Substantive Session of the Special Committee on Peacekeeping Operations, United Nations Headquarters, New York, Monday 24 February, 2014.

67 Raja Reza Raja Zaib Shah, Statement at the General Debate of the 2014 Substantive Session of the Special Committee on Peacekeeping Operations, United Nations Headquarters, New York, Tuesday 25 February, 2014.

68 Lee Chee Leong, Statement on Agenda Item 31: Comprehensive Review of the Whole Question of Peacekeeping Operations in All Its Aspects, at the Fourth Committee of the 63rd Session of the United Nations General Assembly, New York, 28th October 2008.

69 Hussein Haniff, Statement to the United Nations on Agenda Item 53: Comprehensive Review of the Whole Question of Peacekeeping Operations in all its aspect at the Fourth Committee of the 68th Session of the United Nations General Assembly, New York, 30 October 2013.

70 Ng Chin Huat, Statement on Agenda item 33: Comprehensive Review of the Whole Question of Peacekeeping Operations in all its Aspect, at the Fourth Committee of the 64th Session of the United Nations General Assembly, New York, 28th October 2009.

appropriate tasks by those with the specialist knowledge such as the regional organisations, BWIs (Bretton Woods Institutions), and the private sector to ease the pressure on military peacekeepers to focus on their core tasks.[71] Indonesia sees the shift from military to civilian sectors as drawing on the principle of comparative advantage of the different stakeholders in the peacekeeping-peace-building nexus. Indonesia thus sees a multidimensional or comprehensive approach that re-emphasises the civilian dynamic to peace operations and at the same time recognises the importance of the military to be the "first responders" to conflict and instability under a United Nations mandate.[72] What emerges from this comparison between the Indonesian and Malaysian contributions to peace operations is they illustrate a similar cautionary approach to mandate creep through the use of UAVs, the need for stronger pre-deployment training to maintain a global balance of professional contributions, their comparative advantages in this, and a commitment to strengthening the valuable work of United Nations peace operations. Ultimately, the assessment of Indonesia and Malaysia demonstrates the broader trends of how middle or regional powers activate their foreign policy to promote themselves within the international system.

71 Adiyatwidi Adiwoso Asmady, Statement on Agenda Item 34: Comprehensive Review of the whole question of Peacekeeping Operations in all their Aspects at the General Debate of Fourth Committee of the 63rd Session of the United Nations General Assembly, New York, 2 November 2007.

72 Desra Percaya, Statement at open debate of the Security Council: United Nations Peacekeeping: a multidimensional approach, New York, 21 January 2013.

CHAPTER 4

South Asian Regionalism and UN Peacekeeping Missions: A Case of 'and Never the Twain Shall Meet'?

Rashed Uz Zaman and Niloy Ranjan Biswas

Introduction

The title of the chapter contains a line from Rudyard Kipling's famous poem *The Ballad of East and West* which depicts two protagonists and identifies the gap that separates them. Most of us may perceive that South Asian regionalism and the United Nations (UN) peacekeeping are like the two protagonists as depicted by Kipling and destined never to meet.[1] In this chapter, we contradict any such view and argue why South Asian regionalism and UN peacekeeping complements each other.

South Asia as a region is the largest contributor of troops and police to United Nations peacekeeping operations (UNPKO). Nearly 34% of the total troops deployed in UN missions worldwide come from four South Asian countries namely, Bangladesh, India, Nepal and Pakistan.[2] Bangladesh, India and Pakistan are also interchangeably the largest single country contributors to UN missions over the past few years. However, despite the pivotal role played by South Asian countries in sustaining UNPKO globally, there has been little or no coordination among them on this issue. Also, there is a lack of substantial academic discussion in exploring challenges and opportunities for a South Asian regional approach to peacekeeping missions.

This chapter investigates the challenges of participation in UN missions for South Asia as a region. The dominant narrative postulates that structural causes inherent within the historical development of political relations among the countries in the region influence their approach to peacekeeping missions. It is the confrontational nature of politics between South Asian countries, which explains the unilateralism practiced by them with regard to peace missions. The chapter asks: what are the inconsistencies inherent within South

1 To read Rudyard Kipling's *The Ballad of East and West*, visit http://www.kiplingsociety.co.uk/poems_eastwest.htm (accessed 23 February 2014).

2 Philip Cunliffe, *Legions of Peace: UN Peacekeepers from the Global South* (London: C. Hurst & Co., 2013), pp. 9–10.

 | DOI 10.1163/9789004322059_005

Asian trend of regionalism and the UN peacekeeping discourse which hinder the participation of South Asia as a regional organization in such missions? In answering this question, the chapter briefly touches upon the context—why and how South Asian countries address the challenges of current missions. Also, it discusses the challenges emanating from regional political realities. Further, the chapter also examines how regionalism faces challenges within the practices of globalism in the UN.

The chapter is divided into several sections. In the first section, we discuss the relationship between UN and regionalism. This is done with a view to provide an understanding of the challenges and advantages UN faces while dealing with regional organizations on issues related to international security. An attempt is made in the second section to understand the state of regionalism in South Asia. It looks at the rationales behind the birth of South Asian Association for Regional Cooperation (SAARC) and attempts to see how the organization has fared since inception. South Asian countries have, in recent years, emerged as important players in terms of contributing peacekeepers and this section also sees a discussion on the contribution of the region to UN peacekeeping missions. Peacekeeping is an extremely challenging task and peacekeeping countries need to prepare themselves accordingly to meet such challenges. The third section of the chapter looks at the future trends in international peacekeeping and asks what such changes may mean for South Asian troop-contributing countries. The chapter concludes by pointing out the need for a new approach to peacekeeping by South Asian countries.

I United Nations Peacekeeping: Globalism vis-à-vis Regionalism

Since the end of the World War I there has been a general, though not unimpeded, trend towards greater multilateral involvement in the maintenance of international peace and security. The League of Nations was created with the objective of preventing a repetition of the events leading to World War I. However, the failure of League of Nations and the horrors of World War II convinced world leaders that an international organization dealing with peace and security was more necessary than ever.[3] The UN was established to fill this lacuna and consequently, various regional organizations followed in its wake. The security challenges that emerged since the end of the Cold War have

3 Alex J. Bellamy and Paul D. Williams, *Understanding Peacekeeping* (Cambridge, UK: Polity Press, 2nd edition, 2011), pp. 76–81.

further accelerated the trend through the creation of an environment where regional organizations can play a bigger role in peace operations. Such developments have led to an intensification of debate both in the UN and the scholarly literature about the role of regional organizations in the maintenance of international peace and security. This principle of regional organizations playing a prominent role – often identified as the application of the principle of 'subsidiarity'[4] has gained popularity especially as regional organizations are increasingly asked to step in and perform crucial peacekeeping operations. However, the concept has not been without controversy and the pros and cons of the debate are discussed below.

The UN Charter poses critical insights on the positions of 'regional arrangements' in international peace discourse. Gustaf Lind asserts that the contemporary provisions of the Charter only allow the regional organizations to get involved with its own member states and prohibits any involvement beyond these.[5] Chapter VIII of the UN Charter thus stipulates in Article 53.1 that "The Security Council shall, where appropriate, utilize such regional arrangements or agencies for enforcement action under its authority". Article 52.2 states that "The Members of the United Nations (...) shall make every effort to achieve pacific settlement of local disputes through such regional arrangements or by such regional agencies before referring them to the Security Council." Such reading of the UN Charter tends to represent regional organizations as first resort on issues of peaceful resolutions of international conflicts. However, it must also be noted that the UN Charter underlines that different rules apply to the use of non-peaceful means when it states in Article 53.1 that "No enforcement action shall be taken under regional arrangements or regional agencies without the authorization of the Security Council".[6] The ambiguity surrounding regional organizations is further deepened when it comes to defining such organizations. Angel Angelov argues that the term 'regional organisations' is neither mentioned in Chapter VIII nor in the rest of the Charter, which instead refers to regional arrangements and/or agencies. It must be noted that though

4 For the historical evolution of the concept 'subsidiarity', see: Bjørn Møller 'The Pros and Cons of Subsidiarity: The Role of African Regional and Subregional Organisations in Ensuring Peace and Security in Africa', *DIIS Working Paper no. 2005/4* (Copenhagen: Danish Institute for International Studies, 2005), p. 3.

5 Gustaf Lind, 'Chapter VIII of the UN Charter: Its Revival and Significance Today', in Peter Wallensteen & Anders Bjurner (eds.), *Regional Organizations and Peacemaking: Challengers to the UN?* (London: Routledge, 2014), p. 28.

6 Bjørn Møller, 'The Pros and Cons of Subsidiarity', p. 4.

there are references to the latter throughout the Charter, no definition of regional agencies is produced either.[7] One reason behind this evasiveness on part of the UN's founders may be due to the fact that when the conference on a UN Charter convened at San Francisco on April 1945, it witnessed an 'explosive' clash between seemingly incompatible universal and regional tendencies.[8] The inability to reconcile such contradictory views may have induced the international body in adopting such a confusing approach to regional organizations. Boutros-Ghali takes a similar view and points out that such posture was done purposefully so as to allow the UN 'useful flexibility' for collective undertaking in the maintenance of international peace and security.[9]

While the vagaries of Cold War politics prevented regional organizations from playing any role, the situation changed with the end demise of confrontation between United States and Soviet Union. Of course, at the beginning of the 1990s, the co-operation between the UN and regional organizations were somewhat improvised and in a 'state of infancy'.[10] Since then regional organizations, most notably in Africa, have taken responsibility for international peacekeeping missions.

In the post-Cold War era, several African regional and sub-regional organizations conducted peace missions in Africa's troubled zones on their own or in collaboration with the UN where the member-states of the organizations contributed troops and police to attain the mandates of the mission. The African participation is critical for peace and security. Until now, it has contributed approximately 45% of the blue helmets in the region.[11] As of mid-2015, nearly eighty thousand troops and police and fifteen thousand civilians are deployed in

---

7 Angel Angelov, 'Regional Involvement in Peace Operations: an Analysis of the Debate within the UN Security Council', *Conflict, Security & Development*, vol. 10, no. 5, November 2010, pp. 599–623; A similar argument is also made in Oldrich Bures, 'Regional Peacekeeping Operations: Complementing or Undermining the United Nations Security Council?', *Global Change, Peace & Security*, vol. 18, no. 2, June 2006, pp. 83–99.

8 Michael Pugh, 'The World Order Politics of Regionalization', in Michael Pugh and Waheguru Singh Sidhu (eds.), *The United Nations and Regional Security: Europe and Beyond* (Boulder: Lynne Reiner, 2003), p. 33.

9 Boutros-Ghali, *An Agenda for Peace* (New York: United Nations, 1992), Para 61.

10 Richard Jones and Tamara Duffey, 'Sharing the Burden of Peacekeeping: The UN and Regional Organisations', *Peacekeeping and International Relations*, vol. 25, no. 3, 1996, pp. 4–6.

11 Cedric de Coning, 'Will the High-level Independent Panel Manage to Revitalise a New Generation of UN Peace Operations?' *ACUNS Quarterly Newsletter*, 2015, issue 2, pp. 3–4, available at http://acuns.org/wp-content/uploads/2015/05/ACUNS-60-MAY15-ACUNS_Newsletter_2_WEB.pdf (accessed 10 August 2015).

Africa.[12] In recent times, two of the largest African missions consider the involvement of the regional structures in various capacities — the African Union (AU) and UN jointly administer a hybrid operation in Darfur (UNAMID)[13] and the AU-led peacekeeping mission in Somalia (AMISOM).[14] In addition to this, the AU and Economic Community of West African States (ECOWAS) coordinated a joint peace mission in Mali and the mandate had transferred to the UN in 2013 with strong presence of the African forces from the member states of these organizations.[15] Since 2004, with the inception of the AU's Peace and Security Council (PSC), it has mandated nearly sixty five thousand uniformed peacekeepers in Africa.[16] At this moment, the ECOWAS also conducts a minute UN-mandated mission in Guinea Bissau.[17] While historically Asia has not seen regional organizations taking part in the UN peacekeeping missions[18] and small-scale civilian peacekeeping endeavors are conducted by the Organization of American States (OAS) in Americas,[19] regional organizations in Africa have increasingly become an important feature of the contemporary architecture of peace operations.

12 Danielle Renwick, *Peace Operations in Africa*, CFR backgrounders, 15 May 2015, available at http://www.cfr.org/peacekeeping/peace-operations-africa/p9333 (accessed 9 August 2015).

13 Bellamy & Williams, *Understanding Peacekeeping*, p.309.

14 Marika Fahlen, 'The African Union Mission in Somalia', in Wallensteen & Bjurner (eds.) *Regional Organizations and Peacemaking: Challengers to the UN?*, pp. 179–192.

15 Further to the UNSCR 2100 (April 2013), the African-led International Support Mission in Mali (AFISMA) had transferred its authority to the United Nations Multidimensional Integrated Stabilization Mission in Mali (MINUSMA) on June 2013. The AU and ECOWAS contributed to the repackaged mission in Mali. See: African Union, AFISMA Transfers its Authority to MINUSMA, Press release, 1 July 2013, available at http://www.peaceau.org/uploads/afisma-transfers-it-authority-to-minusma-01-july-2013.pdf (accessed 9 August 2015).

16 Renwick, *Peace Operations in Africa*, 2015. For more details of the four different patterns of the involvement of African regional organizations in UN peace missions, see: Walter Lotze, *The Future of African Peace Operations: Time to Adjust the Operational Design*, Policy Briefing (Berlin: *Zif* Center for International Peace Operations, May 2015), available at http://www.zif-berlin.org/fileadmin/uploads/analyse/dokumente/veroeffentlichungen/ZIF_Policy_Briefing_Walter_Lotze_Future_African_Peace_Operations_May_2015.pdf (accessed 9 August 2015).

17 Renwick, *Peace Operations in Africa*, 2015.

18 The League of Arab States (LAS) was permitted by the UN Security Council (6498th meeting, UNSCR resolution 1973, 2011) to be instrumental in ending violence and protecting lives of civilians in Libya, See: Mikael Eriksson, 'Towards Selective Regionalization? The Intervention in Libya and the Emerging Global Order', in Wallensteen & Bjurner (eds.), *Regional Organizations and Peacemaking: Challengers to the UN?*, pp. 217–232.

19 For details, see: OAS Peace Fund, *OAS Peace Missions*, available at http://www.oas.org/sap/peacefund/PeaceMissions/ (accessed 9 August 2015).

The increasing trend of subsidiarity supports provided by the regional organizations in peace operations has led to an extensive debate in the academic community about the wisdom of using such organizations for expanded UN peacekeeping missions. In the following paragraphs we summarize the key arguments for and against subsidiarity/regionalization of peacekeeping.

Arguments for and against Regionalism

The main argument of subsidiarity is that regional and sub-regional organizations should be the 'first point of reference' for problems transcending national boundaries. This will allow the UN and the international community to deal with issues of concern that cannot be solved at the lower level.[20] A number of advantages accrued from using regional organizations in peacekeeping missions can be identified.

Proponents of making more use of regional organizations argue that such an arrangement will help the international community deal with the perennial dilemma between those who espouse a greater salience of norms and institutions in international affairs and those who identify themselves as realists. The greater involvement of regional institutions, argues Michael Hirsh, will prevent the problem of regional powers acting on their own initiative and being identified as a regional hegemonic power whose involvement may aggravate an already fragile international security situation. Greater participation of regional organizations will also allow the UN to act more efficiently in regional conflicts and overcome the problems of military manpower and cash which often seem to grip the international body. All these will help make the UN a more credible organization in dealing with international crises.[21]

Regional organizations are also assumed to be more efficient when it comes to taking and implementing decisions compared to UN which is circumscribed by its universal membership. Supporters of the regional organizations are quick to point out that membership of such organizations is usually limited and members tend to share similar characteristics like language, religion, ethnicity, and tradition. The UN is often limited by its large membership in taking decisions swiftly and even if a consensus is made, it often unable to react quickly to implement the decision.[22]

Regionalism also offers a solution to a problem which all policy-makers have to face: how to convince a sceptical legislature and public that international peacekeeping missions serve national interest. Today's conflicts tend to

20 Bjørn Møller, 'The Pros and Cons of Subsidiarity', p. 4.

21 Michael Hirsh, 'Calling All Regio-Cops: Peacekeeping's Hybrid Future', *Foreign Affairs*, vol. 79, no. 6, November-December 2000, p. 5.

22 Angelov, 'Regional Involvement in Peace Operations', pp. 606–607.

have ramifications far and wide and countries are often unable to escape fall-outs from conflicts in neighbouring countries. Michael Hirsh convincingly argues that while in the past neighbours often took advantage of a kind of geo-political *schadenfreude* – deriving advantages from a war-affected neighbour's predicament – in today's globalized world most countries are aware of the costs caused by economic dislocation and population movement which are results of such conflicts. Regional peacekeeping therefore emerges as a critical tool in the repertoire of countries as they try to ensure national security.[23]

While the reasons for involving regional institutions in peacekeeping operations are many, the subsidiarity norm is not without its problems. In fact, the opponents of this approach have pointed out that such a policy suffers from quite a few drawbacks. Regional institutions derive their advantages from close proximity to conflicts. However, this very closeness may turn out to be a disadvantage for them. Walter Dorn in a hard-hitting article on regionalism and peacekeeping points out these institutions tend to view conflicts in their regions through the coloured glasses of parochial national or regional interests and are thereby unable or unwilling to perform impartial peacekeeping.[24] A similar conclusion is reached by Tavares who studied peacekeeping deployments by ECOWAS and SADC and noted decisions to intervene were often made in national capitals than in the headquarters of regional organizations and that in the majority of cases, national and individual interests rather than any institutional principle, served as the rationale for the interventions.[25] Wallensteen surveys a few significant cases in Africa and concludes that the powerful country/ies in the respective regions dominate the regional organizations in their peace endeavours. The authors refer the role of South Africa in South African Development Community (SADC), Ethiopia in Inter-Governmental Authority on Development (IGAD), and discuss a strategic balance of self-interests between the regional stalwarts like Nigeria and Ghana in the ECOWAS.[26] This, nonetheless, can also arguably be implied considering the role of India in South Asia.

23 Hirsh, 'Calling All Regio-Cops: Peacekeeping's Hybrid Future', pp. 5–6.

24 Walter Dorn, 'Regional Peacekeeping Is Not the Way', *Peacekeeping and International Relations*, vol. 27, no. 4–5, 1998, p. 1.

25 Rodrigo Tavares, 'The Participation of SADC and ECOWAS in Military Operations: The Weight of National Interests in Decision-Making', *African Studies Review*, vol. 54, no. 2, 2011, p. 166.

26 Peter Wallensteen, 'International Conflict Resolution, UN and Regional Organizations', in Wallensteen & Bjurner (eds.), *Regional Organizations and Peacemaking: Challengers to the UN?*, p. 23. In addition to this, more information on African-led missions can be accessed in Adekeye Adebajo, 'UN Peacekeeping and the Quest for a Pax Africana', *Current History*, vol. 113, issue 763, May 2014, pp. 178–184.

Critics are also quick to point out that rarely do regional organizations have the necessary capacity to undertake and sustain peacekeeping missions. Two case studies are worth considering in this regard. First, scholars question the capacity of the League of Arab States (LAS) in the 2011 UN-mandated humanitarian intervention in Libya. Eriksson observes that the LAS failed to provide desired supports to the UN-mandated no flying zone in Libya. He says, "LAS immediately proved itself impotent and, apart from financial support, it could not contribute operationally to enforcing the zone. It simply had no capacity in this regard. It had to rely on UN action."[27] Another interesting example could be the lack of capacity of the contributing members in the Uganda-led African Mission in Somalia (AMISOM). Although from 2011, the AMISOM experienced significant progress in its fight against the terrorist organization—Al-Shabab, initially the mission had been obstructed due to a small supply of troops available on the ground. The AMISOM had suffered from basic military capacities and medical supports for civilians and peacekeepers. Further, a critical component of the AMISOM, maritime peacekeeping unit, still remains unfunded and inadequate to support the overall objectives of the mission.[28]

The tendency to shift the onus of peacekeeping missions upon regional organizations may also lead to accusations of international community neglecting parts of the world not deemed important. Under such circumstances, subsidiarity may be seen as a justification for 'buck-passing', i.e. for neglecting the developing world and asking them to solve problems on their own.[29] Lastly, the UN possesses moral authority of a world body which all regional organizations lack. In spite of many set-backs, the UN peacekeeping forces have achieved a level of legitimacy and acceptability which no regional organizations have been able to emulate. Critics fear too much emphasis on regional peacekeeping may lead to siphoning off of resources, money and attention from the United Nations and have a negative effect on international security.[30]

While the issue regionalism in upholding international peace and security has created a lot of debate, the topic is seldom discussed within the context of South Asia. This is quite remarkable since South Asia suffers from a host of problems pertaining to international security. Moreover, quite a few South

27 Eriksson, 'Towards Selective Regionalization? The Intervention in Libya and the Emerging Global Order', p. 231.

28 Matt Freear and Cedric de Coning, 'Lessons from the African Union Mission for Somalia (AMISOM) for Peace Operations in Mali', *Stability: International Journal of Security & Development*, vol. 2, no. 2, 2013, pp. 1–11.

29 Bjørn Møller, 'The Pros and Cons of Subsidiarity', p. 5.

30 Dorn, 'Regional Peacekeeping is Not the Way', p. 3.

Asian countries participate actively in UN peacekeeping missions and are at the top of the list of troop-contributing countries. Under such circumstances it is imperative we understand the dynamics of South Asian regionalism and how it may affect UN peacekeeping missions in future.

II South Asia: Peacekeeping and Regionalism

South Asia is a populated sub-region in Asia that can be demarcated geographically with the major presence of India at its center. Afghanistan, Bangladesh, Bhutan, India, Maldives, Nepal, Pakistan and Sri Lanka are state-members of the region. These eight countries in South Asia share a common ethnic origin, colonial past, historical ties, religious and cultural traditions, linguistic affinities, and values and social norms.[31] Such commonalities have emerged as both unifying and divisive factors for the region. For example, all countries in the region share major religions—Hinduism, Islam, Buddhism, Sikhism and Christianity. Nevertheless, the history of state formation in South Asia and the impact of overlapping of the religious and linguistic groups across national boundaries have become a source for intra-regional conflicts on several occasions.[32] Therefore, the process of regional integration has been a challenging one for South Asia.

There exists a critical significance of South Asia's geostrategic position in contemporary world politics. Its proximity of central and western Asia, threat of Chinese expansionism in the region, South Asia's increasing trade volume and the intra-state relationship are major contributing factors that define its geostrategic significance. India's supremacy in the region, its rise as an emerging world power, its relations with the United States in the post-9/11 period, and historical legacy of Indo-Pak rivalries add values to the significance of the region. Moreover, South Asia faces non-traditional security threats like cross-border terrorism, internal militancy fuelled by ethnic and religious extremism, separatist movements, proliferation and use of small and light weapons, drugs,

31 Kishore C. Dash, *Regionalism in South Asia: Negotiating Cooperation, Institutional Structures* (London: Routledge, 2008), pp. 45–6.

32 Uttara Shahashrabuddhe, *Regionalisation Processes in South Asia and Southeast Asia: A Comparative Study*, available at http://www.asianscholarship.org/asf/ejourn/articles/Sahasrabuddhe.pdf (accessed 11 February 2014); Arjun Guneratne and Anita M. Weiss (eds.), *Pathways to Power: The Domestic Politics of South Asia* (Hyderabad, India: Orient Black Swan, 2014).

and refugee issues.[33] In addition, democratic political governance is yet to be consolidated in many countries that cause internal political instability in South Asia. Despite all these, the countries of South Asia possess a good track record in keeping peace all over the world under the mandate of the UN. Top troop and police contributing countries (TCCs/PCCs) in the blue-helmet force at UNPKO have been Bangladesh, India and Pakistan interchangeably. These three countries have been continuously generating troops and police in the multinational peacekeeping forces and providing significant contributions to multilateral diplomatic forums in the UN. Apart from the above-mentioned countries, Nepal and Sri Lanka also contribute sizable amount of troops and police in the peacekeeping missions. By combining all the individual contribution of South Asian countries, it is clear that the region demonstrates a stronger commitment to the UN peace operations and to UN principle of multilateralism.[34]

In the latter part of this section, we will draw a short history of regionalism in South Asia and its challenges. These challenges are critical factors to understand the crisis in the formation of a regional peacekeeping force. It is in this context that we discuss the contribution of South Asian countries in UN peace mission as the extent of contribution would help enunciating the significance and challenges of a South Asian regional approach to future UN missions.

South Asian Contribution in UN Peacekeeping

Altogether these five countries—Bangladesh, India, Nepal, Pakistan, and Sri Lanka—have contributed the largest share of troops to UN missions than any other region during the post-Cold War period. Since 1999, South Asia has consistently provided between 20% and 50% of all UN troops. At present, the region contributes 34% of the total deployed troops and police members in the UN missions (see figure 1). The region's police contributions have steadily increased and currently account for 35% of the UN's total police force.[35]

Since 2005, any of these three countries—Bangladesh, India and Pakistan—has provided the most troops among all contributor states to UN missions.

33 C.S.R. Murthy, *Contemporary World Order and Approaches to UN Peace Operations: A South Asian Perspective* (Berlin: Friedrich-Ebert Stiftung, 2012), p. 3.

34 Murthy, *Contemporary World Order and Approaches to UN Peace* Operations, p. 4.

35 See Cunliffe, *Legions of Peace*, pp. 9–10; Adam Smith, 'Recent Developments in UN Peacekeeping and their Implications for South Asian Troop- and Police-Contributing Countries', Keynote Speech presented at a Regional Conference on South Asian Contributions in UN Peacekeeping, organized by Dept. of International Relations, University of Dhaka in collaboration with The American Center, U. S. Embassy Bangladesh, 24–25 August 2013, Dhaka, Bangladesh.

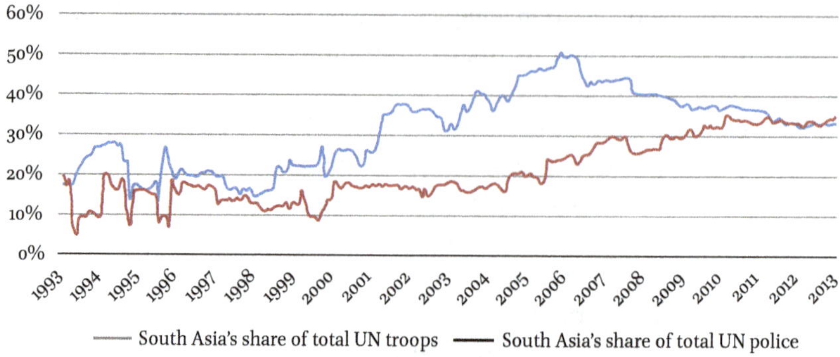

FIGURE 1 *Percentage of total* UN *troops and police contributed by South Asian countries (1993–2013).*

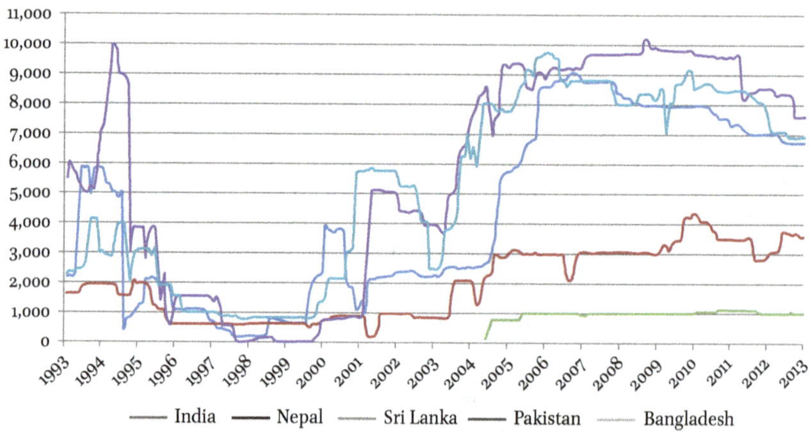

FIGURE 2 *Monthly troop contributions of South Asian countries (1993–2013).*

During this period, Pakistan has contributed an average of 9,234 troops per month, with Bangladesh 8,371 and India 7,673 troops, followed by Nepal with 3,239 troops. Sri Lanka began contributing troops from 2004, at an average of 977 troops per month (see figure 2).[36]

Financial contribution is also critical for the UN missions. Due to financial constraints as developing countries, South Asian countries contribute a relatively small percentage of the UN peacekeeping budget. India contributes the highest among five countries of South Asia. It has paid slightly more than 0.1% of the annual peacekeeping budget, which amounted to US$ 9.9

36 Smith, 'Recent Developments in UN Peacekeeping and their Implications for South Asian Troop- and Police-Contributing Countries', 2013.

TABLE 1 *Contributions by top uniformed personnel contributors from South Asia*

Country	2013 Peacekeeping assessment rate	2013 Expected peacekeeping assessment (in millions)	Uniformed personnel (Dec 2013)	Share of total uniformed personnel (Dec 2013)
Bangladesh	0.0010%	0.07	7,918	8.06%
India	0.1332%	9.90	7,849	7.99%
Nepal	0.0006%	0.04	4,580	4.66%
Pakistan	0.0170%	1.26	8,266	8.42%

million in 2013 (see table 1).[37] On the other hand, as large troop and police contributing countries, South Asian countries receive more money from the UN for troops and equipments than they actually contribute to UN's peacekeeping budget.

The significance of South Asian contribution in UNPKO can be discerned in the fact that one in every four men/women in uniform happens to be from a South Asian country.[38] There is hardly a major operation that has been deliberated without South Asian co-operation to contribute troops and police forces. In addition to the recognition from the UN, both host nations and regional forums have acknowledged the roles of South Asian nations in different missions. Bengali was declared as the second language of Sierra Leone by its government in recognition to Bangladesh's extraordinary contribution in the reconstruction in the wake of Sierra Leone's civil war.[39] Considering India's noteworthy role, the African Union pertinently describes this South Asian state as an exemplary reference point in the area of peacekeeping.[40] This is also critical from the perspectives of individual nations of South Asia. They consider their contribution to peace operations as a symbol of international recognition of their experience in handling

37 Katharina P. Coleman, 'The Political Economy of UN Peacekeeping: Incentivizing Effective Participation', *Providing for Peacekeeping*, no. 7, New York: International Peace Institute, May 2014, p. 23.

38 Murthy, *Contemporary World Order and Approaches to UN Peace Operations*, p. 4.

39 Rashed Uz Zaman and Niloy R. Biswas, 'Bangladesh', in Alex Bellamy and Paul D. Williams (eds.), *Providing Peacekeepers: The Politics, Challenges and the Future of United Nations Peacekeeping Contributions* (Oxford: Oxford University Press, 2013), p. 186.

40 Murthy, *Contemporary World Order and Approaches to UN Peace Operations*, p. 4.

delicate situations of internal unrest and their capacity to provide a positive difference in world politics.[41]

Moreover, there are experts from these South Asian countries who were selected for several international leadership positions in field missions and in UN Headquarters. All three troop and police contributors from South Asia hold Force Commander positions in different missions, such as in the United Nations Mission for the Referendum in Western Sahara (MINURSO), United Nations Disengagement Observer Force (UNDOF), and United Nations Operation in Côte d' Ivoire (UNOCI). Nationals from these countries also held influential civilian posts: Under Secretary-General of Field Support (Bangladesh), Special Adviser of the Secretary-General for Myanmar (India), and Special Adviser to the Secretary-General (Pakistan).[42]

These countries have frequently served at the UN Security Council (UNSC) as non-permanent members. India and Pakistan have each served 14 years at the UNSC, while Bangladesh and Nepal have each served four years, Sri Lanka serving for two years. Individually, these countries have raised their voice with regard to the critical issues of peacekeeping. Bangladesh was the founding chair of the UN Peacebuilding Commission. Further, as regular top contributors to UN peacekeeping missions, Bangladesh, India, and Pakistan have consistently gained seats at the Organizational Committee of the Commission. However, there is no evidence of a concerted regional effort to uphold issues related to peacekeeping missions and rights of peacekeepers. Given the changes taking place in the arena of global peacekeeping, we must raise the question of such absence persists in promoting peacekeeping as a regional agenda in South Asia. To shed light on the absence of South Asian regional approach to UN peacekeeping, we need a critical reflection on regionalism in South Asia and the manifold challenges to regional integration.

Regionalism in South Asia: Formation and Challenges

South Asian Association for Regional Cooperation (SAARC) was the first formal expression of a regional forum in South Asia. SAARC was a result of series of negotiation at the national levels among the governments of its founding state members in 1985. The membership of this organization consisted of seven members during the time of its formation. Later, Afghanistan joined SAARC in 2007. Altogether, these states account for a

41 Kabilan Krishnasamy, 'Recognition for Third World Peacekeepers: India and Pakistan', *International Peacekeeping*, vol. 8, no. 4, 2001, pp. 56–76.

42 Smith, 'Recent Developments in UN Peacekeeping and their Implications for South Asian Troop- and Police-Contributing Countries', 2013.

huge population mass that is just under one quarter of the world's total population.[43] Over the last three decades, SAARC has attempted to address several regional concerns, for example, drug and human trafficking, economic cooperation among South Asian states and most recently efforts have been made to tackle the menace of terrorism in the region.[44] However, SAARC has faced a slow expansion so far as the consolidation of the regional integration is concerned. One can identify various reasons as challenges behind the unimpressive track record of SAARC. Some of these challenges are also critical relating to the potential of a future regional peacekeeping force from South Asia. Therefore, it is important to list the hindrances that SAARC faces in developing regional integration.

According to the SAARC Charter (1985), member states are

> desirous of peace, stability, amity and progress in the region through strict adherence to the principles of the United Nations Charter and Non-Alignment, particularly respect for the principles of sovereign equality, territorial integrity, national independence, non-use of force and non-interference in the internal affairs of other States and peaceful settlement of all disputes.[45]

However, SAARC has never been successful to address its long-term objectives as a regional body and has, for years, grappled with inter-state, intra-state and regional conflicts. Major structural challenges are fourfold. First, South Asian countries lacked a common approach to address international politics during the Cold War. The bipolar world system heavily influenced the intra-regional divisions in South Asia. Moreover, the spirit of regionalism, as practiced in West European or South East Asian integration, is missing in South Asia. The record of South Asian regionalism shows that countries are not too eager to forge links with each other, rather being more pragmatic about their relationship with globally powerful states.[46] Second, a commonly

43 Shiva Hari Dahal, Haris Gazdar, S.I. Keethaponcalan and Padmaja Murthy, *Internal Conflict and Regional Security in South Asia Approaches, Perspectives and Policies* (Geneva: United Nations Institute for Disarmament Research, 2003), p. 3.

44 Zahid Shahab Ahmed and Stuti Bhatnagar, 'Interstate Conflicts and Regionalism in South Asia: Prospects and Challenges', *Perceptions*, Spring-Summer 2008, p. 2.

45 SAARC Charter, available at http://saarc-sec.org/SAARC-Charter/5/ (accessed 11 February 2014).

46 Lok Raj Baral, 'Reconstruction of South Asia: a Precondition for Saarc', *South Asian Survey*, vol. 10, no. 1, 2003, pp. 71–84.

perceived extra-regional threat is absent for the regional state-members. On the contrary, India is perceived as a threat by many countries within the region. This has deteriorated relationship among the member states on several occasions, and hence, impeded regional integration. Third, the historical legacy of the India-Pakistan dispute is a crucial factor to understand the development of regional dynamics in South Asia. The conflict between the two major powers of the region has made developing an effective regional approach nearly impossible. Fourth, India, the leading power of South Asia has hardly relied on multilateralism. Despite its rhetoric of multilateralism in global international affairs, India has generally followed bilateralism in its relations with South Asian neighbours.[47] Nonetheless, when it comes to regional engagement, their bilateral relations have remained strained. Moreover, it is characterized by mistrust and suspicion, and thus making regional cooperation a hostage to bilateral politics.[48] For example, critical issues of cross-border terrorism are addressed at a bilateral level, which is a reflection of the fact that states do not believe developing a regionally integrated mechanism. Being a brainchild of the Cold War period, the founding fathers of SAARC aimed for a cautious approach and avail more time to raise confidence among the member states and thereby the decision to exclude bilateral and contentious issues out of SAARC deliberations emerged. They feared SAARC's role as political score-settling forum would derail any possibility of progress in regional cooperation. However, it is very clear now that the approach of keeping politics out of SAARC deliberations has not fulfilled its intended objective.[49]

As a consequence of all these intertwined factors, there were a few momentums for regional integration in South Asia. South Asia has been both a late starter and a reluctant actor in regionalization process. However, this reluctance may become an issue of concern for South Asian countries. Peacekeeping may undergo changes in the years ahead and it is an imperative that South Asia prepares itself accordingly. In the next section, we examine the future possible trends in international peacekeeping that may affect South Asia's contribution in this sector.

47 Baral, 'Reconstruction of South Asia: a Precondition for Saarc', p. 83.

48 Smruti S. Pattanaik, 'SAARC at Twenty-Five: An Incredible Idea Still in Its Infancy', *Strategic Analysis*, vol. 34, no. 5, 2010, pp. 671–677.

49 Rahul Tripathi, 'Reorienting the Regional Discourse on South Asia: Vision for a People's SAARC', *South Asian Survey*, vol. 13, no. 2, 2006, p. 323.

III Future Trends of Peacekeeping: Challenges and Opportunities for South Asia

We identify four critical factors that explain future trends of peacekeeping activities mandated by the UN. First, the UN *New Partnership Agenda: Charting a New Horizon for United Nations Peacekeeping*[50] report offers ambitious agenda to develop capacities of TCCs and PCCs in bolstering the effectiveness of peacekeeping. This requires a thorough reinforcement and broadening of internal and external partnerships with the UN and regional organizations in future. Second, the idea of peacekeeping itself is expanding and currently it emerges with more robust mandates, such as, use force under Chapter VII, interventions in more perilous operational environments, and the like. It is highly anticipated that the robustness of future peacekeeping will be more demanding so far as the capabilities and will of TCCs and PCCs are concerned. Third, the recent global financial downturn discouraged the top donors of UN missions to facilitate the capacities of individual peacekeeping operations. Fourth, member states, through dint of their membership of regional organizations, may gain a say in international affairs which is difficult to obtain otherwise. Most importantly, future peacekeeping requires more sophisticated technologies and special skills for the uniformed personnel to contribute in peacebuilding activities. Thus the contributing states need to reorient the pattern of their engagements with the future hybrid missions[51] accordingly.

First, *The New Horizon* report suggests reforms in the capability development of the current TCCs/PCCs and other actors who would be potential in meeting the demands of future peacekeeping. This is also critical for South Asian TCCs/PCCs, because it suggests more contributions of personnel and equipment from new and emerging TCC/PCCs. It is identified as broadening the base of troop and police contributing countries that advocates:

> A globally representative mix of contributors is a critically important strength of UN peacekeeping. Broad-based, global participation underpins

50 In short, this report is known as *The New Horizon Report*. See, Department of Field Support (DPKO/DFS), 'A New Partnership Agenda: Charting a New Horizon for UN Peacekeeping', (United Nations: New York, July 2009).

51 Thierry Tardy defines a broader and instrumental meaning of 'hybridity' in peace operations. He presents hybrid peace operations as a coordinated response to the evolving needs of conflict management. He further notes that the future operations in complex conflicts 'require a multiactor, coordinated, and therefore hybrid response'. See: Thierry Tardy, 'Hybrid Peace Operations: Rationale and Challenges ', *Global Governance*, vol. 20, issue 1, 2014, pp. 111–112.

> legitimacy and strong partnership, offering both greater depth and flexibility to deploy the right combination of actors and capabilities in a particular situation. Greater participation enables more collective burden-sharing and helps build a shared understanding of the challenges to be met.[52]

The major challenge in this context is that the UN will not be over-reliant on one or two suppliers of troops and will search the availability of new sources—states or regional bodies. South Asia has already experienced a 17% decrease in its market share of UN troop contributions over the last several years (from 51% in 2006 to 34% in 2013).[53] Given such trends, is it possible for South Asian TCCs/PCCs to reconsider their force-generation policies to cope with the *broadening base* idea of future peacekeeping proposed by the UN?

Second, as per the robust mandates, the UN authorizes its peacekeepers "to 'use all necessary means' to deter forceful attempts to disrupt the political process, protect civilians under imminent threat of physical attack, and/or assist the national authorities in maintaining law and order."[54] Such reforms in the nature of the peacekeeping operation are heavily informed by the Chapter VII of the UN Charter. Further, there is a new development that took place in March 2013. The UN Security Council approved an explicit mandate to favour the robustness of its missions that would allow peacekeepers to use force. The mandate authorized a newly-created 'Force Intervention Brigade' for the UN mission in the Democratic Republic of the Congo to "carry out targeted offensive operations... in a robust, highly mobile and versatile manner... to prevent the expansion of all armed groups, neutralize these groups, and to disarm them."[55] A mission mandated under Chapter VII of the Charter requires more robust participation by the troops, if needs be, than the Chapter VI missions. Nonetheless, the recent transformation in the peace missions has made the robust participation a more explicit tool of peace enforcement. This would hamper the safety and security of the peacekeepers more than from the previous engagements. On the other hand, Paddon identifies the surfacing of a commitment gap between the UN and the TCCs/PCCs due to their involvement in

52 DPKO/DFS, 'A New Partnership Agenda', p. 33.

53 Smith, 'Recent Developments in UN Peacekeeping and their Implications for South Asian Troop- and Police-Contributing Countries', 2013.

54 United Nations, 'United Nations Peacekeeping Operations: Principles and Guidelines', January 2008.

55 UN Security Council Resolution 2098, 28 March 2013, p. 34.

risky robust missions.[56] While the developed states are involved in drafting ambitious mandates for future missions, they are neither involved in taking the risks, nor do they provide sufficient technical and financial support to shoulder the responsibilities.[57] These will create problems in two fronts:

(a) One result of commitment gap between the UN and TCCs/PCCs may be difference in policy options on part of the latter where some countries would be willing to take part in these missions while others may have their doubts. This would affect the partnership between the UNSC with its conventionally committed state contributors who may not be willing to generate enough support to participate in robust missions;

(b) Negligence might increase on part of the permanent members of the UNSC to avoid the involvement of TCCs/PCCs in mandate-drafting. A continuous lack of consultation with TCCs/PCCs would hamper the relationship between the UNSC and the supplier states.[58]

Third, funds for UN peacekeeping enterprise have always faced uneven junctures. It has been clear that due to heavy economic downturns since 2007/08, peacekeepers are asked to perform more with fewer resources. Existing missions are already overstretched due to shortage of personnel and equipments.[59] Moreover, the growing demands for robust missions put more pressure on TCCs/PCCs without any qualitative changes in the pay structure for them. Particularly in countries of South Asia and Africa, there is a feeling that their contributions are not adequately considered by the UN Security Council. This becomes more of an issue when they feel they are expected to perform more and in the difficult missions, while at the same time, questions are raised about the quality of their troops and doubts are being expressed about their effectiveness.[60]

56 Emily Paddon, 'Partnering for Peace: Implications and Dilemmas', *International Peacekeeping*, vol. 18, no. 5, 2011, pp. 516–533.

57 This issue was highlighted by Paul D. Williams in a recent report where he makes the case for more U.S. involvement in peacekeeping missions in Africa. See, Paul D. Williams, *Enhancing U.S. Support for Peace Operations in Africa*, Council Special Report, no. 73, New York: Council on Foreign Relations, May 2015, pp. 1–56.

58 Paddon, 'Partnering for Peace: Implications and Dilemmas', p. 520.

59 Pavan Kapoor, *UN Security Council Briefing on UN Peacekeeping Operations*, 12 December 2012, cited from Smith, 'Recent Developments in UN Peacekeeping and their Implications for South Asian Troop- and Police-Contributing Countries', 2013.

60 Jair van der Lijn and *et al.* (eds.), *Peacekeeping Operations in a Changing World*, Clingendael Strategic Monitor Project (The Hague: Netherlands Institute of International Relations - Clingendael, January 2015), pp. 25–26.

Fourth, a close observation of the participation trends of TCC and PCC contributors under the auspices of the regional organizations in UN missions reflect the fact that a good number of the missions are heavily dependent on large force generation from its member countries. Coleman shows the trend in context of Sub Saharan Africa—Ethiopia, Eritrea, Burundi, Sudan and Somalia in the first decade of the 21st century where majority of troops are contributed from particular African states, e.g. South Africa, Uganda, Nigeria and Rwanda.[61] Individually, these countries are small contributors of peacekeepers in UN-mandated missions. However, jointly, they form bigger force under the regional framework and raise a common voice on matters related to peacekeeping. Nonetheless, the contribution of these regional organizations and its member states are not immune to the levels of technological sophistication that is increasingly required in the future peacekeeping missions.[62] One may question whether the existing regional frameworks could meet the future needs or it requires more coordination among the top troop and police contributing nations from beyond Africa. This global trend would affect South Asian countries. In a more robust peacekeeping scenario, the necessity of excessive force generation will be complemented with the ability of the contributors to generate more sophisticated technologies in carrying out the missions. This could particularly be problematic for the states that have leverage only on the force generation, but fail to forecast the critical other needs of the future peace operations. Thus, for South Asia, the importance of large force generation would possibly become less-demanding if that is not supported by a well-coordinated approach with updated and tailor-made technologies for the missions.

Finally, majority of the South Asian countries are self sufficient in sending large number of troops. There are institutional, normative and financial rationales for such intensive participation of Bangladesh, India, Pakistan and Nepal.[63] Further, these countries do not face major internal or external problems in individual force generation. Needless to say, South Asian troops are professional, well-trained and have proved their worth in carrying out UN mandate, which make them much sought after assets for the UNPKO. Although

61 Katharina P. Coleman, 'Innovations in 'African Solutions to African Problems': the Evolving Practice of Regional Peacekeeping in Sub-Saharan Africa', *Journal of Modern African Studies*, vol. 49, no 4, 2011, pp. 517–545.

62 For details, see: United Nations, *Performance Peacekeeping: Of the Expert Panel on Technology and Innovation in UN Peacekeeping*, 22 May 2014, pp. 3–11, available at http://www.effectivepeacekeeping.org/sites/effectivepeacekeeping.org/files/03/Performance%20Peacekeeping%20Final%20Report_Dec2014.pdf (accessed on 15 August 2015).

63 For details, see, Bellamy and Williams, (eds.), *Providing Peacekeepers: The Politics, Challenges, and Future of United Nations Peacekeeping Contributions.*

the South Asian member states did not experience an official co-deployment in a multilateral or any types of UN peacekeeping missions, they have worked together unofficially in some of these missions. A former peacekeeper from India and a retired officer of the armed forces of India, in an email conversation, opines that a combined deployment is difficult as all these countries have ample supply of forces to meet the demands raised from the mission areas.[64] However, Bangladesh, India, Pakistan and Nepal have experienced working side by side in a mission under a common UN mandate. The 2005 UN Mission in the Democratic Republic of the Congo (MONUC) is a classic example of cooperation among the South Asian nations. In February 2005, rebels killed nine Bangladeshi peacekeepers in a UN mission in Congo and their colleagues from India, Pakistan and Nepal conducted a robust response in retaliation. With immediate offensive operations, a combined force of Nepalese and Pakistani soldiers supported by an Indian attack helicopter mobilized to regain control over Congo's troubled Ituri region and killed almost 50 militiamen.[65] In addition, the members of the armed forces of these nations work together in the DPKO and in other commanding level capacities across the missions' headquarters. This experience places an added emphasis on the UN governance that would underscore the necessity of a South Asian regional force to be active in robust peacekeeping missions.

Amidst challenges for a regional cooperation in South Asian contribution in the UNPKOs, discussions have started in different platforms that bring in experts and policymakers to explore the challenges and opportunities of such venture.[66] A major demand of cooperation has emerged in the drafting of mandates for peacekeeping missions. The top contributors want to make their

---

64 Authors' interview with Major General (Retd.) Dipankar Banerjee [online through email], 20 May 2014.

65 Victoria K. Holt and Tobias C. Berkman, 'Protecting Civilians on the Ground', *The Impossible Mandate? Military Preparedness, The Responsibility to Protect and Modern Peace Operations*, (Washington DC: The Henry L. Stimson Center, 2006), p. 165; Indian Express, 'Indians, Pakistanis Join Hands in Congo Battle', 5 March 2000, available at http://zeenews.india.com/home/indians-pakistanis-join-hands-in-congo-battle-the-indian-express_205236.html (accessed on 9 August 2015).

66 Three such meetings and conferences are worth mentioning in this regard. First, Stockholm International Peace Research Institute (SIPRI) and Friedrich-Ebert-Stiftung (FES) organized a dialogue in Katmandu, Nepal in 2012. Second, Department of International Relations, University of Dhaka, in collaboration with US Embassy, Dhaka, organized a regional conference on peacekeeping and South Asia in August 2013 in Dhaka, Bangladesh. The third of its kind was organized by South Asian University and FES in February in New Delhi, India. All these three platforms brought together a range of leading experts, government officials

voices heard in decision making on mission mandates. Here, South Asian countries, a major troops contributing region, may think of building a common platform that provides them a comparative advantage in formulating mandates and operational policies of UNPKOs.[67] The South Asian diplomats from the top TCC and PCCs have long been advocating for a substantial rise of the rate of reimbursement. A recent development in the May-July 2014 UN Fifth Committee meetings expose a multilateral agreement on the pay hike of the troop reimbursement to the contributing nations.[68] The representatives from the South Asian top contributors played critical roles along with other G77 members to raise common concerns in regard to the challenges faced as contributors in the UN missions and the relevance of a pay rise for the peacekeepers. The 2014 pay rise is considered as a progress of combined diplomatic maneuvers by these countries in the UN platform. Similarly, a collective role of South Asian countries in the UN Peacebuilding Commission would be significant to enhance its regional endeavor in effective policymaking with regard to future UNPKOs. South Asian policymakers can also emphasize on regional cooperation to build training facilities for other troop and police contributing countries who would be deployed to missions operated by regional organizations in collaboration with the UN.[69] Provided that some of the South Asian countries already have the capacity and infrastructure to provide world-standard training, a joint regional effort would attract others to consume such services. While SAARC has its own limitations, policymakers can think of forming *ad hoc* platforms with special mandates that would oversee the potentials of cooperation in regard to peacekeeping ventures of the United Nations.

It must be borne in mind that regional cooperation on any issue largely depends on the will and the commitment of the regional powers. It is not yet clear whether the regional actors would like to commit their resources in

---

and academia and international development partners to discuss challenges and opportunities for South Asian contributors in the future global peacekeeping landscape.

67 Xenia Avezov, 'The New Geopolitics of Peace Operations: A Dialogue with Emerging Powers: South Asia Dialogue', *Journal of International Peacekeeping*, vol. 17, issue: 1–2, 2013, pp. 149–161.

68 For details, see, United Nations, *Concluding Second Resumed Session, Fifth Committee Approves Texts on Peacekeeping Budget, Increasing Troop Reimbursement Rates*, Sixty Eight General Assembly, Fifth Committee, 47th Meeting, 3 July 2014, available at http://www.un.org/press/en/2014/gaab4116.doc.htm (accessed 9 August 2015).

69 Avezov, 'The New Geopolitics of Peace Operations', p. 154. Such cooperation has already started among the ASEAN member states. For this, see: Carl Thayer, 'ASEAN and UN Peacekeeping' *The Diplomat*, 25 April 2014, available at http://thediplomat.com/2014/04/asean-and-un-peacekeeping/ (accessed 31 October 2015).

exploring the potentials of regional cooperation in global peacekeeping operations. India is no longer contented with its position as a regional power. It is gradually harboring doubts on contributing a large mass of troops or police in peacekeeping missions. However, India is more interested to play an effective role in policy levels of the UN. If the trend persists, it would be difficult to imagine India as the flag-bearer for the region on peacekeeping issues and to represent the voices of the south who are the top troop and police contributing states.[70] India, as emerging global power, may be interested to deviate from its heavy contribution policy and be more pragmatic to get share in the UN leadership in these matters.[71] Of course, a more wise policy would be if India carries a collective voice in UN platforms that serves the mutual interest of all the players of the region.

Concluding Remarks

This chapter argues that subsidiarity is a critical factor in UN peacekeeping operations in the contemporary period. The High-Level Independent Panel on Peace Operations led by former President Jose Ramos-Horta of Timor Leste also argues that the United Nations must play a leading role in forming a vision for a stronger global-regional partnership.[72] However, the growing patterns of the engagement of regional actors in UN-mandated missions raise several issues that indicate the potentiality of reforms in UN governance structure. For example, the definition of regional organization, according to the UN charter, is incomplete and it raises debates about the nature of regionalism. Moreover, the global trend reflects that the regional organizations involved in peacekeeping ventures are state-based organizations and deployment of forces are undertaken by its member-states. It is imperative to consider a scope for regional cooperation beyond the state both at the policy-level and in the service providing sector in which the existing global peacekeeping governance may be more accommodative.

The chapter also engages with the challenges that South Asian countries might experience in future in light of the ongoing transformations taking place in the structures of UNPKOs. While the regional trend in South Asia may pose a bleak feature at this moment with regard to harnessing a regional voice in

70 Coleman, 'The Political Economy of UN Peacekeeping', p. 32.

71 Avezov, 'The New Geopolitics of Peace Operations', p. 150.

72 *Uniting Our Strength for Peace – Politics, Partnership and Peace*, Report of the High-Level Independent Panel on Peace Operations, New York: United Nations, 16 June 2015, p. xii.

future UN missions, the short term strategy should focus in developing consensus on peacekeeping issues on an ad hoc basis. However, the long term goal should be developing a regional approach on peacekeeping issues within the framework of SAARC. A recent example showed that at a high-level meeting on the issue of a pay-raise to UN peacekeepers held at the UN India was pointedly absent. India has shown its clear dissatisfaction on the role of the developed countries who usually finance peacekeeping missions while sidelining the troop contributing countries from the decision making process. Through this action, India sent a message to the global forum "to accept that nations sending most troops to the world's most troubled hotspots should be overruled by countries that finance the global body but aren't risking soldiers."[73] With India taking such a decisive role, it is time that South Asian countries as a whole project a common voice in UN forums as large troop and police contributing countries.

This chapter has also discussed some basic challenges of regionalism in South Asia that hampers the possibilities of cooperation among the armed forces of SAARC member countries. For a common regional force, this cooperation seems like far-fetched, however, is not entirely impossible. The leadership, professionals and academia from South Asia and abroad should engage in constructive dialogue on the forms and modalities of such cooperation. Furthermore, the engagement of the regional actors in upcoming robust peacekeeping missions requires more commitments for longer stay and steady contributions on the nation/state building processes. The chapter has also highlighted the futuristic trends of less-troop-intensive missions. All South Asian TCCs/PCCs will face the crisis and they need to increase their strength otherwise to overcome this specific challenge. Under the purview of SAARC, state leadership should extend their cooperation to incorporate actors like—NGOs, justice sector, law-enforcement agencies, human rights experts and academia to form regional expert groups for increasing peacebuilding efforts of South Asian countries. South Asian expert groups on peacebuilding can be more functional and effective to address the global needs in post-conflict zones anywhere in the world due to the experiences gathered from their long standing contribution in this sector.

One may question the viability of such a new approach to peacekeeping by South Asian countries. Indeed, given the present state of SAARC, one may argue that making SAARC effective and co-operative on UNPKO issues may be too ambitious. However, we agree with Guehenno that peacekeeping has

73 Charu Sudan Kasturi, 'India Snubs UN on Peace Troops' Pay', *The Telegraph*, 23 February 2014, available at http://www.telegraphindia.com/1140223/jsp/nation/story_18012289.jsp#.UwxfBnnivIV (accessed 23 February 2014).

undergone changes in the last twenty five years and shall experience more changes in the years ahead.[74] This brings us back to Kipling. An attentive reader of the poem knows that Kipling did not write-off such a meeting and so goes our argument in light of the evidence presented here: South Asian regionalism and UN peacekeeping missions may stand poles apart right now but in a changed context the two may meet and find to their surprise that one complements the other.

Acknowledgements

The authors would like to thank the anonymous reviewers for their detailed comments and suggestions. An earlier version of this chapter was presented at a conference on *United Nations Peacekeeping: South Asian Perspectives* organized by the Department of International Relations, South Asian University (SAU), New Delhi, India on 1 March 2014. Authors are grateful to Dr. Soumita Basu of SAU and Friedrich Ebert Stiftung (India) for inviting them to attend the conference and speak on South Asian regionalism and peacekeeping missions.

74 Jean–Marie Guehenno, *The Fog of Peace: A Memoir of International Peacekeeping in the 21st Century* (Washinton D.C.: Brookings Institution Press, 2015), p. 309.

CHAPTER 5

Australia and Peacekeeping

Peter Londey

Australia and Peacekeeping

Australia can lay claim to the proud record of having had peacekeepers in the field every single day since 14 September 1947. Yet while Australian political support for peacekeeping has generally been unwavering, there have been marked shifts in Australian governments' willingness to commit actual troops on the ground. A recent publication by the Australian Department of Foreign Affairs and Trade, detailing the history of Australian contributions to the United Nations, includes a chapter by Moreen Dee, titled 'Australia and UN peacekeeping: steady and unwavering support'.[1] The truth is not quite so simple.

Over the 67 years since Australian peacekeepers first entered the field in Indonesia, there have only been four periods when Australia displayed a marked commitment to peacekeeping.[2] The first three, in the late 1940s, the mid-1970s and the early 1990s, coincided with left-leaning Australian Labor Party (ALP) governments, with individuals in them who were strong enthusiasts for the United Nations. These individuals were, respectively, Dr Herbert V. Evatt, Minister for External Affairs from 1941 to 1949; Gough Whitlam, Prime Minister from 1972 to 1975; and Gareth Evans, Minister for Foreign Affairs from 1988 to 1996. In contrast to the first three periods the fourth was under a conservative Liberal Party government (in coalition with the National Party), and the global aspirations evinced by Evatt, Whitlam and Evans were replaced with

1 Moreen Dee, 'Australia and UN Peacekeeping: Steady and Unwavering Support' in J. Cotton and D. Lee (eds.), *Australia and the United Nations* (Canberra: Department of Foreign Affairs and Trade, 2012), pp. 228–264.

2 For an overview of all Australian peacekeeping from 1947 to 2004, see Peter Londey, *Other People's Wars: a History of Australian Peacekeeping* (Sydney: Allen and Unwin, 2004). See also David Horner, Peter Londey and Jean Bou (eds.), *Australian Peacekeeping: Sixty Years in the Field* (Melbourne, Cambridge University Press, 2009). A multi-volume official history of Australian peacekeeping is in preparation, but so far only two volumes have appeared: David Horner, *Australia and the 'New World Order': from Peacekeeping to Peace Enforcement: 1988–1991* (Melbourne: Cambridge University Press, 2011); and David Horner and John Connor, *The Good International Citizen: Australian Peacekeeping in Asia, Africa and Europe, 1991–1993* (Melbourne: Cambridge University Press, 2014).

 | DOI 10.1163/9789004322059_006

a tight regional focus, as Australia took the lead, for about 10 years from 1998, in large peacekeeping operations in Bougainville (Papua New Guinea), East Timor, and Solomon Islands.

In between have been periods when Australian governments saw the world in Cold War rather than multilateral terms; retreated into military isolationism; or shared in the general decline in peacekeeping after the debacles of Somalia, Rwanda and Yugoslavia. In recent years, as Australian commitments in the Middle East, especially Iraq and Afghanistan, have stretched the capacity of the Australian Defence Force (ADF), peacekeeping has again taken a back seat. In what follows, I will examine Australian motivations for engaging in peacekeeping, and the nature of the commitments which have resulted. Because both motivations and results have varied markedly from period to period, the organization will be chronological.

1 The 1940s: Evatt and the UN

Dr Herbert V. Evatt (1894–1965) was a jurist who, as both Minister for External Affairs and Attorney-General in the ALP government of (successively) John Curtin and Ben Chifley, took a moderately high-profile role in the 1945 San Francisco Conference on International Organization, which drew up the UN Charter. Evatt promoted the interests and influence of middle powers, and foresaw some of the problems the Security Council veto would cause.[3] Evatt remained committed to the UN ideal and was President of the General Assembly in 1948–49. From 1947 he was supported by the youthful Secretary of the Department of External Affairs, John Burton.

In 1947, the opportunity arrived to put Evatt and Burton's multilateral ideals to work. The Second World War had provided a major impetus for Australians to see the Asia-Pacific as their prime area of interest. Their chief military engagement in the immediate post-war period was to take the lead role in the British Commonwealth Occupation Force, which under overall American leadership had its own area of operations in southern Japan. But now came a crisis which seemed to offer a diplomatic role for the UN. Since the end of the war, the Dutch had never been able to regain full control of their colonial possession, the Netherlands East Indies, modern Indonesia. The nationalist Indonesian Republicans, led by Sukarno, had been placed in nominal power as a parting gesture by the wartime Japanese occupiers, and the Dutch were never

3 For an excellent account, see W.J. Hudson, *Australia and the New World Order: Evatt at San Francisco – 1945* (Canberra: Australian National University, 1993).

able to regain control over the whole territory. The conflict simmered along, until in July 1947 the Dutch had had enough, and used their considerably greater military strength to invade Republican territory on Java and Sumatra.

Militarily the action was successful, and the Dutch made major gains. Politically, despite the Dutch attempt to paint the invasion as a 'police action', the move was disastrous, since it led directly to United Nations intervention. India and Australia competed with each other to refer the matter to the Security Council, and the latter set up a Committee of Good Offices (UNGOC) to bring the parties to the negotiating table, and, as an interim measure, a Consular Commission to monitor the ceasefire which had been forced on the parties by international pressure.[4]

Australia's representative on the six-man Consular Commission was its Consul-General in Batavia, Charles 'Moth' Eaton, a wartime Royal Australian Air Force pilot who seems to have brought his wartime experience to bear on his new task. It quickly became apparent that it was difficult for the diplomats who made up the Consular Commission to get a clear enough understanding of what was happening on the ground to determine whether the parties were adhering to the ceasefire. In particular, it seemed that the Dutch were carrying out considerable mopping up operations in unpacified areas on their side of their unilaterally declared ceasefire line, the 'Van Mook Line'. On 1 September 1947 the Commission, very possibly at Eaton's behest,[5] called on its six member governments to provide 'military officers' to be attached to the two sides as 'observers', to gather information for the Commission. All six countries responded. The Australians were the first to arrive in Batavia, on 13 September, and without waiting for the others to arrive deployed into the field the following day. They were arguably the first United Nations peacekeepers.[6]

Over the period 1947–1951, about 70 Australian observers served with UNGOC and its successor, the UN Commission for Indonesia.[7] In the first six months of the operation, the observers from all the countries worked together, on the basis of minimal instructions from home governments or from New York, more or less to invent multinational peacekeeping. Many of the principles

4 UN Security Council Resolutions 27 (1 August 1947); 30 and 31 (25 August 1947); 32 (26 August 1947); 36 (1 November 1947).

5 A week later Eaton wrote to Canberra suggesting the need for an 'international police force' to maintain order; see Londey, 'The Invention of Peacekeeping', p. 19.

6 On Australian peacekeeping in Indonesia, see especially Londey, *Other People's Wars*, pp. 12–28; Londey, 'The Invention of Peacekeeping', pp. 18–20.

7 For a comprehensive list of the numbers of Australian peacekeepers in individual operations, see Horner, Londey and Bou, *Australian Peacekeeping*, pp. 273–280.

which have subsequently governed UN peacekeeping were set out in a document produced by a conference of observers in March 1948: the need to work in multinational teams, the need for impartiality, the fact that they were not in a position to give orders, but rather must 'assist in bringing both parties into agreement through the use of initiative, a sense of fair play, ingenuity and common sense'.[8]

Despite Evatt and Burton's undoubted sympathies with such a multilateral approach, the Australian government's motives were not quite so simple. Even at a disinterested level, the Indonesian question presented an early, clear example of the conflict between two often incompatible principles, both enshrined in the UN Charter: sovereignty, and self-determination. In this case, Indonesian desire for self-determination ran counter to what many (in Australia, as elsewhere) regarded as legitimate Dutch sovereignty over its colonial territory. Even in the post-colonial era, the incompatibility continues to exist in any state faced with an active separatist movement: the recent conflicts over Bougainville and East Timor, in both of which Australia became heavily involved, are good examples. I have argued elsewhere that this incompatibility was a more important driver for the development of peacekeeping than was the stasis of the Cold War.[9] For Australia the problem was greatly compounded by geographical proximity, which made the future relationship with whoever controlled the area a matter of national security. Although the Japanese never, it seems, intended to invade Australia, their advance to the chains of islands immediately to the north had prompted something close to national panic. The Dutch failure to defend their territory had exposed Australia to danger even more than British failures in Malaya and Singapore.

The result was a series of Australian attempts to become a player in the future of the Netherlands East Indies, attempts which, however, were fatally undermined by a refusal to commit any substantial resources at all to the project.[10] During the war Evatt had suggested a Dutch–Australian partnership

8 UNGOC Milex [Military Executive Board] instruction, 'General instructions for military observers, Committee of Good Offices', 20 March 1948, National Archives of Australia (NAA): A10158, 62. For discussion, see Londey, 'Inventing peacekeeping', pp. 20–21.

9 Londey, 'Inventing Peacekeeping', pp. 17–18. On the incompatibility of the ideals, cf. Coral Bell's comments at C. Bell (ed.), *The United Nations and Crisis Management: Six Studies* (Canberra: Australian National University, 1994), pp. 3–6. On H.V. Evatt's rather creative response to the problem in the Indonesian case, see Londey, *Other People's Wars*, p. 16.

10 On all this, see Margaret George, *Australia and the Indonesian Revolution* (Melbourne: Melbourne University Press, 1980). For a useful succinct account, see Peter Dennis, 'Australia and Indonesia: the Early Years', in David Lowe (ed.), *Australia and the End of Empires* (Geelong: Deakin University Press, 1996), pp. 43–52.

in developing the territory after the war, or even that Australia should lease the NEI from the Netherlands; in 1945 he suggested that the territory should come under a UN trusteeship. The Dutch resisted these overtures, and when Australia did have a chance to play a major role in bringing order to Indonesia after the sudden of the war, Prime Minister Ben Chifley refused to commit the necessary ground-troops. As Peter Dennis has commented, 'Evatt's grand plans dissolved against the background of Australian inaction.'[11] As I have commented elsewhere, a further reason for the development of peacekeeping was nations' general unwillingness to commit the necessary resources to implement any sort of effective collective security regime.[12] So in this case: Australia actually had what it perceived as vital national interests at stake in the Indonesia question, but was unwilling to devote the military resources which might have made it a serious player. So in August and September 1947 we may reasonably see Evatt and Burton's eager embrace of the Consular Commission, of UNGOC, and of a role for the Australian military observers, as a chance for the Department of External Affairs to get involved in the Indonesia question, with only a minimal defence force contribution: foreign policy on the cheap.

That is certainly not to say that Evatt had no interest in genuine multilateralism. He strongly believed in a role for the United Nations, and himself played a major part in the partition of Palestine.[13] During his term as Minister for External Affairs, Australia was a member of the UN Special Commission on the Balkans (UNSCOB), the UN Temporary Commission on Korea (UNTCOK), and the UN Commission on Korea (UNCOK); Evatt also offered Australia's services as a mediator in Kashmir. Although under Evatt Australia's presence in these missions was diplomatic rather than military, they did set Australia up as a middle power with a distinctly broad-ranging view of its place in the world.

2 1949–1972: the Liberal-Country Party Government

In December 1949, the Labor government was defeated by a conservative coalition of the Liberal and Country Parties, led by Robert Menzies. The Coalition remained in power until 1972, with Menzies as Prime Minister until 1966. The new government was generally more interested in maintaining Australia's alliance with the United Kingdom and the United States, and did not share Evatt's

11 Dennis, 'Australia and Indonesia: the Early Years', p. 51.

12 Londey, 'Inventing Peacekeeping', pp. 14–16.

13 See Daniel Mandel, *H.V. Evatt and the Establishment of Israel: the Undercover Zionist* (London: Frank Cass, 2004).

enthusiasm for the United Nations. Nevertheless, Australia remained involved in several regions. As one example, initiatives begun by Evatt to have Australia involved in the conflict over Kashmir led to the appointment, in April 1950, of Australian judge Sir Owen Dixon as UN mediator. Dixon ultimately departed, frustrated and unsuccessful, but a legacy of his efforts was that Australia was invited to contribute a new Chief Military Observer to the UN Military Observer Group in India and Pakistan (UNMOGIP). Major General (later Lieutenant General) Robert Nimmo commanded UNMOGIP from 1950 till his death in early 1966. Nimmo, a Gallipoli veteran, was almost 57 when he arrived, and might easily enough have treated the position as a pre-retirement sinecure. Instead, he threw himself into the task to the extent that by the mid-1960s members of the UN Secretariat were calling him 'by far the most successful United Nations observer ever'.[14]

The year after his arrival, Nimmo asked for more observers, and was probably instrumental behind the scenes in getting the United Nations to invite Australia to contribute. Prime Minister Menzies threw himself behind the request, but for reasons which no longer had much to do with the ideals of UN multilateralism, but rather with British Commonwealth solidarity and Cold War concerns: 'It is of great importance to Commonwealth relations and to the defence of the Middle East and South-East Asia that hostilities should not break out again over Kashmir.'[15] In 1952 Australia duly supplied an initial eight observers, a commitment which continued unbroken until 1985.[16] Yet for many years, until the mid-1970s, these were consistently either army reserve officers or regular officers on the retired list. For the regular army, the real business remained the Cold War conflicts in Korea and Vietnam, and what Australia perceived as critical regional conflicts: the Malayan Emergency, and 'Confrontation' with Indonesia over the creation of Malaysia.[17]

Indeed, this set of priorities was already starkly apparent in the case of Korea in 1950. In early 1950 Australia, which had already been diplomatically involved in UN efforts to resolve the Korean issue, agreed to supply two military

---

14 Cable, Australian Mission in New York to Canberra, 'Kashmir Military Observers', 2 December 1964, NAA: A3688, 871/R3/6.

15 Menzies to McBride, 29 November 1951, NAA: A5954, 2277/4.

16 Londey, *Other People's Wars*, pp. 38–57; Pauline Dawson, *The Peacekeepers of Kashmir: the UN Military Observer Group in India and Pakistan* (London and New York: Hurst and Company/St Martin's Press), 1994.

17 For a useful summary of Australian concerns over this period, see Peter Edwards, *Crises and commitments: the Politics and Diplomacy of Australia's Involvement in Southeast Asian Conflicts 1948–1965* (Sydney: Allen and Unwin, 1992).

observers to UNCOK. But when New York came back with a request for one more observer and a more senior officer to command the whole observer mission, despite the potential prestige of the latter role the services pleaded that they had no more personnel to spare, and the request was refused. Yet when war broke out in June 1950, and the United Nations (partly on the basis of a report by the two Australian observers in the field) authorised the US to lead forces to defend South Korea, suddenly Australia had forces available. It was now a matter of supporting allies (the US and Britain) and of fighting communism. In the end, 17,000 Australians fought in Korea.[18]

Australia was not one of the countries which provided military observers to the UN Truce Supervision Organization (UNTSO) when it was set up, but Australian observers did arrive in 1956, and have remained part of UNTSO ever since. As noted above, Australia had been involved diplomatically in the United Nations' partitioning of Palestine and endorsement of the state of Israel. The arrival of the Australian observers happened before the Suez Crisis, and does not seem to have been connected with it. Most likely, Australian membership on the Security Council led to a sense that some participation in Middle East peacekeeping was necessary.[19] The Suez Crisis which broke out in late 1956 saw Australia isolate itself as one of only five countries in the General Assembly to vote against the withdrawal of British and French troops (the others were Britain, France, Israel, and New Zealand). Prime Minister Menzies had been sent as an envoy to negotiate with Egypt's President Nasser, but Menzies' abrasive manner undermined any chances of success. The crisis became an important milestone in the history of peacekeeping, as Canada's Lester Pearson proposed a buffer force which would occupy territory between the parties: this became the UN Emergency Force. Australia was keen to contribute, but understandably the Egyptians vetoed Australian participation.[20]

The United Nations' greatest peacekeeping operation until the 1990s was the UN Operation in the Congo (ONUC), but Australia contributed only a small number of observers and medical personnel. There were similarly small contributions to the UN Temporary Executive Authority (UNTEA) in West New Guinea and the UN Yemen Observation Mission (UNYOM). In 1964, however,

18 Robert O'Neill, *Australia in the Korean War 1950–53*, vol. I *Strategy and Diplomacy* (Canberra: Australian War Memorial, 1981), esp. pp. 12–15, 35–61; Londey, *Other People's Wars*, pp. 29–37; Londey, 'The Invention of Peacekeeping', pp. 15–16.

19 I am not aware, however, of any documents which make this explicit.

20 For a brief account, Londey, *Other People's Wars*, pp. 67–70. For a full account of Menzies' role, see W.J. Hudson, *Blind Loyalty: Australia and the Suez Crisis, 1956*. (Carlton: Melbourne University Press, 1989).

Australia made a substantial contribution of 40 civilian police to the UN Peacekeeping Force in Cyprus (UNFICYP). The contingent size later peaked at 50, but has steadily dropped away since then, though even today there is still a small Australian contingent of police in Cyprus. Yet this long-standing presence obscures the fact that the initial deployment was essentially a triumph of the bureaucracy over a rather unwilling government. The government was quick to offer financial support to UNFICYP, but rejected a request for troops: Australian eyes were now firmly on the troubled south-east Asian region. Down the track, a request for police came in. Again the government refused. This time, the internationalists in the Department of External Affairs took up the cudgels. First Assistant Secretary Patrick Shaw wrote to the minister, pointing out that Australia needed to be in the peacekeeping game if it were to have any future influence in the area, and be seen as a supporter of the collective security ideal; that Cyprus was part of the Commonwealth; that the eastern Mediterranean was of strategic importance to Australian trade through the Suez Canal; and that Greek and Turkish harmony was important to NATO. Most importantly, and getting to the heart of why nations may contribute to peacekeeping, was the problem – very deeply felt in Australia – of Indonesian 'Confrontation' with Malaysia: if the Malaysia question were ever brought to the United Nations, 'Australia will have a need for all the credit with the U.N. which it can attract to itself beforehand.'[21] The government gave in, and the police were despatched.

3 1972–1983: Whitlam and Fraser

The Labor Party finally returned to power for a brief three years (1972–1975), under Prime Minister Gough Whitlam. In the Evatt mould, Whitlam was a firm internationalist. In 1974 he told the General Assembly: 'we wish Australia to be always among the first nations from which the UN would ask for peacekeeping forces: we shall be among the first to respond.'[22] Whitlam quickly reversed a decision by the previous government to pull out of Cyprus, but found few opportunities in his brief term of office to make good on his pledge to the

---

21 Patrick Shaw to Minister for External Affairs [Sir Garfield Barwick], 20 April 1964, NAA: A1838, 913/5/1 pt 1. In 1965 Shaw began a five-year period as Australian Permanent Representative to the United Nations.

22 Address by Prime Minister of Australia, E.G. Whitlam, to UN General Assembly, 30 September 1974, p. 7 (text available at http://pmtranscripts.dpmc.gov.au/transcripts/00003410.pdf (accessed 5.7.14)).

General Assembly. When the UN Emergency Force II was set up after the Yom Kippur War in 1973, the government was very keen to participate, but was stymied by the need for political balance across the force. Nor was Australia asked to take part in the UN Disengagement Observer Force (UNDOF), though Australian observers with UNTSO regularly worked with UNDOF and, later, with the UN Interim Force in Lebanon (UNIFIL).[23]

Australia's chance to contribute to UNEF II came soon after Whitlam lost office in late 1975. Early the following year, UN Secretary-General Kurt Waldheim visited Australia and surprised his hosts by asking for helicopters for UNEF, which had recently had its area of operations greatly increased. The government agreed, and four Iroquois helicopters flew in the Sinai from 1976 to 1979.[24] In this case, the conservative government was more or less manoeuvred into a commitment by the enthusiasm for the operation shown by its predecessors. Prime Minister Malcolm Fraser was not necessarily a great enthusiast for the United Nations *per se*, but he did have an abiding and deeply felt personal interest in decolonisation in southern Africa. He played an influential role within the British Commonwealth in pushing Britain towards accepting majority rule in Zimbabwe (formerly Southern Rhodesia), and as a result Australia was one of five nations which formed the Commonwealth Monitoring Force (CMF), a non–UN British Commonwealth force which monitored the situation in Rhodesia in the run-up to elections in March 1980. The CMF was armed, but vastly outnumbered by the Rhodesian Security forces on the one hand and the Patriotic Front guerrilla armies on the other. Despite some scares, all went reasonably smoothly, but in fact this was probably one of the most dangerous peacekeeping operations in which Australians have served.[25]

Fraser's government also saw Australia agree to join another non–UN operation, the American-led Multinational Force and Observers (MFO), which eventually took over UNEF II's role in the Sinai, in the wake of the Camp David accords. The USSR professed opposition to the accords, if only to keep its Middle Eastern allies happy, so a UN force was impossible. The Labor Party in opposition vigorously attacked the proposed participation in the MFO, enunciating the principle (understandable after Vietnam) that in future overseas military engagement should only ever be under the UN flag, or at very least not under American leadership. (Opposition to Australian participation in the CMF had been more muted: sentimentally, Australians still preferred British

23 Londey, *Other People's Wars*, pp. 6, 97–100, 107–108.

24 Londey, *Other People's Wars*, pp. 100–106.

25 Londey, *Other People's Wars*, 126–132.

leadership.) Labor also raised unfounded fears about the likely dangers of the operation: in fact, Egypt and Israel had every interest in the MFO's success, and this was a far less hazardous operation than the CMF. The government held strong, and eight Australian and New Zealand Iroquois helicopters arrived in the Sinai in 1982.[26]

4 1983–1996: Two Faces of the Labor Party

Labor returned to power in 1983, and remained in government for 13 years, under two Prime Ministers: Bob Hawke (1983–1991) and Paul Keating (1991–1996). From the point of view of Australian peacekeeping, the more important figures were the successive Ministers for Foreign Affairs, Bill Hayden (1983–1988) and Gareth Evans (1988–1996). Hayden, who had been a minister in the Whitlam government, was a representative of post-Vietnam Labor, deeply suspicious of overseas military adventures. Coming to office he was faced with the *fait accompli* of Australian participation in the MFO but, despite visiting the Sinai and finding the contingent eager to continue, he pulled them out as soon as he decently could, in 1986. Despite UN disappointment, in 1985 he also terminated the 35-year participation of Australian observers in Kashmir. Small groups of Australians remained in UNTSO and in Cyprus, but that was about all.[27] Nevertheless, at the very end of his five-and-a-half years as Foreign Minister, Hayden approved his first peacekeeping contribution: the deployment of observers to the UN Iran–Iraq Military Observer Group (UNIIMOG). He had his reasons: Australia had long supported UN efforts to bring an end to the Iran–Iraq war; Australia had trade interests in the Middle East; and he saw this deployment as a possible 'alibi' if Australia were inclined to avoid potentially more dangerous operations in Namibia and Cambodia.[28] Australians stayed with UNIIMOG until late 1990, shortly before it was wound up as the Gulf moved towards war in the wake of Iraq's invasion of Kuwait.[29]

26 Londey, *Other People's Wars*, pp. 108–114. Appropriately, given the presence of a joint Australian–New Zealand unit, Israel completed the handover of the Sinai and the MFO became fully operational on 25 April, Anzac Day.

27 Londey, *Other People's Wars*, pp. 92–93, 116–120; Horner, *Australia and the 'New World Order'*, pp. 36–39.

28 Horner, *Australia and the 'New World Order'*, pp. 144–175; on the 'alibi' (Hayden's word), see p. 174.

29 On Australians in UNIIMOG, see Horner, *Australia and the 'New World Order'*, pp. 176–205.

Much changed when Gareth Evans became Foreign Minister. Evans' arrival did, of course, coincide with the thawing and end of the Cold War, a time when the United Nations suddenly found itself with the opportunity to act more freely on the world stage. But Evans, like Evatt before him, was also deeply engaged with the question of how to make the United Nations more effective. With assistance from his department, he wrote *Cooperating for peace*, a lengthy and detailed disquisition on the mechanisms by which the international community might achieve peace in the conflict-ridden post–Cold War world.[30] Evans' commitment to peace led, after he retired from politics, to his heading the International Crisis Group (2000–2009), and playing major roles on the International Commission on Intervention and State Sovereignty and the International Commission on Nuclear Non-proliferation and Disarmament. Evans' presence ensured that, when UN peacekeeping greatly expanded after the end of the Cold War, Australia was a full participant.

Soon Australia was involved in several peacekeeping operations. The largest in the early period was in Namibia, where Australia contributed 300 engineers to the UN Transition Assistance Group (UNTAG). In this case the original commitment had been made a decade earlier in 1979, by the Fraser government, when the operation was first mooted. Some in Australia had seen Namibia as a useful excuse for getting out of what they saw as the more dangerous operation in Rhodesia.[31] Finally in 1989 the end of the Cold War made it possible for the United Nations to proceed with UNTAG, and Australia honoured its original commitment, sending two contingents of engineers for a total of 12 months from April 1989 to April 1990. The operation opened dramatically with incursions by SWAPO fighters, repelled with significant casualties by South African forces; Australian engineers were put to work as ceasefire monitors. In the latter part of the operation, the Australians played a major role in ensuring that elections ran smoothly.[32]

---

30 Gareth Evans, *Cooperating for Peace: the Global Agenda for the 1990s and beyond* (Sydney: Allen and Unwin, 1993). The book is dedicated to the memory of H.V. Evatt. Canberra gossip liked to describe it as a lengthy job application for the position of Secretary-General, but it was a serious contribution to the subject at a time when, perhaps more so than today, the subject was being taken seriously. The empirical basis of *Cooperating for peace* was a series of case studies, mostly by members of the Department of Foreign Affairs and Trade, which were later published in Kevin Clements and Robin Ward (eds.), *Building International Community: Cooperating for Peace Case Studies* (Sydney: Allen and Unwin, 1994).

31 Horner, *Australia and the 'New World Order'*, p. 58.

32 Horner, *Australia and the 'New World Order'*, pp. 53–143.

More commitments quickly followed. Also in 1989, Australia began a commitment to the UN Mine Clearance Training Team (UNMCTT), teaching mine awareness and later mine clearance techniques to Afghan refugees in Pakistan (and later in Afghanistan itself).[33] In the wake of the Gulf War, Australian medical personnel worked with Operation Habitat, assisting Kurdish refugees in northern Iraq,[34] while Australians also played key roles with the UN Special Commission (UNSCOM), inspecting for and destroying nuclear, chemical and biological weapons in Iraq.[35] Before and after the Gulf War, Australian ships formed part of the Maritime Interception Force (MIF) patrolling the Persian Gulf.[36] In other parts of the world, from 1991 to 1994 Australia provided signallers to the UN Mission for the Referendum in Western Sahara (MINURSO),[37] and from 1992 small numbers of personnel to the UN Protection Force (UNPROFOR) and subsequent operations in the former Yugoslavia.[38] What is striking about Australian peacekeeping in this period is its geographical unboundedness, and the broad range of capabilities being offered. More was to follow.

Gareth Evans took a particular interest in the problem of Cambodia, a million of whose people had been killed by the genocidal Khmer Rouge regime in the 1970s. Subsequently, rather cynical Western intransigence against the Vietnamese-installed regime which had succeeded the Khmer Rouge kept Cambodia in a state of conflict. Once again, the end of the Cold War gave the United Nations – previously hamstrung by differences on the Security Council – the chance to act. Evans, with the pragmatic Australian desire for a solution, rather than endless negotiation, put forward a set of concrete proposals in 1990: for an interim period, all four major factions in the conflict should share power, while the United Nations itself would oversee administration in the country and the holding of elections.[39] Ultimately this led to the formation of the UN Transitional Authority in Cambodia (UNTAC, 1992–1993), one of

33 Horner, *Australia and the 'New World Order'*, pp. 206–237.

34 Horner and Connor, *The Good International Citizen*, pp. 395–426.

35 Horner and Connor, *The Good International Citizen*, pp. 427–500, 518–525.

36 For detailed accounts of Australian naval operations around Iraq, see Horner, *Australia and the 'New World Order'*, pp. 269–498; Horner and John Connor, *The Good International Citizen*, pp. 501–533. For an effort to distinguish between robust peacekeeping, before and after the Gulf War, and the war itself (which was certainly not peacekeeping), see Londey, *Other People's Wars*, pp. 156–157.

37 Horner and Connor, *The Good International Citizen*, pp. 267–330.

38 Horner and Connor, *The Good International Citizen*, pp. 333–391.

39 Department of Foreign Affairs and Trade, *Cambodia: an Australian peace proposal: working papers prepared for the informal meeting on Cambodia, Jakarta, 26–28 February 1990* (Canberra: AGPS, 1990).

the most complex UN peacekeeping operations to that time. UNTAC was commanded by an Australian, Lieutenant General John Sanderson, while Australia contributed over 500 personnel, including the force's signallers.[40] Despite serious threats of intimidation by the Khmer Rouge, the elections in May 1993 were unimpeded and saw a very high voter turn-out. No peacekeeping operation is completely successful, but UNTAC was clearly one of the more successful ones.[41]

At the same time as the UNTAC involvement, Australia was sending a battalion to take part in the American-led Unified Task Force (UNITAF, 1992–1993) in Somalia, while also contributing smaller numbers to the UN operations which preceded and followed UNITAF, the UN Operation in Somalia I and II (UNOSOM, 1991–1995). As is well known, UNOSOM ended badly, yet the role of the Australian battalion in 1993, protecting humanitarian relief operations in and around Baidoa in south-west Somalia, was by and large highly successful.[42] In 1994, Australians found themselves back in Africa, providing medical support to the UN Assistance Mission for Rwanda (UNAMIR). Seeing the way things were going bad in Somalia, the government actually shared the international reluctance to get involved in Rwanda, but public opinion, swayed understandably by the horrific images of genocide coming out of the country, pushed hard for Australian involvement. It was, it seems to me, a period in which the sense that 'we' should 'do something' was much stronger in Australia than it is today. In the event, despite the all-too-apparent dangers, the only serious casualties the Australian contingent suffered were psychological. Many Australians saw traumatising sights, but none more so than a small group who witnessed but were unable to prevent the massacre in April 1995 of several thousand displaced persons at a camp at Kibeho. The group treated and evacuated as many as possible, and helped count the bodies. One of them was a visiting Australian artist, George Gittoes, one of whose many works deriving from Kibeho, *The preacher*, later won the Blake Prize for religious art.[43]

---

40 Australia had also made a smaller contribution to UNTAC's predecessor, the UN Advance Mission in Cambodia (UNAMIC).

41 The literature is vast. For a full account of Australia's role, see Horner and Connor, *The Good International Citizen*, pp. 41–263.

42 The best account is Bob Breen, *A Little bit of Hope: Australian Force – Somalia* (Sydney: Allen and Unwin, 1998).

43 On Australians in Rwanda. Londey, *Other People's Wars*, pp. 194–213; Kevin O'Halloran, *Rwanda: Unamir 1994/95* (Canberra: Army History Unit, 2012). On Gittoes' Rwanda work, G. Fry, *George Gittoes* (North Ryde: Craftsman House, 1998); on his earlier work with peacekeepers, D. Hart, *The Realism of Peace: George Gittoes* (Darwin: Museum & Art

After disastrous failures in Somalia and Rwanda, Australia shared the world's temporary loss of enthusiasm for peacekeeping. There were small commitments to Mozambique and Haiti, and later to Guatemala, and a noticeable commitment to de-mining in both Cambodia and Mozambique, but in general there was a lull: by the end of 1995, Australia had fewer than 100 peacekeepers around the world.[44]

5 1996–2003: Regional Engagement

In 1996 the conservative coalition of Liberals and Nationals returned to power, and John Howard became Prime Minister for the next 11 years. The first part of this period saw a clear upsurge in Australian peacekeeping, but with a notable difference from the Evans years. Under Evans, Australia's peacekeeping efforts had been diverse and far-flung. Now the operations remained diverse, but they were tightly focused on Australia's own region, and seen almost entirely as a contribution to regional stability. Very small numbers of peacekeepers still went to Cyprus, to Israel, Syria and Lebanon, and to the Balkans, Eritrea, Sierra Leone, to Iraq (as weapons inspectors), and to the Sudan. But the big operations were in Bougainville, East Timor, and Solomon Islands, all part of what Australian analysts liked to hype as the 'arc of instability'.[45]

Bougainville was a province of Papua New Guinea (PNG), a product of colonial boundary-drawing which became independent in 1975. Bougainvilleans considered themselves ethnically closer to the people of the neighbouring Solomon Islands, and had resented being part of PNG. Resentment flared into a full-scale separatist movement from 1988 on. In the mid-1990s New Zealand led the way towards a negotiated settlement, with Australia, somewhat hampered by being viewed as too close to the PNG government, tagging along behind. The negotiations, which finally did achieve peace, led first to the New Zealand–led Truce Monitoring Group (TMG, 1997–1998), and then the following year to the larger, Australian-led Peace Monitoring Group (PMG,

Gallery of the Northern Territory, 1995). Twenty years later, Gittoes is still trying to find ways to express in art what he saw at Kibeho: cf. Christiana Spens, 'Community, War and the Role of Art: an Interview with George Gittoes', *Studio International*, 2 September 2013 (http://studiointernational.com/index.php/george-gittoes, accessed 7.7.14).

44 Londey, *Other People's Wars*, pp. 143–145 (Mozambique, Eritrea and Sierra Leone), 211–213 (Haiti and Guatemala); Horner and Connor, *The Good International Citizen*, pp. 225–263 (de-mining in Cambodia), 371–391 (former Yugoslavia).

45 See comments at n. 52.

1998–2003).[46] These monitoring groups were innovative in peacekeeping terms, with monitoring teams formed of a mix of military, police and civilian personnel going out to often remote villagers, talking up the peace process.[47]

Australia's largest ever peacekeeping operation was in East Timor, from 1999. East Timor had been a Portuguese colony, taken over by Indonesia at a time of Portuguese instability in 1975. Many Australians opposed this, partly because of fond memories for East Timorese help to Australian soldiers fighting the Japanese in World War II; but Australian governments regarded placating Indonesia as a prime foreign policy goal.[48] Pressure for action built in the 1990s, and in 1999 a period of political change in Indonesia gave Australian Prime Minister Howard the opportunity to press for the East Timorese to be allowed to vote on their own future. Possibly to Australian surprise, the Indonesians agreed, and an unarmed peacekeeping mission, the UN Mission in East Timor (UNAMET), mainly composed of police, oversaw a plebiscite in August 1999.[49] Following an overwhelming vote for independence, a wave of violence by Indonesian-supported militia broke out, catching Australia and the United Nations completely unprepared. With UN blessing, Australia hastily put together a peacekeeping force, the International Force East Timor (INTERFET), which began landing at Dili on 20 September 1999, after widespread international pressure on Indonesia forced it, somewhat unwillingly, to accept the need for the force. Over half of INTERFET's 10,000 personnel were Australian, and an Australian, Major General Peter Cosgrove, was in

---

46 Londey, *Other People's Wars*, pp. 214–225; Reuben Bowd, *Doves over the Pacific: in Pursuit of Peace and Stability in Bougainville* (Loftus, NSW: Australian Military History Publications, 2007). There had been an earlier, small-scale peacekeeping effort, the South Pacific Peace–Keeping Force (SPPKF), facilitating and protecting an abortive peace conference in 1994: see Bob Breen, *Giving Peace a Chance: Operation Lagoon, Bougainville, 1994: a Case of Military Action and Diplomacy* (Canberra: Strategic and Defence Studies Centre, ANU, 2001).

47 For a fascinating account, see Monica Wehner and Donald Denoon (eds.), *Without a Gun: Australians' Experiences Monitoring Peace in Bougainville, 1997-2001* (Canberra: Pandanus Books, 2001).

48 For a huge collection of Australian documents relating to the Indonesian takeover, see Wendy Way, Damien Browne and Vivianne Johnson (eds.), *Australia and the Indonesian Incorporation of Portuguese Timor, 1974–1976* (Melbourne: Melbourne University Press, 2000), a volume in the Department of Foreign Affairs and Trade's Documents on Australian Foreign Policy series, published just as there was great interest in Australia in re-visiting what exactly had happened in 1975.

49 On UNAMET, see Ian Martin, *Self-determination in East Timor: the United Nations, the Ballot, and International Intervention* (Boulder: Lynne Rienner, 2001); David Savage, *Dancing with the Devil: a Personal Account of Policing the East Timor Vote for Independence* (Melbourne: Monash University Press, 2002).

command. INTERFET quickly brought order to East Timor, before handing over to the UN Transitional Administration in East Timor (UNTAET) in February 2000. Many Australian soldiers simply donned blue berets and carried on. Though not without frictions, INTERFET was outstandingly successful in cowing the militia and putting an end to violence. A series of UN missions followed, as East Timor started on the long road to recovery, development and self-sufficiency.[50] Australians remained until 2005, and then were called back the following year to help quell new civic unrest.[51]

The third element in the 'arc of instability' was Solomon Islands, an ethnically diverse state independent since 1978. As in many places, Western institutions did not sit well with local cultural expectations, and by the late 1990s there was widespread social disorder and violence. Peace talks led to a ceasefire and a low-key, Australian-led peacekeeping operation, the unarmed International Peace Monitoring Team (IPMT, 2000–2002). The IPMT attempted to disarm the rival groups, but was ultimately unsuccessful in curbing the spiral into violence. In Australia there was much (patronising) talk about the dangers of 'failed states'.[52] Wary of appearing neo-colonialist, Australia

50 UNTAET (2000–2002) was followed by the UN Mission of Support in East Timor (UNMISET, 2002–2005); UN Office in Timor-Leste (UNOTIL, 2005–2006); and the UN Integrated Mission in Timor-Leste (UNMIT, 2006–2012). Following the troubles in 2006, the Australian-led International Stabilisation Force (ISF) helped restore order; the last Australians left in 2013.

51 The literature is large; among others, see: Clinton Fernandes, *The Independence of East Timor: Multi-Dimensional Perspectives – Occupation, Resistance, and International Political Activism* (Eastbourne, UK: Sussex Academic Press, 2011); James Cotton, *East Timor, Australia and Regional Order: Intervention and Its Aftermath in Southeast Asia* (London: Routledge Curzon, 2004); Department of Foreign Affairs and Trade, *East Timor in Transition 1998–2000: An Australian Policy Challenge* (Canberra: DFAT, 2001); David Connery, *Crisis Policymaking: Australia and the East Timor Crisis of 1999* (Canberra: ANU E-Press, 2010); Michael G. Smith and Moreen Dee, *Peacekeeping in East Timor: The Path to Independence* (Boulder: Lynne Rienner, 2003). For a succinct account, Londey, *Other People's Wars*, pp. 230–261.

52 On the use of terms such as 'failed state' and 'arc of instability', see the comments of Steven Ratuva, 'Australia's New Assertiveness in the Pacific: the View from "the Backyard"', in Greg Fry and Tarcisius Tara Kabutaulaka (eds.), *Intervention and State-building in the Pacific: the Legitimacy of 'Cooperative Intervention'* (Manchester: Manchester University Press, 2008), pp. 87–101, especially at p. 90: 'The term "arc of instability" ... is not only an attempt at political categorisation and image construction, at the policy level; it also serves as an ideological justification for intervention.' Ratuva quotes a June 2003 interview by the Australian Minister for Foreign Affairs, Alexander Downer, warning of the dangers of allowing 'Solomon Islands to become a failed state and a failed state to fester off the coast of Australia.'

nevertheless ultimately took up the challenge, and mounted the multinational Regional Assistance Mission to Solomon Islands (RAMSI) in 2003. RAMSI was unusual in being led by police and civilians, though with a substantial military component for security. It was successful in settling the situation, but its overbearing attempt to impose Western cultural values was viewed unfavourably by some of the local population. Though much diminished in scale, RAMSI continues in 2014.[53]

6 From 2003 to the Future

After 2003, Australia was too much taken up with fighting wars in Iraq and Afghanistan to do much peacekeeping. Even the return of a Labor government from 2007 to 2013 did little to alter this situation. Some existing missions kept going, but there was little attempt to do anything new. There are some problems with definition, but today (in 2014) it is probably true that Australia once again has fewer than 100 peacekeepers in the field, in the Middle East (UNTSO and the MFO), Cyprus (UNFICYP), the Sudan (UNMISS), and Solomon Islands (RAMSI). Australia has over the years produced many effective, technically skilled, emotionally engaged peacekeepers. The country has also produced notable proponents of the Responsibility to Protect (R2P), including Gareth Evans, who co-chaired the International Commission on Intervention and State Sovereignty, and Professor Ramesh Thakur, now at the Australian National University, who was a member. But three things are particularly striking.

First, Australia is well advanced towards producing an ambitious, multivolume Official History of its peacekeeping, yet at a more general level there is very little public discourse about peacekeeping in Australia today, and little attempt to differentiate peacekeeping from war-fighting.[54] To take one example, the official website for Australia's current Security Council membership makes the following claims: 'More than 65 000 Australians have served in over 50 United Nations and other multilateral peace operations in Africa, the Asia-Pacific, Central America, Europe, and the Middle East since 1947. This tradition continues today, with more than 3100 Australians serving in peace and security operations around the globe.'[55] It is hard to calculate the total number of

53 Londey, *Other People's Wars*, pp. 225–229; Fry and Kabutalauka, *Intervention and State-building in the Pacific*; Sinclair Dinnen and Stewart Firth (eds.), *Politics and State Building in Solomon Islands* (Canberra: ANU E-Press and Asia Pacific Press, 2008).

54 See my remarks at Londey, 'The Invention of Peacekeeping', pp. 12–13.

55 http://australia-unsc.gov.au/australia-and-the-unsc/peacekeeping/ (accessed 14 September 2014).

Australians who have served in peacekeeping operations. The best attempt of which I am aware is that in the Appendix to *Australian peacekeeping*:[56] the total is certainly fewer than 40,000. The larger number, often touted, reflects inclusion at very least of all Australians who served in the Korean War (which may have had UN badging, but was no peacekeeping operation). The current figure of 3,100 includes all Australians serving overseas, whether fighting wars (the great majority) or serving as peacekeepers (fewer than 100, as noted above).

Secondly, a number of commentators have noted the powerful influence in Australia of an Anzac mythology which focuses on the imagined deeds of Australian soldiers in World War I as a foundational myth of Australian nationhood.[57] These views are not restricted to left-wing academics. Former army officer, James Brown, has commented recently that Australian soldiers in Afghanistan are scarred by the sense that they cannot match 'the heroic giants of Anzac', that they do not want 'glory bestowed by a society that fetishises war but doesn't know the first damn thing about fighting it'.[58] A military mythology which intimidates even those fighting wars has little place for peacekeepers. There are small exceptions. In 2013, after many years' resistance, the Australian War Memorial added peacekeepers who had died on operations to the Roll of Honour, an inscribed list of all Australia's war dead. A site has been allocated for a memorial to peacekeepers in Anzac Parade, the main national locus of military commemoration; but lack of funding has prevented any progress towards building it. The Australian Defence Force, stretched hugely by its recent Middle East commitments, maintains a low-key interest in peacekeeping. The enthusiasm which led all three services, eager to highlight their activities in Cambodia and Somalia, to contribute financially to the Australian War Memorial's first peacekeeping exhibition in 1993 is long past. The ADF Peace Operations Training Centre,[59] set up in 1992, continues to operate, but the major centre for peacekeeping training in Australia is now the Australian Federal Police's International Deployment Group (IDG) in Canberra.[60] The

56 Horner, Londey and Bou, *Australian Peacekeeping*, Appendix 1.

57 For a comprehensive statement, see Marilyn Lake and Henry Reynolds (eds.), *What's Wrong with Anzac? The Militarisation of Australian History* (Sydney: University of New South Wales Press, 2010), with contributions by Joy Damousi, Mark McKenna, and the two editors.

58 James Brown, *Anzac's Long Shadow: the Cost of Our National Obsession* (Collingwood, Vic.: Redback, 2014), p. 4.

59 http://www.defence.gov.au/adfwc/peacekeeping/index.htm (accessed 14 September 2014).

60 http://www.afp.gov.au/en/policing/international-deployment-group.aspx (accessed 14 September 2014).

IDG, set up in 2004, provides regular courses for civilian police, to ensure a pool of trained members available for deployment overseas.

Thirdly, as noted above, all of Australia's large-scale recent peacekeeping has been in its own neighbourhood, reflecting a general shift (very apparent in Africa) towards regionally based peacekeeping. This shift abandons some of the original ideas behind UN peacekeeping. As Patrick Shaw put it in his 1964 memo to the Minister for External Affairs (emphasis in original):

> The Secretary-General, in selecting countries for approach for help in Cyprus, has been guided by the principle, frequently stated by the Secretary-General, that in any such operation, countries with a specific interest should if possible be excluded. Australia has much to gain by establishing this principle, and by establishing a general duty of United Nations members to help solve distant disputes in which they are not strategically concerned. (Thus, Pakistan supplied troops for the United Nations' team which supervised the transfer of power to Indonesia in West New Guinea.)[61]

The principles embodied in those remarks have largely been lost sight of in Australia. In the 1990s Australian peacekeeping reflected Shaw's ideals, under the umbrella of what Gareth Evans liked to term 'good international citizenship'.[62] There is little talk of that in the modern Australia, where the dominant political discourse focuses on keeping refugees away, and avoidance of action on climate change. The climate for peacekeeping, in Australia, has become rather bleak.

61 Patrick Shaw to Minister for External Affairs [Sir Garfield Barwick], 20 April 1964, NAA: A1838, 913/5/1 pt 1.

62 See, for example, a speech by Evans in Canberra on 6 March 1990, 'Foreign policy and good international citizenship', accessible at http://gevans.org/speeches/old/1990/060390_fm_fpandgoodinternationalcitizen.pdf (accessed 7.7.14).

CHAPTER 6

RAMSI Ten Years On: From Post-conflict Stabilisation to Development in Solomon Islands?

Sinclair Dinnen

Introduction

The Regional Assistance Mission to Solomon Islands (RAMSI) was deployed in mid-2003 following a request from the beleaguered Solomon Islands government (SIG). A low-level conflict, known locally as 'the tension', had erupted on the main island of Guadalcanal in late 1998. Groups of young Guadalcanal men, calling themselves the Isatabu Freedom Movement, launched a campaign of violent harassment directed mainly at settlers from the neighbouring island of Malaita.[1] Around 35,000 of these settlers were forcibly evicted from their homes in rural Guadalcanal and the peri-areas surrounding the national capital, Honiara.[2] This provoked the emergence of a rival militia – the Malaita Eagle Force – and over the following two years armed skirmishes occurred between bands of militants claiming to represent the interests of the two islands. Attempts by SIG to restore order were unsuccessful and the Royal Solomon Islands Police Force (RSIPF) fractured along ethnic lines.[3] A *de facto* coup in June 2000 mounted by Malaitan militants, supported by elements of the police, forced the resignation of the incumbent Prime Minister, Bartholomew Ulufa'alu.[4] The Australian and New Zealand governments brokered a peace agreement between the main militia groups in October 2000. While the Townsville Peace Agreement (TPA) ended the spectre of an all-out ethnic war, the country remained militarised and ex-militants and rogue police engaged in collective and opportunistic violence in Honiara and parts of rural Guadalcanal and Malaita. Government revenues dropped dramatically with the closure of major commercial enterprises, essential services ground to

1 Matthew Allen, *Greed and Grievance: Ex-Militants' Perspectives on the Conflict in Solomon Islands, 1998–2003* (Honolulu: University of Hawai'i Press, 2013).

2 Amnesty International, *Solomon Islands – A Forgotten Conflict* (London, 2000).

3 In the absence of a standing military force, the police constitute the principal enforcement agency of the Solomon Islands state.

4 Sinclair Dinnen, 'Winners and Losers: Politics and Disorder in the Solomon Islands 2000–2002,' *The Journal of Pacific History*, vol. 37, issue 3, 2002, pp. 285–298.

 | DOI 10.1163/9789004322059_007

a halt in many areas, while the compensation process adopted as the main instrument of peacemaking became rapidly corrupted.[5] Confronted with national bankruptcy, lacking any independent enforcement capacity, and viewed by many of its own citizens as deeply compromised, it became clear that SIG on its own was incapable of resolving the crisis.

The arrival of RAMSI in mid-2003 under the auspices of the Pacific Islands Forum (PIF), the premier grouping of regional states, was welcomed by most Solomon Islanders who were tired of the violence, insecurity and disruption of the previous five years. Regional in character, the mission was led by Australia, which also supplied the bulk of funding (recently estimated at $AUD2.6 billion in real terms between 2003 and 2013),[6] personnel and other resources. Smaller but significant contributions came from New Zealand and other Forum member states. The restoration of law and order was entrusted to the mission's police, the Participating Police Force (PPF), comprising around 330 police officers with security and logistical support provided by approximately 1,800 military personnel. RAMSI evolved considerably over a ten year period in terms of its operational priorities, organisation and manner of engagement. Consistent with liberal peace orthodoxies, restoring security was linked to an ambitious and longer-term state-building exercise aimed at strengthening the central agencies of the Solomon Islands' state and creating an enabling environment for investor-led growth.[7] Ten years later, the mission is in its final phase of transition and drawdown. This has entailed a progressive reduction in its size and range of activities, including the complete withdrawal of all remaining military personnel in 2013. Over a four year period – 2013–2017 – RAMSI's development programs are being absorbed into regular aid arrangements managed by bilateral and multilateral donors, including Australia.[8] RAMSI's remaining presence consists of a slimmed down PPF continuing capacity-building work with the RSIPF, primarily in Honiara.

---

5 Jon Fraenkel, *The Manipulation of Custom: From Uprising to Intervention in the Solomon Islands* (Wellington: Victoria University Press, 2004).

6 Jenny Hayward-Jones, *Australia's Costly Investment in Solomon Islands: The Lessons of RAMSI* (Sydney: Lowy Institute for International Affairs, Analysis, May 2014), *available electronically at: http://www.lowyinstitute.org/publications/lessons-ramsi.*

7 Matthew Allen and Sinclair Dinnen, 'The North Down Under: Antinomies of Conflict and Intervention in Solomon Islands,' *Conflict, Security & Development*, vol. 10, issue 3, July 2010, pp. 299–327.

8 Nicholas Coppel, 'Transition of the Regional Assistance Mission to Solomon Islands', Australian National University, SSGM Discussion Paper 2012/10, pp. 1–19, available electronically at: http://ips.cap.anu.edu.au/ssgm.

While RAMSI's early success in restoring security has rightly attracted praise, much remains to be done in order to fulfil the mission's longer-term goals for a stable, secure and self-sufficient Solomon Islands. Outstanding concerns include the sustainability of gains made over the last decade and the extent to which the island nation's own leaders and institutions can maintain and build on these. Many of the factors that contributed to the original tension in the late 1990s remain and pose a potential threat to future stability. Some of the underlying stresses are likely to become more pronounced in light of projected demographic and economic trends. These include the misalignment between Solomon Islands' small and constrained formal economy and the expectations of its rapidly growing population, the conflict stresses that may follow as the economy shifts from logging to mining, as well as the consistently poor service delivery and development outcomes associated with current forms of political leadership.

These issues will be examined in the context of Solomon Islands' recent history, present circumstances and likely future. The first section looks at some of the main factors and dynamics that contributed to the original tension and that need to be addressed in order to achieve durable peace and stability. Section two looks at RAMSI's activities, impacts and evolution since 2003, while the final section considers the country's prospects in the post-RAMSI era, with a particular view to the implications for international actors.

Background to the Tension

Solomon Islands has never had a fully functioning Weberian state, either in terms of institutional capabilities or the ability to project authority across the length and breadth of the territory. Although the tension and subsequent breakdown of order from 2000–2003 exacerbated the fragility of the state to the point of collapse, the events that unfolded from the late 1990s were as much a consequence of this underlying fragility as they were a source of it. The state inherited from Britain at independence in 1978 has struggled to consolidate within Solomon Islands' socially diverse and geographically fragmented environment. With an estimated population of 555,000 people,[9] speaking

9 Solomon Islands country brief. Australian Government: Department of Foreign Affairs and Trade, *available electronically at*: http://www.dfat.gov.au/geo/solomon_islands_brief.html#site-header.

around 64 languages,[10] Solomon Islands comprises a double chain of six main islands, lying 1,800 kilometres off Australia's north-east coast. The population is widely dispersed across the archipelago, with around 82% living in rural areas. Individual identities remain relentlessly localised, with little sense of 'nation' or shared political community. A former Prime Minister, Solomon Mamaloni, famously declared that Solomon Islands was "a nation conceived but never born".[11] Contemporary forms of 'community' revolve around complex interplays of kinship and exchange relations, friendships, church membership and myriad claims to customary land. While under enormous pressure in many places owing to the pace of change, local forms of informal or customary governance retain high levels of legitimacy among rural Solomon Islanders. Most people continue to live on the margins of the modern state and formal economy, relying on these local systems for their welfare and security needs, and on a mix of subsistence agriculture, fishing and cash cropping for everyday survival.

The centralisation of political and administrative power was actively contested in many areas during colonial times.[12] Widespread dissatisfaction with the workings of the government system has continued throughout the post-independence period, feeding into debates around political devolution and provincial autonomy, including current proposals for a federated system. Frustrations are expressed regularly about the uneven and poor quality of government service delivery, particularly in rural localities where most citizens live. Many older Solomon Islanders share a perception of the progressive withdrawal of government from rural areas during the post-independence period and of a widening gap between Honiara and the rest of the country. While provincial governments were established in 1981, the relationship between them and national tiers of government has never been clear, with confusion over the allocation of responsibilities and functions, and perennial underfunding.[13] The dissolution of Area Councils in the 1990s saw the

---

10 D.H. Tryon and B.D. Hackman, *Solomon Islands Languages: An Internal Classification* (Canberra: Department of Lingusitics, Research School of Pacific and Asian Studies, Australian National University, 1983).

11 Solomon Mamoloni, 'The Road to Independence', in Ron Crocombe and Esau Tuza (eds.), *Independence, Dependence, Interdependence – The First 10 Years of Solomon Islands Independence* (Honiara: Government Printing Press, 1992), at p. 14.

12 David W. Akin, *Colonialism, Maasina Rule, and the Origins of Malaitan Kastom* (Honolulu: University of Hawai'i Press, 2013).

13 John Cox and Joanne Morrison, 'Solomon Islands Provincial Governance Information Paper' (Canberra: AusAID, 2004).

effective demise of the official local–level government system and an important mechanism for the delivery of government services and public works to rural communities.[14] Under pressure from the donor community to reduce government expenditure, Area Councils were defunded in 1993 and disbanded altogether between 1996 and 1997.

The Area Councils derived from an older colonial system of indirect administration introduced by the British that also included local courts and officials such as the 'area constables' as part of a devolved administrative system that sought to coordinate a range of agency and services functions at local levels. Following the removal of Area Councils, area constables disappeared in all provinces, with the exception of Renbel. These officials used to assist in the enforcement of council by-laws and local court decisions, performing an important role in dispute resolution and order maintenance, as well as serving as critical intermediaries between customary and state authorities at local levels. Although they still exist in many areas, local courts have, for the most part, become moribund in the absence of adequate government support.[15] While many factors contributed to the tension,[16] it is worth pointing out that the conflict in Guadalcanal occurred shortly after the dissolution of Area Councils. An association between these events has been drawn by some observers who suggest that the demise of "the local policing and justice systems removed restraints on anti-social behaviour that were formerly available".[17] The retreat of state from rural Solomon Islands provides an important aspect of the broader context of increasing local grievances, contestation and instability in recent decades.

Understanding the political economy behind this retreat is important not only for the light it can shed on the origins of the tension but also for developing a better understanding of what is required to prevent future conflict and instability. Solomon Islands' post-independence political culture and the

---

14 Sinclair Dinnen and Matthew Allen, 'Paradoxes of Postcolonial Police-building,' *Policing & Society*, vol. 23, issue 2, 2013, pp. 222–242.

15 Daniel Evans, Michael Goddard with Don Paterson, *The Hybrid Courts of Melanesia: A Comparative Analysis of Village Courts of Papua New Guinea, Island Courts of Vanuatu and Local Courts of Solomon Islands* (Washington DC: World Bank, Justice and Development Working Paper Series, no. 13, 2011), at p. 11.

16 Matthew G. Allen, *Greed and Grievance: Ex-Militants' Perspectives on the Conflict in Solomon Islands 1998–2003* (Honolulu: University of Hawai'i Press, 2013).

17 Ian Scales, 'The Flourishing of Local Level Governance after the Coup in Solomon Islands: Lessons for Reform of the State'. Unpublished Paper Presented at the *Symposium on Governance in Pacific States: Reassessing Roles and Remedies*, 30 September – 2 October 2003, Canberra, The Australian National University.

actions of its political leaders are deeply implicated in these developments. The latter have consistently failed to address the need for effective systems of government administration at provincial and local levels. In many respects, they have actively sought to monopolise the distribution of public resources at the centre, thereby neutralising potential rivals at lower levels. In fairness, their actions have also been facilitated, as mentioned, by pressure from international donors wedded to neo-liberal frameworks to reduce public expenditure. Alternative approaches devised by political actors to satisfy the demands of local constituents, primarily through off-budget discretionary funds, have made the task of administrative reform all the more challenging. They have also accentuated patterns of uneven development and accompanying perceptions of relative deprivation.

The political culture that has evolved in Solomon Islands during the post-independence period shares many characteristics with that of its Melanesian neighbours.[18] A strong party system based on policy or ideological differences has failed to take root. Instead a fluid and personalised style of 'big-man' politics prevails. In addition to large numbers of independent MPs with no stated affiliations, parties appear to serve primarily as vehicles for the ambitions of individual leaders rather than for the pursuit of distinct policy agendas.[19] Accessing and redistributing funds through patronage networks based on kinship animates the relationship between elected politicians and their voter base. 'Money politics' has become pronounced in political behaviour at the national level and been fuelled by a corrosive nexus between elements of the political elite and the notoriously corrupt Asian-dominated logging industry.[20] Financial and other forms of inducement are integral to the messy (and expensive) process of stitching together loose coalition governments following elections, as well as in the actions of leaders to consolidate or undermine these coalitions once in office.[21]

Needless to say this kind of politics is not conducive to stable and effective government, or to equitable and sustainable development outcomes. Political

18 Bill Standish, 'The Dynamics of Papua New Guinea's Democracy: an Essay', *Pacific Economic Bulletin*, vol. 22, no. 1, March 2007, pp. 135–157.

19 Jeffrey S. Steeves, 'Unbounded Politics in the Solomon Islands: Leadership and Party Alignments', *Pacific Studies*, vol. 19, no. 1, 1996, pp. 115–138.

20 Judith Bennett, *Pacific Forest: A History of Resource Control and Contest in Solomon Islands, c. 1800–1997* (Cambridge and Leiden: White Horse Press and Brill Academic Publishers, 2000).

21 Sinclair Dinnen, 'The Solomon Islands Intervention and the Instabilities of the Post-Colonial State', *Global Change, Peace and Security*, 20 (3), October 2008, pp. 339–55.

patronage has been further institutionalised since the mid-1980s with the introduction of various forms of discretionary funds.[22] These are provided to individual members of parliament for spending in their constituencies with limited control or oversight over their use. The amount of funding available to each member has grown steadily with each new government.[23] Funds are typically deployed in the lead-up to elections by sitting members seeking to secure electoral advantage over other candidates. Such acts of political gifting inevitably create divisions between beneficiaries and those who lose out at the constituency level. Their usage corrodes bureaucratic service delivery systems and diverts scarce public resources to partisan political ends. Decisions around the distribution of these funds are driven primarily by short-term and parochial political considerations rather than by any larger planning or policy framework. Despite generally unimpressive outcomes in terms of development and service delivery, these funds and other informal sources available to political leaders are now an important aspect of how power actually works in Solomon Islands, and are jealously guarded by their political patrons. Some scholars have argued that the potential disruption to political patronage networks posed by the declining demand for log exports during the Asian financial crisis in the late 1990s and the election of a reformist government, provoked deliberate acts of destabilisation by vested political and business interests and that these, in turn, contributed to the subsequent tension.[24]

The more familiar narrative of the tension highlights the social stresses associated with internal migration. Solomon Islands' small formal economy – logging, fishing and, increasingly, mining – has failed to match the needs and expectations of its rapidly growing and youthful population.[25] Spatial inequalities associated with longstanding patterns of uneven development

---

22 Jon Fraenkel, 'The Atrophied State: A Supply-Side Perspective on Politician 'Slush Funds' in Western Melanesia' in R. Duncan (ed.), *The Political Economy of Economic Reform in the Pacific* (Mandaluyong City, Philippines: Asian Development Bank, 2011), pp. 303–326.

23 The media reported in April 2013 that SIG had agreed to increase the size of the constituency development funds for each of Solomon Islands' 50 constituencies to SBD$6 million (approximately AUD$800,000), *available electronically at* http://www.radioaustralia.net.au/international/radio/program/pacific-beat/call-for-greater-accountability-for-solomon-mps-discretionary-funds/1111958.

24 Shahar Hameiri, 'The Trouble with RAMSI: Re-examining the Roots of Conflict in Solomon Islands', *Contemporary Pacific*, vol. 19, issue 2, 2007, pp. 409–441; 'Risk Management, Neoliberalism, and the Securitisation of the Australian Aid Program', *Australian Journal of International Affairs*, vol. 62, issue 3, 2008, pp. 357–371.

25 Annual population growth in 2012 was 2.3%. The 2009 census records around 41% of the population under the age of fifteen. See, Allen, *Greed and Grievance*, at p. 37.

dating back to colonial times have encouraged internal migration from less developed regions to areas offering better employment and economic prospects, and improved access to services. Migration from the densely populated and undeveloped island of Malaita to Honiara and adjacent areas in rural Guadalcanal over many years served to accentuate cultural differences between 'settlers' and 'indigenous' groups. Local resentments have been directed at the perceived monopolisation of employment and other opportunities by Malaitans, and their involvement in land transactions viewed as contrary to Guadalcanal customs.[26] These resentments were most acutely felt among the inhabitants of the remote and poorly developed southern Weather Coast and it was mainly young men from that area who started attacking and intimidating Malaitan settlers.

The Regional Assistance Mission to Solomon Islands (RAMSI)

Solomon Islands' authorities had issued several unsuccessful requests for Australian assistance prior to 2003.[27] An approach to the UN in September 2002 was abandoned after it became clear that any Security Council vote was likely to be vetoed by China owing to Solomon Islands' diplomatic recognition of Taiwan.[28] The Australian government's decision to act when it did resulted from a confluence of strategic considerations. Concerns about regional instability had been growing since the late 1990s following political upheavals in Indonesia, East Timor, Papua New Guinea, Fiji and Solomon Islands.[29] These were intensified further after the 9/11 attacks against the United States in 2001.The 'war on terror' provided a new lens that linked instability and conflict in failed states to the generation of threats to regional and global

26 Tarcisius Kabutaulaka, 'Beyond Ethnicity: the Political Economy of the Guadalcanal Crisis in the Solomon Islands', Working Paper 01/01, Canberra: State Society and Governance in Melanesia Project, Research School of Pacific and Asian Studies, Australian National University, 2001.

27 These included requests by Prime Minister Ulufa'alu and his successor Manasseh Sogavare, the first as early as 1999 and later during the Commonwealth Heads of Government Meeting (CHOGM) in 2002. Rebecca Lineham, 'The Regional Assistance Mission to Solomon Islands and democratic accountability'. Wellington, NZ: Unpublished Master of Strategic Studies thesis, Victoria University of Wellington, March 2006, pp. 1–148.

28 Richard Ponzio, 'Solomon Islands: The UN and Interventions by Coalitions of the Willing', *International Peacekeeping*, vol. 12, no. 2, summer 2005, pp. 173–188.

29 Robert Ayson, 'The 'Arc of Instability' and Australia's Strategic Policy', *Australian Journal of International Affairs*, vol. 61, issue2, 2007, pp. 215–231.

security.[30] Applying this lens to events in Solomon Islands between 1998–2003 provided a compelling case for intervention.[31] The proposed remedy was a liberal peace intervention with a strong accent on security, state-building and economic reform.[32] Each element is reflected in the three pillars around which RAMSI was organised: law and justice; the machinery of government; and economic governance.

Australian leadership of the regional mission was contingent on securing the consent of Solomon Islands' authorities and member states of the Pacific Islands Forum (PIF). Forum Foreign Ministers endorsed Australia's plan of intervention, while the Solomon Islands Parliament unanimously passed the Facilitation of International Assistance (FIA) Act 2003, setting out the powers and immunities of mission personnel. Described as a form of "co-operative intervention" by the then Australian Foreign Minister,[33] RAMSI was to operate through Solomon Islands national laws and respect the island nation's sovereignty.[34] Under the FIA Act, the Solomon Islands Parliament was to review RAMSI annually and could, in theory, terminate the mission by revoking its consent.

The mission's wide-ranging mandate combined security and development objectives:

- Ensure the safety and security of Solomon Islands;
- Repair and reform the machinery of government, improve government accountability and improve the delivery of services in urban and provincial areas;
- Improve economic governance and strengthen the government's financial systems;
- Help rebuild the economy and encourage sustainable broad-based growth; and
- Build strong and peaceful communities.[35]

30 See, for example, *The National Security Strategy of the United States of America* (Washington DC: White House, 2002), p. iv.

31 Australian Strategic Policy Institute, *Our Failing Neighbour: Australia and the Future of Solomon Islands* (Canberra: Australian Strategic Policy Institute, 2003).

32 Julien Barbara, 'Antipodean Statebuilding: The Regional Assistance Mission to Solomon Islands and Australian Intervention in the South Pacific', *Journal of Intervention and Statebuilding*, 2008, 2:2, pp. 123–149; Allen and Dinnen, 'The North Down Under'.

33 Alexander Downer, 'Our Failing Neighbour: Australia and the Future of the Solomon Islands'. Address at the launch of the ASPI Report, Sydney, 10 June 2003.

34 Michael Fullilove, 'RAMSI and State Building in Solomon Islands', *Defender*, Autumn 2006, at p. 33.

35 As listed on the RAMSI website: http://www.ramsi.org/about/what-is-ramsi.html.

RAMSI's initial phase, led by the PPF, focused on the restoration of law and order and involved mission police in an executive policing role. This was to be followed by a period of consolidation and institutional reform, and, finally, the building of sustainability and self-sufficiency among Solomon Islands' own institutions. In addition to the highly visible police and military presence, civilians from a range of Australian government departments[36] were placed as advisers in various ministries and agencies. In this regard, RAMSI has been described as "the most comprehensive whole of government strategy towards a fragile state of any donor to date".[37] As well as Australia's substantial commitment of funds and personnel, no fixed exit date was specified. The mission was coordinated in Solomon Islands by a Special Coordinator's Office, headed by a senior Australian diplomat, while Australian-based agencies operated through an interdepartmental committee in Canberra.

Security was restored quickly and peacefully. Large numbers of firearms were handed over to mission personnel, while well-known militant leaders were apprehended to be processed subsequently through the criminal courts. This intensive period of law enforcement placed considerable pressure on other parts of the fragile criminal justice system, and the mission placed a number of international personnel in relevant agencies, including as magistrates, lawyers, clerks and prison officials. In addition to their executive policing role, the PPF also began the longer-term task of cleaning up and rebuilding the RSIPF.[38] Over 400 officers resigned or were removed, amounting to more than one quarter of the total workforce. Other early achievements included restoring stability to government finances. Improvements in public financial management and tax collection saw government revenues increase by around 170% during RAMSI's first three years.[39] Legislative and policy provisions were enacted to support private sector investment, while measures were taken to

---

36 Australian government departments participating in RAMSI included: the Departments of Prime Minister and Cabinet, Foreign Affairs and Trade, AusAID, Defence, Australian Federal Police, Attorney-General's, Customs, Treasury, and Finance and Administration.

37 Stewart Patrick and Kaysie Brown, *Greater than the Sum of its Parts? Assessing "Whole of Government" Approaches to Fragile States* (New York: International Peace Academy, 2007), at p. 87.

38 Sinclair Dinnen, 'State-Building in a Post-Colonial Society: The Case of Solomon Islands', *Chicago Journal of International Law*, vol. 9, no. 1, Summer 2008, pp. 51–78; Clive Moore, 'External Intervention: The Solomon Islands Beyond RAMSI' in M. Anne Brown (ed.), *Security and Development in the Pacific Islands – Social Resilience in Emerging States* (Boulder & London: Lynne Rienner Publishers), pp. 169–196.

39 See, 'Careful planning puts archipelago in the sun', *The Australian*, 15 June 2007.

strengthen Solomon Islands' accountability mechanisms, including the Office of the Auditor-General, the Ombudsman, and the Leadership Code.[40]

Inevitably, there were also set-backs. Serious public disturbances occurred in Honiara in April 2006 following national elections.[41] Two days of rioting and opportunistic looting destroyed much of the capital's Chinatown and served to highlight the underlying fragility of the peace. Manasseh Sogavare's subsequent election as Prime Minister heralded a dramatic deterioration in bilateral relations between the Solomon Islands' and Australian governments. A staunch nationalist and critic of the mission, Sogavare sought to reassert his government's control over RAMSI and curb what he viewed as Australia's dominant influence. This, in turn, provoked strong resistance from political leaders in Canberra.[42] Although these differences were fought out at the highest levels of the two governments and did not necessarily affect operational relationships, they inevitably cast a shadow over the future of the mission. In doing so, they also exposed the inherent vulnerability of the 'co-operative intervention' model to the vagaries of shifting local political allegiances.

Changes of government in Australia and Solomon Islands in late 2007 provided a much-needed circuit breaker. Improved relations with the Melanesian countries – Solomon Islands and PNG in particular – were a high priority for the new Australian government led by Kevin Rudd. Although there was no radical change in substantive policy, there was a distinct change in tone with Australian pronouncements now couched in the more constructive language of 'partnership', 'mutual respect' and 'mutual responsibility'.[43] RAMSI's evolution and capacity for learning were most apparent in this later period.[44] A recurring criticism raised by local and regional observers during the first phase of the mission related to Australia's dominance of key decision-making

40 Evaluations of these various initiatives suggest mixed results. See, for example, John Braithwaite, Sinclair Dinnen, Matthew Allen, Valerie Braithwaite, and Hilary Charlesworth, *Pillars and Shadows: Statebuilding as Peacebuilding in Solomon Islands* (Canberra: ANU E Press, 2010), pp. 56–58. See also Jon Fraenkel, Joni Madraiwiwi and Henry Okole, *The RAMSI Decade: A Review of the Regional Assistance Mission to Solomon Islands, 2002–2013* (Honiara: Solomon Islands Government and the Pacific Islands Forum, July 2014), pp. 68–74.

41 Sinclair Dinnen, 'Dilemmas of Intervention and the Building of State and Nation', in S. Dinnen and S. Firth (eds), *Politics and State Building in Solomon Islands* (Canberra: Asia-Pacific Press and ANU E Press, 2008), pp. 1–38.

42 *Ibid*, pp. 17–26.

43 This change in tone was expressed most clearly in the Australian and Papua New Guinean Governments' *Port Moresby Declaration* of 6th March 2008.

44 John Braithwaite et al, *Pillars and Shadows*, pp. 156–162.

and the perceived marginalisation of Solomon Islands' and regional stakeholders. While to a large extent an inevitable consequence of the asymmetry in resources and capabilities between the different stakeholders, as well as the initial prioritisation of RAMSI's security agenda, the period since 2007 saw the creation of more space for Solomon Islander and regional voices to actively participate in the shaping and implementation of the mission.

New consultative arrangements included the 2009 Solomon Islands-Australia Partnership for Development that sought closer collaboration between the two governments in meeting agreed development goals. A Forum Ministerial Standing Committee (FMSC) was established,[45] as was a 'triumvirate group' comprising senior officials from SIG, PIF and RAMSI,[46] while a Partnership Framework was designed to increase alignment between the mission's work and the priorities of SIG.[47] These mechanisms reflected a growing sensibility to local concerns and priorities that had previously been overlooked. The earlier emphasis on law enforcement was broadened through support to locally-led reconciliation processes, including the establishment of a Truth and Reconciliation Commission (TRC) in 2009. There was also a lessening of the mission's initial reluctance to facilitate national dialogue around issues of political decentralisation.

Transition and Beyond — Solomon Islands' Future Prospects

As it marked its tenth anniversary in July 2013, the mission still enjoyed high levels of popular support. The People's Survey 2013 revealed that that 86% of Solomon Islanders surveyed continued to support RAMSI's presence.[48] This is unusual for a prolonged international intervention and an indication of the strengths of local perceptions about the important contribution of the mission. Although uneven across sectors, there is evidence of improvements in government service delivery. A substantial amount of public debt has

45 The FMSC comprises past, present and future Foreign Ministers of Forum Chair countries, as well as the Foreign Ministers of Solomon Islands, Australia, and, since 2009, PNG.

46 The 'triumvirate group' comprises the Solomon Islands Government Permanent Secretary to RAMSI, the Honiara-based PIF Representative to Solomon Islands, and the RAMSI Special Coordinator.

47 Progress under the Framework is monitored by a Joint Performance Oversight Group co-chaired by the Special Coordinator and Solomon Islands Prime Minister.

48 The Peoples Surveys, commissioned by RAMSI and undertaken by the Australian National University, have been gauging local views across the Solomon Islands since 2006 on a range of social, economic and development issues. They can accessed on the RAMSI website: http://www.ramsi.org/

been retired, while the formal economy has been growing consistently, with GDP growth averaging around 7% since 2004.[49] Rumours of renewed ethnic tensions in Guadalcanal in early 2012 were dismissed unequivocally by spokespersons for the two former rival militias.[50] The RSIPF successfully managed protests associated with the change of government in November 2011, while reported incidents of serious crime remain low by regional and international standards.

While an indicator of the success of the mission, the high levels of popular support also suggest a continuing lack of confidence by Solomon Islanders in their own institutions and anxiety about a possible return to conflict without the presence of RAMSI. For example, according to the 2011 People's Survey, 65% of respondents believed that the country was not yet ready for RAMSI to scale back its activities, while only 19% said it was. An unintended consequence of the mission's success in restoring security and administrative functionality has been to induce high levels of dependency among many Solomon Islanders, rendering RAMSI indispensable in their eyes to the country's continuing stability. This dependency has been evident in varying degrees across different sectors of government, as well as extending from the highest levels of political leadership to citizens in rural localities. This in turn suggests that the task of rebuilding local capabilities and self-sufficiency on the part of Solomon Islands actors and institutions still has a long way to go.

The mission's extensive police-building engagement illustrates some of these dilemmas,[51] many of which are common to all large interventions.[52] Although there have been some positive signs, successive People's Surveys indicate that Solomon Islanders still have limited confidence in their own police force.[53] While in large part a legacy of the earlier tension, there is also evidence that many Solomon Islanders are now evaluating the local police in relation to the much better resourced and highly professional mission police.[54] The RSIPF inevitably come off worse in such comparisons. An irony here is

49 Matthew Allen, *Long-term Engagement: The Future of the Regional Assistance Mission to Solomon Islands* (Canberra: Australian Strategic Policy Institute, 2011), p. 6.

50 'Ex-militants warned of false information', *Solomon Star*, 5 April 2012.

51 The following discussion draws on Dinnen and Allen, 'Paradoxes'.

52 See, for example, Michael Ignatieff, 'The Burden', *New York Times Magazine*, 5 January 2003, p. 162.

53 For example, 60% of respondents in the 2013 People's Survey stated that they were not satisfied with RSIPF response to a reported crime.

54 Dinnen and Allen, 'Paradoxes', pp. 228–233.

that the continuing presence of the PPF, whose primary task for some time has been to rebuild the RSIPF, may have served inadvertently to accentuate this lack of confidence on the part of many citizens. Likewise RAMSI's substantial financial and other support to the RSIPF – around two-thirds of the total costs[55] – may have reduced the incentive for SIG to adequately resource its own police force.

With much of RAMSI's development work focused on central government agencies in Honiara, many rural Solomon Islanders still face major problems of access to state services. Despite improvements in some areas of service delivery over the past ten years, the country remains in the low human development category and is currently ranked 143 out of 187 countries in the UN's Human Development Index.[56] Difficulties experienced by rural citizens in accessing government services can also be illustrated in relation to state police and justice systems. According to 2010 figures, the RSIPF had some 28 police stations and posts located outside of Honiara in the provinces.[57] The former are usually based in provincial capitals, leaving a scattering of smaller police posts in selected rural areas. Significant disparities exist in the distribution of police personnel and other assets in different parts of the country. For example, just over half the total number of RSIPF officers were stationed in Honiara which is home to less than 20% of the total Solomon Islands population. By contrast, only 7.5% of the police were located in Malaita province with around 30.3% of the national population. It is only recently that more attention has been given to the development of a model of community policing that will be able to extend the reach of the RSIPF across the archipelago and that will be sustainable in light of the fiscal constraints facing SIG.

The limited presence and reach of state agencies in rural communities means that the latter remain largely dependent on their own informal mechanisms and processes. In addition to the findings of People's Surveys, recent research by the Ministry of Justice and Legal Affairs and the World Bank's Justice for the Poor Program demonstrates the extent to which rural Solomon Islanders continue to rely on their own village-based mechanisms

---

55 J. Gouy and M. Harding, *'True Cost' of Policing in the Solomon Islands. Identifying Policing and Security Expenditures and Costs Borne by External Agencies*. Final Report, 9th March 2011.

56 UNDP: Human Development Report 2013. *The Rise of the South: Human Progress in a Diverse World*. Explanatory note on 2013 HDR composite indices. Solomon Islands. http://hdr.undp.org/sites/default/files/Country-Profiles/SLB.pdf.

57 Martin Goode, *Mekim Senis – Resourcing Change 2010–2013* (Honiara, Royal Solomon Islands Police Force).

for managing everyday disputes and ensuring community safety.[58] Different configurations of three broad and overlapping justice systems – *kastom*,[59] church and state systems – are found in different areas, with the former (*kastom*) being most commonly used to resolve local disputes. Rather than being archaic remnants of a pre-modern past, local systems are highly dynamic and manifestly capable of adaptation. Although weakening in many places under the weight of rapid change and new forms of disputation, and while they may suffer from lack of accountability and inconsistency with human rights standards, they retain a high level of legitimacy among most Solomon Islanders.[60]

RAMSI's singular focus on strengthening government systems in Honiara has largely neglected the role of local non-state actors and informal types of governance. Whether these local systems are a product of necessity or choice on the part of villagers, their prevalence in rural localities presents an opportunity for complementing the top-down approach to state-building with bottom-up approaches that build on existing local strengths. This would entail a focus on developing linkages between the different forms of authority and layers of governance, from Honiara down to the most local levels. Support for this kind of multilayered approach is provided by the World Bank research which makes a strong case for engaging with the realities of legal pluralism in Solomon Islands and deliberately nurturing linkages between different security and justice providers. This would potentially enable greater alignment between the diverse sources and forms of regulation at local levels. It could also lead to the development of more socially attuned and fiscally sustainable approaches to managing disputes, as well as helping to prevent the kind of conflict escalation that occurred in the late 1990s. In the long term, it could make an important contribution to the larger task of nation-making in the archipelago.

RAMSI has been sensitive to local concerns about the potentially destabilising effects of its drawdown and eventual departure. The current Partnership Framework provides the master transitional strategy of graduated withdrawal and the mission's drawdown is calibrated according to the completion of

---

58 Matthew Allen, Sinclair Dinnen, Daniel Evans, and Rebecca Monson, *Justice Delivered Locally– Systems, Challenges, and Innovations in Solomon Islands* (Washington DC: World Bank, Justice for the Poor Research Report, August 2013), available electronically at: http://www.worldbank.org/en/news/featue/2013/10/18/justice-delivered-locally-in-solomon-islands.

59 The term '*kastom* system' is used here to refer to local rule systems whose authority lies in appeals to locally-specific bodies of *kastom* (custom) or tradition, and that are typically administered by local 'chiefs'.

60 Allen et al., *Justice Delivered Locally*, pp. 34–65.

agreed objectives in relation to different activities rather than being bound by strict timelines. It is clear that some form of external security guarantee will be required for the foreseeable future. Since 1st July 2013, RAMSI's three development pillars (law and justice, machinery of government and economic governance) have shifted across to bilateral development programs managed out of the Australian and New Zealand High Commissions. During the next four years, RAMSI will consist primarily of a small contingent of Honiara-based PPF providing capacity-development assistance to the RSIPF. This switch in the modality of external assistance signifies the transition from post-conflict stabilisation to a more regular development assistance approach.[61]

The continuing need for long-term international support is premised on an appreciation of the structural challenges facing the island nation, including its relatively poor economic prospects and the conflict stresses these might induce. Many of the underlying factors that contributed to the original tension remain unaddressed. A recurrence of conflict remains a real risk with international evidence confirming the cyclical character of many conflicts in fragile states.[62] Analysis by the World Bank[63] demonstrates how economic growth in Solomon Islands since 2003 (average *per capita* growth of 3.6 *per annum*)[64] has been largely driven by the influx of aid flows associated with the regional mission (38% of GDP on average since 2003)[65] and unsustainable levels of logging. Set against an annual population growth rate of around 2.6%, even these growth rates have been unable to bring incomes back to pre-tension levels. According to recent forecasts, commercial logging stocks are expected to be exhausted by 2015, leading to a dramatic anticipated drop in government revenues. Planned new projects in fisheries, mining, tourism and agriculture, even if successful, are unlikely to make up for the shortfall that will result from such a development. As well as the impact on revenue and jobs, the demise of the notoriously corrupt logging industry "is likely to place pressure on local patronage networks and exacerbate socioeconomic grievances, thereby partly

61 Coppel, 'Transition of the Regional Assistance Mission to Solomon Islands'.

62 World Bank, *World Development Report 2011 – Conflict, Security and Development* (Washington DC: World Bank), pp. 2–6.

63 World Bank, *Solomon Islands Growth Prospects: Constraints and Policy Priorities* (Washington DC: World Bank).

64 Tobias Haque, 'Economic Transition in Solomon Islands', In Brief 2013/16, Canberra: State Society and Governance in Melanesia Program, College of Asia and the Pacific, Australian National University, 2013, available electronically at: http://ips.cap.anu.edu.au/ssgm.

65 *Ibid.*

recreating conditions that contributed to the original outbreak of violence in the late 1990s".[66]

Projections indicate that likely medium-term economic growth will increasingly be concentrated around Honiara, which will attract increasing numbers of migrants from rural areas and around enclave resource development, especially mining. This is likely to deepen historical patterns of uneven development and associated grievances over relative deprivation. Rapid and unplanned urban growth in Honiara, typically involving informal settlements on customary or state land, has considerable potential for generating conflict over land use, as well as entrenching real and perceived inequalities in the distribution of incomes and services, with accompanying social problems including crime. Likewise, experience in Papua New Guinea and the neighbouring island of Bougainville attests to links between extractive projects and new patterns of rent-seeking and local level conflict.[67]

The likely constraints on Solomon Islands' future growth prospects provides the context for increasing calls for Australia to open up its own labour markets to temporary labour migration schemes for the islands.[68] For young Solomon Islanders this would create an opportunity to earn an income, while acquiring new skills and expanding personal horizons. As well as a source of remittances, such a scheme could contribute to domestic stability by providing a much needed safety valve in the face of the growing constituency of unemployed and underemployed youth. While Solomon Islanders have some access to both a New Zealand labour migration scheme and a pilot Australian scheme, the numbers accepted to date remain modest. Unlike their counterparts in Polynesia, where agreements with former colonial powers provide the possibility for short-term and long-term migration, Solomon Islanders have limited opportunities for working or settling overseas. Strict restrictions on labour mobility imposed by metropolitan neighbours, notably Australia, represent a lost opportunity for development in Solomon Islands and for relieving growing social stresses.[69]

---

66 Allen, *Long-Term Engagement*, p. 2.

67 Sinclair Dinnen, Doug Porter, and Caroline Sage, 'Conflict in Melanesia: Themes and Lessons' (Washington DC: World Bank, Background Paper, World Development Report 2011), available electronically at: http://documents.worldbank.org/curated/en/2010/11/14265804/conflict-melanesia-themes-lessons.

68 Allen, *Long-Term Engagement*, pp. 11–13.

69 David Craig, Richard Bedford, David Gegeo, Patricia Rodi, Rebecca Miller and Ward Friesen, *Labour Mobility and Diaspora: An Overview of Solomon Islands' Historical Regulatory Experience, 1850s–2013* (Waikato, NZ: University of Waikato, National Institute of Demographic and Economic Analysis, Working Paper No. 6 January 2014).

Longer-term challenges include the need for Solomon Islands' political and economic elites to provide the leadership and institutional arrangements necessary to achieve positive development outcomes and lasting stability as the country moves into the post- RAMSI future. It is clear that the short-termism, personalised and informal character of 'national' politics as it has evolved during the post-independence period is neither conducive to development nor stability. This includes the corrosive impact on formal delivery systems of the rise of parallel informal institutions such as the constituency development funds. RAMSI's focus on formal institutions and its adoption of a deficit perspective – identifying existing deficiencies and seeking to fix them – has to a large extent neglected local political realities and the way in which power actually works in Solomon Islands. Development scholars increasingly recognise that the manner in which power is exercised by local elites in fragile and post-conflict settings like Solomon Islands is largely through informal institutional arrangements including patronage and the monetisation of politics. Growing attention is being given to the nexus between politics and institutional reform, with a view to improving understanding of the power relationships that shape statebuilding processes, as well as the formal and informal institutions that underpin institutional inclusiveness, performance and stability.[70] Ensuring alignment between institutions and political power is a necessary basis for building accountable and legitimate institutions capable of delivering public goods on a sustainable basis.[71] In the case of Solomon Islands, development partners need to accept the reality of critical informal institutions such as the discretionary funds available to MPs and devise ways of engaging with them in order to develop accountability mechanisms and improve development outcomes.

RAMSI undoubtedly succeeded in its initial task of restoring security and stability to Solomon Islands but the outstanding challenge remains to sustain and build on these achievements in the years ahead. While the security phase

70 See, for example: Adrian Leftwich, *States of Development – On the Primacy of Politics in Development* (Cambridge, UK: Polity, 2000); Sam Hickey, *Thinking about the Politics of Inclusive Development: Towards a Relational Approach* (Manchester: University of Manchester, Effective States and Inclusive Development Research Centre (ESID) Concept Paper, 2011), 1–33, available electronically at: http://www.effective-states.org/_assets/documents/esid_wp_01_hickey.pdf. Daron Acemoglu and James Robinson, *Why Nations Fail: The Origins of Power, Prosperity and Poverty* (New York: Crown Publishers, 2012).

71 *World Development Report 2011*, pp.8–16; Department for International Development (DFID). *The Politics of Poverty*. London: DFID, 2010.

was relatively straightforward, long-term development is much more complex and challenging. It is now acknowledged that while RAMSI will disappear, substantial international engagement will be needed for many years to come in the form of development assistance tailored to Solomon Islands changing circumstances and needs. Fortunately this appears to be recognised by the new Australian government in Canberra, as it was by its predecessor.

CHAPTER 7

All-Japan Approach to International Peace Operations

Yuji Uesugi

Introduction

This chapter sheds light on a largely neglected aspect of Japan's policy and activities in international peace cooperation (IPC)[1] by discussing the development and features of the All-Japan approach that can be restated as integrated inter-agency/civil-military coordination. The All-Japan approach has now been placed in Japan's IPC policy, and has a potential to constitute Japan's unique contribution to international peace operations as the All-Japan approach can match with the Abe administration's policy on "proactive contribution to international peace and security." This chapter provides a review of Japan's IPC policy, paying special attention to inter-agency/civil-military nexus. It argues that the All-Japan approach can offer a framework for better coordination among Japanese actors on the ground, and thus it can make Japan's contribution more 'visible' to the local community and populations concerned.

At the same time, it also seeks to present a warning that such an approach may jeopardize the unity of the mission, especially if it is a UN peacekeeping operation (PKO), and disturb the coherence of multilateral efforts on the ground. In addition, one must be aware of the inherent danger of promoting such a top-down approach. In fact, the All-Japan approach can blur decision-making of Japanese actors on the ground because of the unspoken pressure from their government to formulate All-Japan projects.

1 The term "international peace cooperation" or IPC in this chapter represents a policy terminology of the Japanse govermennt. This term covers a wide range of activities aimed at contributing to international peace and security, including but not limited to military contribution to United Nations Peacekeeping Operations (UN PKOs). Recently, the UN sometimes uses "peace operations" in lieu of "peacekeeping operations" in order to encompass diverse activities ranging from humanitarian assistance to peacebuilding now undertaken by the different UN actors in the field. Nevertheless, in Japan, the acronym, "PKO", is still widely used in political and academic discourse as well as in the media since the term is well recognized in the general public.

 | DOI 10.1163/9789004322059_008

To examine the prospect of the All-Japan approach, this chapter will first explore the development of the concept/policy of the All-Japan approach and then its actual implementation on the ground in Timor-Leste, Iraq, Haiti and South Sudan. In essence, this chapter is normative in that it recommends better coordination between agencies and between the civil and military sectors. At the same time, it also seeks to discuss the implications of the All-Japan approach for Japan's current debate and action regarding the relaxation of the constitutional constraints on the use of the Self Defense Force (SDF) in overseas activities, which have been undertaken under the rubric of "proactive contribution to international peace and security." Before turning to a main discussion revolving around the All-Japan approach, a brief history of the development of such a concept/policy is in order.

Concept/Policy of the All-Japan Approach

International Context

The emphasis on inter-agency/civil-military coordination is not unique to Japan. Faced with complex and difficult challenges of post-conflict statebuilding and peacebuilding, both within and outside of the UN, more systematic approaches have been called for. For example, in 2000 the UN put forward two proposals for structural integration of various UN initiatives. First, integration between UNPKOs and UN Country Teams (UNCTs) on the ground and establishment of the Integrated Mission Task Forces at the headquarters were proposed in the *Report of the Panel on United Nations Peace Operations* (so-called Brahimi Report).[2] Then, the UN Secretary-General published his *Note of Guidance on Integrated Missions*, in which the promotion of structural integration between a UN PKO and a UNCT through a 'triple hatted' appointment of a Deputy Special Representative of the Secretary-General (DSRSG)/Resident Coordinator/Humanitarian Coordinator.[3] In addition to such an initiative to

2 *Report of the Panel on United Nations Peace Operations* (UN Doc. A/55/305-S/2000/809, 21 August 2000) paras. 198–217.

3 *Note of Guidance on Integrated Missions*, December 2000. This note from the Secretary-General was revised in 2006 to address some concerns about the integrated mission of the humanitarian community (*Note of Guidance on Integrated Missions*, 17 January 2006). Also, *Integrated Mission Planning Process Guideline* was issued in 2006 (revised in 2010) to outline mission planning process and mechanisms in the headquarters and the field. In 2008, the Secretary-General Decision on Integration (Decision No. 2008/24—Integration) defined scope of integration and the requirement for an Integrated Strategic Framework, http://www.undg.org/docs/9898/Integration-decision-SG-25-jun-08.pdf, 26 June 2008.

integrate the UN's political, security, development, human rights and humanitarian agencies under one UN integrated mission, a more system-wide coherence in the activities of the UN family working in the humanitarian and development areas was sought under the slogan of 'Delivering as One' and/or 'One UN.'[4]

Similar development has also been witnessed outside of the UN. The North Atlantic Treaty Organization (NATO), the European Union (EU), the Organization for Economic Co-operation and Development (OECD) and several western governments have coined comparable concepts such as 3D (diplomacy, development and defense), Whole-of-Government, and Comprehensive approaches.[5]

The military forces of the major western countries were employed to provide protection and escort for their civilian counterpart working in a non-permissive environment in Iraq, Afghanistan and elsewhere. Furthermore, a mode of civil-military cooperation in which humanitarian and development aid was used as 'force multipliers' to supplement military efforts to bring stability and to win hearts and minds of the people was introduced as a new strategy in non-UN operations in Iraq and Afghanistan. Against the backdrop of addressing the challenges of failed and fragile states, 3D, Whole-of-Government and Comprehensive approaches were invented and promoted by the United States and its allies in NATO with an aim of utilizing humanitarian and development aid as peace dividends to contribute to stability and/or counter-insurgency operations.[6]

Later on in 2010, such a trend was also reflected in the policy of the UN PKOs, *Civil-Military Coordination in UN Integrated Peacekeeping Missions* (UN-CIMIC), in which indirect assistance of the military was encouraged to "exploit advantages that may serve as a 'multiplier' to civilian efforts to improve local

---

4 UN, *Delivering as One, the Report of the Secretary-General's High-Level Panel on System-wide Coherence*, A/61/583 (New York, 2006); Karsten Friis and Pia Jarmyr (eds.), *Comprehensive Approach: Challenges and Opportunities in Complex Crisis Management* (NUPI Report, 2008), pp. 5–6.

5 Friis and Jarmyr (eds.), *Comprehensive Approach: Challenges and Opportunities in Complex Crisis Management*, pp. 4–5; NATO, *Riga Summit Declaration* (Issued by the Head of State and Government participating in the North Atlantic Council in Riga, 29 November, 2006) para. 10; OECD/DAC, *Whole of Government Approaches to Fragile States* (Paris: DAC Reference Document, OECD, 2006); The United States Joint Forces Command, *The Comprehensive Approach: A Conceptual Framework for MNE 5* (Suffolk, VA: United States Joint Forces Command, 6 April 2009) http://www.dtic.mil/dtic/tr/fulltext/u2/a592375.pdf, 6 September 2014.

6 Department of the Army, *FM 3–24 MCWP 3–33.5: Insurgencies and Countering Insurgencies*, May 2014, http://fas.org/irp/doddir/army/fm3-24.pdf, 6 September 2014.

capacity" and Quick Impact Projects (QIPs) were expected to be used "to establish and build confidence in the mission, its mandate, and the peace process, thereby improving the environment for effective mandate implementation."[7] While the direction of the 'multiplier' effect in UN-CIMIC is different from the usage of non-UN military community such as NATO and EU where civilian efforts are supposed to complement the military objective of fighting a war among people,[8] both attempts sought to identify and exploit opportunities for civil-military synergy.[9] Furthermore, as recent UNPKOs are given a mandate to protect civilians caught up in armed conflicts,[10] closer civil-military coordination has become the *modus operandi* for UN PKOs operating in a non-permissive environment.

Birth of the Concept

Against the backdrop of such a trend, a prototype of the All-Japan concept can be found in a report published in December 2002 by the Advisory Group on International Cooperation for Peace chaired by Yasushi Akashi, a former Special Representative of the Secretary-General (SRSG) for the United Nations Transitional Authority in Cambodia (UNTAC) and the United Nations Protection Force (UNPROFOR) in former Yugoslavia.[11] This landmark report recommended the promotion of coordination and cooperation between the SDF and civilian organizations including NGOs. It also advocated for the collaboration amongst the Japanese actors, both civilians and military, as well as both governmental and non-governmental organizations by arguing that coordination and cooperation with civilian organizations (by the SDF) should be envisioned in a manner that represents a coherent intent of (the government of) Japan. Furthermore, underlining the importance of a more holistic

7 United Nations Department of Peacekeeping Operations and Department of Field Support (UNDPKO and DFS), *Civil-Military Coordination in UN Integrated Peacekeeping Missions* (*UN-CIMIC*) (October 2010) p. 6 (para. 14), p. 7 (para. 16).

8 Rupert Smith, *The Utility of Force: The Art of War in the Modern World* (New York: Penguin, 2006).

9 UNDPKO and DFS, *Civil-Military Coordination in UN Integrated Peacekeeping Missions* (*UN-CIMIC*), p. 6 (para. 13) and p. 8 (para. 22).

10 Victoria Holt and Glyn Taylor with Max Kelly, *Protecting Civilians in the Context of UN Peacekeeping Operations: Successes, Setbacks and Remaining Challenges*, Independent study jointly commissioned by the Department of Peacekeeping Operations and the Office for the Coordination of Humanitarian Affairs (New York: United Nations, 2009).

11 *The Report of the Advisory Group on International Cooperation for Peace*, 18 December 2002 (executive summary of the report is available in English at http://www.mofa.go.jp/policy/un/pko/report0212.pdf, 6 September 2014).

approach, the report suggested that coordination with Official Development Assistance (ODA) be incorporated in Japan's civil-military coordinated efforts in international peace operations.[12]

Judging from the first landmark report, it can be said that, initially, the All-Japan approach was conceived as a way to fill a gap between peacekeeping (a short-term measure) and development (a long-term measure) based on the assumption that this gap has prevented effective Japanese involvement in peacebuilding since the comparative advantage of Japanese assistance was seen in the phase of development, particularly in the area of infrastructure and human resource development. For example, the Japan International Cooperation Agency (JICA) that manages Japan's ODA projects in developing countries, can demonstrate their fuller potential in a permissive environment, but it was not accustomed to operating in failed or fragile states, much less in a war zone. This coincided with a view presented in the so-called Brahimi report of 2000 that advocated for a closer relationship between peacekeeping and peacebuilding, and peacebuilding as a gap filling strategy between peacekeeping and development.[13] Later on, this gap filling strategy came to be known as 'seamless' assistance in Japan's IPC policy.

At the same time, it is also true that the All-Japan concept/policy was given birth as a Japanese version of response to international calling for a more systematic approach in an environment where inter-agency/civil-military coordination were increasingly recognized as a necessary development for effectively addressing the challenges of post-conflict state-building and peacebuilding. While the All-Japan approach was given birth in the same environment as 3D, Whole-of-Government and Comprehensive approaches, Japan's approach has grown differently from the similar approaches of the UN, NATO, EU, OECD and other western governments.

This is partially due to the legal and political constraints on the activities of the SDF operating in overseas missions.[14] The SDF units were not given a mandate to lead stability or counter-insurgency operations, nor were they provided with sufficient capacity to assume such tasks.

---

12 Saya Kiba and Atsushi Yasutomi, 'Jieitai ni yoru "Ohru Japan" gata Kokusaikyouryoku no Kadai: NGO tono Renkei no Jirei kara' [JSDF-NGO Cooperation: Issues and Challenges in JSDF's "All-Japan" International Cooperation Policy], *Journal of International Cooperation Studies*, vol. 21, no. 1, 2013, p. 125.

13 *Report of the Panel on United Nations Peace Operations*, A/55/305-S/2000/809.

14 Chiyuki Aoi, 'Beyond "Activism-Lite"?: Issues in Japanese Participation in Peace Operations', *Journal of International Peacekeeping*, vol. 13, no. 1–2, 2009, pp. 1–29.

Another reason can be found in the Japanese way of thinking about cooperation between PKOs and ODA. In Japan, such cooperation was conceived not based on the mentality of counter-insurgency operations, which was predominant in western countries' approach.[15] Hence, Japan's temptation to use humanitarian and development aid for reaching security-oriented goals was circumvented. Rather, it sought to utilize SDF's capacity on the ground for the purpose of meeting humanitarian and development needs. Such an attitude originated in the philosophy of Japanese policy makers and aid workers that socio-economic development was a key to peace consolidation.

It is true that Japanese ODA projects were introduced as peace dividends for the people of Iraq and to a certain degree they were used to provide better community reception and force protection of the SDF units deployed in Iraq. In addition, QIPs were used by the SDF to win hearts and minds of the people in the mission area. At the same time, however, ODA projects were not reduced to a mere tool for the SDF, nor were they introduced as an integral part of the US counter-insurgency strategy, of which even the SDF was not a part. In short, utilizing humanitarian and development aid directly and solely in support of the security-oriented mission of the SDF did not exist.

This way of thinking was dominant in the initial discourse of Japan's contribution to peacebuilding, and a hybrid usage of SDF troops participating in a UN PKO was explored. That is, while serving as an integral part of a UN PKO performing key peacekeeping functions, SDF troops were also expected to serve as a gap filling measure and as an agent of peacebuilding that can bring seamless involvement of Japanese assistance to the country concerned.

Mainstreaming of the Policy

Three important policy documents that shaped the course of All-Japan policy development were issued during the administration of the Democratic Party of Japan (DPJ) between 2009 and 2012. The first landmark document was published in August 2010 by the Council on Security and Defense Capabilities in the New Era, entitled *Japan's Visions for Future Security and Defense Capabilities in the New Era*. In this report, the term All-Japan Structures appeared in the section A—Establishing New Structures that Facilitate Cooperation among Various Actors in Japan. It argued, "Japan should overcome sectionalism in

15 Yoshiyuki Sakaemura, *A New Role for Armed Forces in a Non-permissive Environment- On the Coordination between the Japan Self-Defense Forces' International Peace Cooperation Operations and the Official Development Assistance in Iraq*, p. 14, http://www.mod.go.jp/js/jsc/jpc/research/image/eng04.pdf, 15 July 2013.

order to carry out All-Japan international cooperation."[16] In addition, underlining the importance of Civil-Military Cooperation (CIMIC) as an agenda for peacebuilding, it also stated that Japan should improve its peacebuilding capabilities through concrete practices of CIMIC.[17] This report gave the All-Japan concept a clear policy orientation and paved the way for the concept to be placed firmly in the Japan's IPC policy.

Reflecting the direction of the discussion of the first document, Japan's Ministry of Defense published the *National Defense Program Guidelines for FY2011 and Beyond* in December 2010, in which two key points were maintained. First, the strategic and effective use of ODA to resolve root causes of conflicts was articulated.[18] Second, inter-agency coordination including cooperation with not only government ministries but also with NGOs was stipulated, stating "Japan will participate in ... international peace cooperation activities, in a more efficient and effective manner, with government ministries and agencies cooperating not only with each other but also with non-governmental organizations and other entities."[19]

In July 2011, the Study Group on Japan's Engagement in UN PKOs, an inter-ministerial group headed by the Senior Vice Minister of the Cabinet Office, Shozo Azuma, issued its *Interim Report*. The report proclaimed the need for further and greater coordination among Japanese actors, including not only governmental organizations but also NGOs, for information sharing and decision-making as a coherent All-Japan engagement.[20] More specifically, the report highlighted the importance of (1) strategic and effective coordination with diplomatic efforts (including ODA) and (2) promotion of CIMIC on the ground between SDF units and civilians engaging in humanitarian assistance and/or socio-economic rehabilitation/development.[21] As a new strategy for the Japanese participation in PKOs, the report underlined the practical use of

16 The Council on Security and Defense Capabilities in the New Era, *Japan's Visions for Future Security and Defense Capabilities in the New Era: Toward a Peace-Creating Nation* (August 2010) p. 55.

17 The Council on Security and Defense Capabilities in the New Era, *Japan's Visions for Future Security and Defense Capabilities in the New Era*, p. 55.

18 *The National Defense Program Guidelines for FY2011 and Beyond*, (17 December 2010) p. 9.

19 *The National Defense Program Guidelines for FY 2011 and Beyond*, p. 6.

20 *Interim Report of the Study Group on Japan's Engagement in UN Peacekeeping Operations*, (July 2011) p. 7 (in Japanese version), http://www.pko.go.jp/pko_j/info/pdf/20110704.pdf (a provisional translation in English is available at http://www.pko.go.jp/pko_e/info/pdf/20110711_report.pdf, 6 September 2014).

21 *Interim Report*, p. 7.

PKOs in Japan's holistic IPC efforts (in conjunction with the application of ODA, and cooperation with NGOs and private sectors).[22] Such a holistic approach, which links conflict prevention, conflict resolution, peacekeeping and peacebuilding to longer-term efforts such as post-conflict reconstruction and development, was labeled as the All-Japan approach. In other words, the All-Japan approach in this report was not just a way to fill in the existing gap between peacekeeping and development, allowing seamless involvement of Japan's assistance in the transition process from war to peace, but it was also conceived as a peacebuilding strategy, which allows effective application of military forces (with engineering capacity) to civilian-led post-conflict reconstruction and development.[23]

This trend of placing the All-Japan approach in the center of Japan's IPC policy was carried over by the succeeding government of the Liberal Democratic Party (LDP) led by Shinzo Abe. On 17 December 2013, the Japanese government issued two key documents regarding its policy on international security and national defense, in which its stance towards IPC was stipulated. The document entitled the *National Security Strategy* indicated clearly Japan's will to step up its cooperation with the UN PKOs more proactively, and stated that:

> ... when participating in PKO, Japan will endeavor to ensure effective implementation of its operations, through coordination with other activities, including ODA projects. Moreover, in order to implement seamless assistance in security-related areas, including through further strategic utilization of ODA and capacity building assistance, as well as coordination with non-governmental organizations (NGOs), Japan will develop a system that enables assistance to potential recipient organizations that cannot receive Japan's assistance under the current schemes.[24]

This emphasis on the coordination between PKO and ODA projects, and PKO and NGOs can also be found in the other key document issued by the Japanese government, entitled the *National Defense Program Guidelines for FY2014 and Beyond* as follows:

22 *Interim Report*, p. 10.

23 Tomoaki Honda, *Heiwa Kouchiku to Jieitai—Kokusaiheiwakyouryoku no Jissou to Nipponnryu Shien no Keisei* [Peace-building and Japan Self-Defense Forces: An Actual Modality of International Peace Cooperation and a Formation of "Japan Model Peace-building Policy"], a doctoral dissertation submitted to Keio University, 2013.

24 *National Security Strategy* (17 December 2013), p. 30.

> Working in partnership with non-governmental organizations and other relevant organizations, Japan will actively engage in international peace cooperation assignments and emergency relief activities to meet diverse needs, from peacekeeping to peacebuilding …[25]

While these official documents effectively avoided the usage of the term All-Japan approach, which can be recognized as a 'trademark' of Japan's IPC policy during the DPJ era, these statements quoted above in fact outlined the essence of such a concept and policy, *i.e.*, inter-agency/civil-military coordination for Japan's coherent effort towards IPC with special focus on the coordination between the SDF and ODA projects, as well as the SDF and NGOs. As have examined above, such an orientation towards the All-Japan approach was not a new phenomenon developed in the recent administrations. In fact, the sprit of the All-Japan approach constituted a key attribute of Japan's IPC policy since early 2000, and both the LDP and DPJ governments nurtured the concept, crafting it as a policy.

Surviving two consecutive regime changes, it can be said that the All-Japan approach has now been placed firmly in the mainstream of Japan's IPC policy. To sum up, the characteristics of the All-Japan approach can be restated as follows: strategic and effective coordination and cooperation between the SDF capacity (military) and ODA projects (civilian) aimed at promoting better inter-agency synergy, and between the SDF peacekeepers (military) and NGO aid workers (civilian) aimed at realizing greater civil-military synergy to increase Japan's presence in the field. As a result, the SDF peacekeepers will be sent to the mission area as an agent of the Japanese government and be expected and instructed to realize collaboration with Japanese ODA and 'visible assistance' as a part of All-Japan initiatives.[26] To validate this from the vantage point of policy implementation on the ground, let us turn to a case study of the application of the All-Japan approach.

Case Studies of the All-Japan Approach

Since the introduction of the All-Japan concept in early 2000, the Japanese government has begun to operationalize the concept in both UN and non-UN missions, in Timor-Leste, Iraq, Afghanistan, Haiti and South Sudan. The concept was refined and clarified after repeated trial and error, from a haphazard,

25 *National Defense Program Guidelines for FY 2014 and Beyond* (17 December 2013), p. 17.
26 Kiba and Yasutomi, 'Jieitai ni yoru "Ohru Japan" gata Kokusaikyouryoku no Kadai', p. 123.

ad hoc reaction to the needs on the ground to a more planned response. One of the purposes of this chapter is to demonstrate a path through which the All-Japan concept was crystallized into a concrete practice in the field. Hence, the pathway of trial and error will be explored in details in this section.

Initial Stage of Japan's Contribution to UN PKOs

The *de facto* debut of Japanese SDF to a UN PKO was in 1992 when Japan sent its engineering battalion to UNTAC. As a beginner, the most important priority of the Japanese contingent was to accomplish its mandate and return home safely. There was no idea to seek the synergy of PKO and ODA within the framework of UNTAC at that time. However, this experience set a precedent for the later development of the All-Japan concept. Since this first mission, the prime task of Japanese SDF has revolved around so-called 'mission support activities', repairing basic infrastructure such as roads and bridges to facilitate the activities of fellow peacekeepers. This nature of the task has shaped the composition of the SDF units deployed to UN PKOs, and it has been engineers that served as a core of expeditionary units of Japanese SDF. This practice allowed for the current All-Japan approach, that is, essentially an application of the SDF's engineering capacity to the ODA's reconstruction projects, to be possible in the first place.

When the SDF was deployed to the United Nations Mission of Support in East Timor (UNMISET) in 2002, the core expeditionary force consisted of engineers following the 'traditional' path laid by Japan's experience in UNTAC. In UNMISET, the SDF engineering unit provided technical support to a project called the Recovery, Employment, and Stability Program for Ex-combatants and Communities in Timor-Leste (RESPECT) organized by the United Nations Development Programme (UNDP) and funded by the Japanese government. RESPECT was introduced to prevent the relapse of violence by appeasing the frustration of ex-combatants by allowing them to be involved in reconstruction projects, offering them an opportunity to generate income. This peacebuilding nature of the program made it possible for the Japanese SDF units operating under the auspice of UNMISET to participate in a UNDP-led program, as the objective of RESPECT was recognized to fall within the parameters of the mandate of UNMISET. It was not a coincidence that such collaboration emerged under the circumstances in which a Japanese senior official, Sukehiro Hasegawa, served as a DSRSG of UNMISET and the head of UNCT/UNDP in Timor-Leste. This is the first sign of emergence of the All-Japan approach.

Different activities that may have constituted precedents for the All-Japan approach were also detected during UNMISET era. The Japanese government came up with a handover strategy; that is, construction equipment such as bulldozers and power shovels that were brought from Japan and used by the

SDF engineering unit for UNMISET mission would be donated to the Timorese government at the end of the SDF deployment. With this handover in sight, the SDF engineering unit began to train local staff in how to operate and maintain construction equipment. After the departure of the SDF, this training was handed over to JICA, which initiated a technical cooperation project called 'Project for Capacity Building in Road Maintenance'.[27] Also, a Japanese NGO called the Japan Demining and Reconstruction Assistance Center (JDRAC), which was an implementing agent of Japan's Grant Assistance for Grassroots Human Security Project (GGP), succeeded a part of the training involving the handling of container houses donated by the SDF in Timor-Leste.[28] These handover cases of Japanese assistance from the SDF to Japanese ODA projects set another precedent for later development of similar efforts in Iraq, Haiti and South Sudan.

Nevertheless, because the concept of the All-Japan approach was not articulated in the Japanese policy of IPC in the first decade of Japan's contribution to UN PKOs, the collaboration between the SDF units and ODA projects was not implemented formally and systematically.

'A Pair of Wheels' Approach in Iraq: Convergence of PKO and ODA (Top Down)

Japan has contributed its troops, as well as its civilians, not only to UN operations but also to non-UN operations to assume its responsibility for maintaining international peace and security. The most significant juncture of Japan's IPC policy was the September 11 (9.11) attack in 2001. More precisely, it was Prime Minister Junichiro Koizumi's bold and impulsive decision in the aftermath of 9.11 to deploy the SDF to Iraq outside the legal framework of the UN PKO Law. This decision has forced Japan to cross the Rubicon. It set the stage for the SDF's more proactive engagement in overseas operations and constituted a prototype of Japanese style CIMIC. Indeed, it was the first organized attempt by Japan to combine the SDF's overseas operations and ODA activities.[29]

27 JICA, 'Purojekuto no Gaiyo' [Outline of the Project], http://www.jica.go.jp/project/easttimor/001/outline/index.html, 6 September 2014.

28 JDRAC, 'Kumitate Hausu Purojekuto' [Prefabricated House Project], http://www.jdrac.org/page01/gaimu02.html, 6 September 2014.

29 Eijiro Imamura, 'Jieitai no Kokusaiheiwakyouryokukatsudou nikansuru Ichikousatsu' [A Study Concerning the International Peace Cooperation Operations by the Self-Defense Forces] *Land Warfare Research* (Japan Ground Self-Defense Force Staff College, November 2005), p. 6; Masahisa Sato, *Iraku Jieitai Sentouki* [The SDF Operations Diary in Iraq] (Tokyo: Kodansha, 2007), pp. 148–152; Sakaemura, *A New Role for Armed Forces in a Non-permissive Environment*, p. 1.

In 2003, the Japanese Diet enacted the Iraq Special Measures Law,[30] which was designed specifically to permit the dispatch of the SDF to Iraq. This law allowed Japan to act on its own initiative and not serve under the auspices of the UN. Although the SDF was deployed to Iraq as a part of the US-led multinational force, the primary mandate of the operation, known as Humanitarian and Reconstruction Assistance (HRA), was different from that of the other participants in the multi-national force. In this way, the SDF operating in Iraq was able to enjoy the operational independence to implement the HRA mandate and support Japanese ODA activities in Iraq as 'a pair of wheels,'[31] which means that the SDF and the ODA are the two wheels of the same vehicle (Japanese assistance) and that the two should work together.

Under the HRA operation, two different groups were sent: (1) Reconstruction Support Group (RSG), a main unit consisting of about 500 personnel responsible for engaging in HRA such as water supply, reconstruction and medical assistance; and (2) Task Planning and Liaison Unit (TPLU), a support unit responsible for assisting the operation of the RSG. In the past, the size and capacity of the support unit were limited in UN PKOs to the task of coordination with its national headquarters in Tokyo and only around 10 officers were assigned to this support unit.[32] This time in Iraq,[33] however, because the Japanese contingent had to operate independently from the multi-national force, a robust support unit with the strength of about 100 was dispatched alongside the main unit. The tasks of the TPLU included the needs assessments of the local communities used for formulating reconstruction projects, and the coordination with different levels of local authorities and tribal leaders.[34] The TPLU also served as an interlocutor for inter-agency/civil-military coordination amongst the Japanese actors on the ground. For example, the CIMIC staff of the TPLU, in

30 The Law is known as the Concerning Special Measures on the Implementation of Humanitarian and Reconstruction Assistance Activities and Support Activities for Ensuring Security in Iraq.

31 Sakaemura, *A New Role for Armed Forces in a Non-permissive Environment*, p. 4.

32 Shigeru Handa, *'Senchi' Haken Kawaru Jieitai* [Dispatch to the War Zone, Changing SDF] (Tokyo: Iwanami, 2009), p. 65.

33 The Ground SDF units that assumed the main task of the HRA operation were deployed to Iraq from December 2003 to July 2006. The Air SDF units that were sent to Iraq to provide transportation support continued their operation until December 2008.

34 Masahisa Sato, 'Goran Kogen kara Iraku he: Ichi Jieitai Shikikan no Chuto Keiken' [From Golan Heights to Iraq: Experience in Middle East of a SDF Commander], *PKO no Shiteki Kensho* [Historical Review of the PKO], vol. 42, no. 3 and 4, 2007, p. 310.

cooperation with actors related to Japanese ODA activities, planned a rehabilitation of the comprehensive water supply system in Al-Muthanna Province, and the SDF contingent and the staff of Japanese Ministry of Foreign Affairs (MOFA) in Al-Samawah City, where the SDF contingent was stationed, complemented each other as 'a pair of wheels' through mutual cooperation.[35]

Unlike previous deployments to UN PKOs such as UNTAC and UNMISET, where the engineering unit was the main component of the Japanese contingent with the strength of between 500 and 700, in Iraq the engineering unit constituted one of five units in the RSG and it had only 50 staff members.[36] Such composition was, off course, largely due to a more volatile security environment in Iraq, requiring a more robust guard unit for force protection, and as a result forced the other units to operate with limited human resources. At the same time, this composition reflected 'a pair of wheels' policy in which HRA tasks of the SDF would be supplemented by inter-agency/civil-military cooperation. In UNTAC and UNMISET, the SDF engineers carried out directly the reconstruction of roads and bridges by themselves. In Iraq, rather than undertaking the reconstruction work by themselves, the SDF engineers acted as a 'project manager' providing supervision, monitoring, oversight and technical advice, whereas local contractors carried out the implementation of the project that was funded by different schemes of ODA such as the GGP.

A combined effort between the SDF's 'soft' aid and the ODA's 'hard' aid was seen in the rehabilitation project of the hospital in Al-Samawah City. The MOFA liaison team donated, through an ODA scheme, medical equipment, ambulances and a radio system to the hospital, while the medical unit of the SDF contingent provided technical assistance for local medical staff so that they would be able to operate the hardware.[37] In addition, the CIMIC staff of the TPLU supervised local constructors to rehabilitate the facility of the hospital and the engineering unit installed power generators to sustain the medical equipment of the hospital.[38] According to Yoshiyuki Sakaemura who served in the CIMIC section of the TPLU, the SDF served as a "development facilitator" by offering peace dividends to local population in the immediate aftermath of the warfare, which contributed to fostering a better relationship with local people and Japan.[39]

---

35 Sakaemura, *A New Role for Armed Forces in a Non-permissive Environment*, p. 8.

36 Honda, *Heiwa Kouchiku to Jieitai*, p. 160.

37 Sakaemura, *A New Role for Armed Forces in a Non-permissive Environment*, p. 9.

38 Sakaemura, *A New Role for Armed Forces in a Non-permissive Environment*, p. 9.

39 Sakaemura, *A New Role for Armed Forces in a Non-permissive Environment*, pp. 13–15.

Civil-Military Cooperation Imperative: Natural Disaster Twist in Haiti

As a response to the policy of promoting more active involvement of Japan in IPC, the Japanese government established a Central Readiness Force (CRF) within the structure of Ground SDF in March 2007. The CRF is a specially designated group for international missions designed to improve the quality and rapid deployment of troops. The rapid deployment capability of the CRF was demonstrated for the first time in 2010 when Japan decided to respond to the appeal of reinforcement of the United Nations Stabilization Mission in Haiti (MINUSTAH) after a great earthquake hit Haiti on 12 January 2010.

Nevertheless, an initial response of the Japanese government to the earthquake in Haiti started as an emergency disaster relief.[40] The Japanese government dispatched a Japan Disaster Relief (JDR) Team composed of 26 civilian medical experts to Haiti as its first group of responders who were responsible for relief operations in the immediate aftermath of the disaster, operating from the 16th to the 25th of January on the ground.[41]

Later, a medical team of the SDF, which operated under the command of the CRF, was deployed under the JDR system and joined the JDR Team in Haiti. The SDF medical team acting as an integral part of the JDR team succeeded the venue, facility, equipment as well as patients from the first badge, and became a primary responder in the JDR Team after civilian medical experts left the scene.[42] When the SDF medical team terminated its emergency relief

40 Japan Disaster Relief (JDR) Teams often include members from the MOFA, National Police Agency, Fire and Disaster Management Agency, Japan Coast Guard, JICA (doctors, nurses, civilian experts, coordinators) and SDF (unarmed). This system of emergency disaster relief was run by the JICA that also has a role as the primary operator of Japan's ODA. Two legal foundations exist that allows the Japanese government to send its SDF to overseas operations: the first one is the PKO Law (for disaster caused by conflict) and the other one is the JDR Law (for other types of disaster such as natural disaster). As has been reviewed in the previous section, the third way also exist. If a special measures law is enacted, the Japanese government will be able to deploy its SDF to overseas operations, as it was the case with the SDF deployment to Iraq in 2003.

41 An initial assessment team (3 personnel) was dispatched on 14 January and returned to Japan on 16 January 2011. The JICA medical team (26 personnel) was dispatched on 16 January and returned to Japan on 29 January. The SDF medical team (183 personnel in total) was operating from 16 January and 18 February 2011, http://www.jica.go.jp/jdr/case.html, 6 September 2014.

42 JICA, *Japanese Civilian and Self Defense Force Medical Experts Help Victims at the Epicenter of Haiti's Earthquake*, http://www.jica.go.jp/english/news/field/2009/20100127_01.html, 27 January 2010; and So Shiokawa, 'Jieitai niyoru Kokusaikinkyuuenjokatudou no Deguchi

operation, it handed over its activity to a medical team of Japanese Red Cross that was operating for a much longer duration than the JDR Team.[43] The JDR Team in Haiti is a good example of the All-Japan approach in natural disasters. In fact, it has been more than a decade since the All-Japan approach was established as a common practice of the JDR system for natural disaster relief operations, and we have witnessed inter-agency/civil-military coordination in the JDR Team deployed to the Philippines (2013), Indonesia (2006), Pakistan (2005), and elsewhere.[44]

The case of Haiti was quite unique in that SDF peacekeepers were deployed in the area where another SDF unit was already operating as a part of the JDR Team. The SDF peacekeepers deployed to MINUSTAH assumed the task of post-earthquake recovery and reconstruction such as the removal of rubble and repair of roads, which was understood as an extension of the disaster relief initiated by the JDR Team. Hence, it was rather natural for the SDF in MINUSTAH to succeed the All-Japan character of the JDR Team operated in Haiti.[45] The fact that both SDF units fell under the command of the CRF also helped to carry over this character and allowed better coordination and seamless transition.

Moreover, to meet increasing demands on the ground and to facilitate coordination of various actors including foreign armed forces operating outside of the auspice of the UN, MINUSTAH created a Joint Operation Tasking Center (JOTC).[46] The establishment of the JOTC within MINUSTAH allowed the SDF unit to engage in and implement All-Japan projects as official tasks of MINUSTAH. For example, the SDF units deployed to Haiti under MINUSTAH and a Japanese NGO called the Peace Winds Japan (PWJ) operating in Haiti in the aftermath of earthquake have agreed to collaborate in a community park development project in which the SDF unit would be responsible for eliminating the rubble on the premises, while the PWJ carried out the task of developing community park in the cleared area.[47] The request for assistance was

Senryaku' [Exist Strategy of the International Emergency Assistance Activities by the SDF], *Journal of International Security*, vol. 38, no. 4, 2011, p. 30.

43 Shiokawa, 'Jieitai niyoru Kokusaikinkyuuenjokatudou no Deguchi Senryaku', p. 32.

44 JICA, 'JDR no Haken Jirei' [Cases of JDR Dispatch], http://www.jica.go.jp/jdr/case.html, 6 September 2014; and JICA, 'JDR no Ayumi' [History of JDR], http://www.jica.go.jp/jdr/history2.html, 6 September 2014.

45 JICA, 'JDR toha?' [What is JDR?], http://www.jica.go.jp/jdr/about.html, 6 September 2014.

46 *Report of the Secretary-General on the United Nations Stabilization Mission in Haiti* (UN Doc. S/2010/200, 22 February 2010) para. 30.

47 Norihisa Urakami, 'Haichi haken wo keiki to shita Nippon gata Kyouryoku Sisutemu no Keisei' [Chapter 7: Development of Japanese Style Cooperation Triggered by the

submitted by the PWJ to the JOTC and then MINUSTAH gave the task order to the Japanese SDF engineering unit.

Using the same procedure, another type of All-Japan projects, *i.e.*, cooperation between the SDF and ODA projects, was also implemented. For example, the SDF unit in MINUSTAH together with the Japanese embassy in Haiti undertook the construction of the buildings of a girls' dormitory and storage in an orphanage, which was a part of a much larger project of rehabilitating the orphanage including the construction of an elementary school and a vocational school.[48] This project was made possible by combining the QIP funds of MINUSTAH allocated to the SDF engineering unit and Japan's ODA (GGP).

Systematic Coordination in South Sudan (Vertical and Horizontal)

The most recent deployment of the SDF to a UN PKO is to the United Nations Mission in South Sudan (UNMISS). Due to the deteriorating security situation in South Sudan in December 2013, civilian actors from Japanese organizations have had to leave or scale down their operations in South Sudan. While the SDF unit remains in South Sudan, the current situation does not allow for the All-Japan approach to develop fully.

However, since January 2012, about 330 Japanese SDF engineers have been deployed to UNMISS together with 40 members of the Assistance Coordination Local Office (ACLO), and several All-Japan projects were implemented before the deterioration of the security situation in December 2013. For example, one All-Japan project was a collaborative effort of the SDF engineering unit and Japan's ODA project (GGP) called 'Project for Building a Community Road in Juba-Nabari.' In this project, the local government purchased construction materials by funds allocated by Japan's GGP and with those materials, the SDF engineering unit undertook construction of a community road as an official task of UNMISS.[49] The SDF units were also able to undertake All-Japan projects with JICA (a filtration plant project in Juba) and a Japanese NGO called the Japan Center for Conflict Prevention (a human resource development project) in South Sudan.[50]

Deployment to Haiti] in Shinichi Yamamoto, *et al* (eds.), *Kokusaiheiwakatsudou niokeru Houkatsuteki Apurochi* [Comprehensive Approach in International Peace Operations] (Tokyo: Naigai Shuppan, 2012), pp. 202–204.

48 Urakami, 'Haichi haken wo keiki to shita Nippon gata Kyouryoku Sisutemu no Keisei', pp. 200–202.

49 Norihisa Urakami, *Activities of the GSDF in United Nations Mission in the Republic of South Sudan (UNMISS)*, a presentation provided to the ICRC on 31 July 2013.

50 Honda, *Heiwa Kouchiku to Jieitai*, pp. 182–183.

One of the most peculiar arrangements is the use of the ACLO as an adjunct to the main engineering unit. The ALCO was established to "develop projects on behalf of the engineering unit and to conduct coordination tasks necessary for the SDF engineering unit's deployment."[51] In other words, the ACLO was set up to identify projects through which UNMISS and Japan can collaborate so that Japan can appeal its All-Japan approach to South Sudan and the international community.[52] The ACLO is outside the command and control of UNMISS (*i.e.*, a National Command Element), and headed by a colonel (who is the national contingent commander), whereas the main engineering unit serving for UNMISS is led by a lieutenant colonel.

In South Sudan, the ACLO, on behalf of the SDF engineering units deployed to UNMISS, initiated coordination with other civilian Japanese actors including the Japanese embassy, JICA and NGOs in order to formulate All-Japan projects whenever deemed appropriate. Once a seed for All-Japan project was identified as a result of coordination between the ACLO and a civilian counterpart, Japanese SDF's engineer staff in UNMISS headquarters undertook necessary coordination within the headquarters so that particular task orders were given to the Japanese SDF engineering unit to carry out All-Japan projects as official duties of UNMISS.[53] In other words, for Japanese actors in South Sudan, All-Japan approach has been considered to be a means to collaborate with UNMISS.[54]

Discussion: a Cautionary Review of the All-Japan Approach

As discussed in the previous sections, the All-Japan approach has been conceived and implemented to meet the daunting challenges of peacekeeping and peacebuilding on the ground. First, it was invented to fill the gap between peacekeeping and development. The second motive behind the promotion of the All-Japan approach was to realize a more effective application of Japanese resources, both human and financial, in peacebuilding operations. The Japanese government also anticipated a ripple effect of the All-Japan approach

51 Secretariat of the International Peace Cooperation Headquarters, http://www.pko.go.jp/pko_j/result/s_sudan/s_sudan02.html, 6 September 2014.

52 Toru Ikutame, quoted from Kiba and Yasutomi, 'Jieitai ni yoru "Ohru Japan" gata Kokusaikyouryoku no Kadai', p. 126.

53 Secretariat of the International Peace Cooperation Headquarters, http://www.pko.go.jp/pko_j/faq/faq_s_sudan.html, 6 September 2014.

54 Kiba and Yasutomi, 'Jieitai ni yoru "Ohru Japan" gata Kokusaikyouryoku no Kadai', p. 126.

in the area of diplomacy, *i.e.*, Japan's contribution would be more 'visible' to the local as well as the international community.

To fill the gap between peacekeeping and development from the development side, JICA started intervening in the immediate aftermath of the conflict delivering emergency grant aid projects in Timor-Leste, Afghanistan, Iraq, and elsewhere. In July 2005, JICA formulated a 'fast-track' system based on the lessons from its involvement in post-conflict peacebuilding and disaster relief operations.[55] This system allows JICA to be operated more effectively in the post-conflict environment with much simpler procedures for disbursing funds, and thus addressing the problem of time lag.

From the peacekeeping side, the SDF sought to fill the gap by engaging themselves in humanitarian and reconstruction activities taking advantage of their engineering capability. Such an engagement was possible because Japan's troop contribution to UN PKOs has been limited mainly to the area of engineering due to its domestically imposed legal and political restrictions.[56] These restrictions has prevented Japan from developing a strategy that allows humanitarian and development workers to operate in a non-permissive environment under the protection provided by the SDF units deployed in the field. Hence, the recent debate about the change of the legal and political restrictions on the SDF operating in UN PKOs will affect this composition of Japanese strategy.

Indeed, a prelude to such a proactive usage of the SDF units was found in a non-combatant evacuation operation carried out by the SDF upon the deterioration of the security situation in South Sudan in December 2013, using a chartered commercial aircraft hired for the replacement of the SDF troops in South Sudan to evacuate Japanese aid workers operated there. While this type of cooperation is beyond the scope of the existing All-Japan approach, this incident in South Sudan proved the utility of the SDF in extending protection for Japanese civilians operating in non-permissive environment, and facilitated a current discussion by the Abe administration on the use of the SDF to protect Japanese nationals caught in open conflicts around the world.

The previous case studies illustrate the fact that the All-Japan approach has evolved in circumstances in which Japanese military contribution to UN PKOs has been concentrated in the area of engineering. Because of such a focus, collaboration between troops on the ground and aid workers undertaking ODA projects in the vicinity of SDF's area of operation has been possible and

55 JICA, *JICA Annual Report 2006*, http://www.jica.go.jp/about/report/2006/spe01_01.html, 6 September 2014.

56 Aoi, 'Beyond "Activism-Lite"?', pp. 1–29.

reasonable. This implies that if the Japanese government decides to shift the emphasis of their troop contribution from engineering to other functions, anticipated multiplier effects and existing complementarity of capacity may no longer be attainable. Hence, one must be cautious of the current discussion on a more proactive contribution of the SDF to UN PKOs. If the SDF units were given a mandate to protect civilians, they would more likely to be composed of infantry, not engineers, and thus losing the capacity required for taking part in All-Japan projects.

Both attempts in UNMISET introduced in the case study can be acknowledged for their original intent and innovative design of bridging the gap between peacekeeping (security) and development measures. The notion of RESPECT, an UNDP-led project that provided a platform for peacekeepers and a development project to collaborate, matched the 'One UN' approach. However, they were far from being an effective and 'seamless' form of assistance that could bring expected outcomes on the ground. The application of SDF peacekeepers to RESPECT was too limited in terms of its visible contribution to the mid-term development, though it represented a turning point in Japan's approach to peacebuilding. The other attempt, the handover strategy, was expected to serve as an effective gap filling measure, but it acted merely as a public relations tool aimed at domestic audience back in Japan. In short, these cases have demonstrated that linking two Japanese actors or Japanese aid schemes would not necessarily and automatically guarantee that cooperation would result in synergy and 'seamless' assistance. In other words, these cases remind us that pursuing the All-Japan approach is not a panacea. Overemphasis on cooperation between the SDF and other actors may only increase the coordination cost while the original purpose of the gap filling remains unachieved.

The tactical alliance between the SDF's 'soft' aid and the ODA's 'hard' aid in Iraq emerged out of necessity in which the SDF had limited funding and disbursement of its funding was confined to 'repair' or 'recovery,' whereas the non-permissive environment prevented for civilian development actors to operate on the ground. In short, a prototype of the All-Japan approach was formulated as a marriage of necessity. As the mandate of the SDF operations was to contribute to the humanitarian assistance and reconstruction in Iraq, the arranged marriage between the SDF and ODA projects was less problematic. However, it created a negative precedent that ODA projects could be used as 'force multipliers' to support the overseas mission of the SDF, which might sideline the needs of the true beneficiaries on the ground.

Furthermore, due to the perceived 'success', from the perspective of the Japanese government, of the arranged marriage between the SDF and ODA projects in Iraq, the Japanese government found it difficult to resist the temptation to apply this formula, which was possible under the non-UN operation where the SDF enjoyed operational independence from the rest of the multinational force, to UN PKOs where the SDF units would be expected to be placed under the operational command and control of the UN, and act coherently with the rest of the mission.

This temptation was further amplified when another 'success' story was delivered from Haiti. The All-Japan approach was possible and perhaps appropriate because MINUSTAH had the dual functions of peacekeeping and post-earthquake recovery. In fact, the SDF engineering unit in MINUSTAH was authorized to take part in All-Japan projects because tasks such as removal of rubbles were considered to be within the parameters of MINUSTAH's mandate. One has to be aware of the fact that Japanese SDF's unique engagement in its 'national' endeavors was acceptable to the UN under these special circumstances.

The circumstances under which the SDF engineering unit was deployed to UNMISS were quite different from those of the Iraq and Haiti cases. The SDF engineering unit was deployed to a UN PKO, which had a more security-oriented mandate such as to provide support for peace consolidation, protection of civilians, and security sector reform (SSR).[57] Nevertheless, the Japanese government decided to promote the All-Japan approach and to place the SDF unit in UNMISS within Japan's ODA efforts for recovery and reconstruction efforts in South Sudan.[58]

As the case of South Sudan shows, vigorous effort to promote the All-Japan approach in the policy circle and senior leadership in Tokyo can be misinterpreted by the government actors on the ground. In particular, SDF units may feel compelled to adhere to the strict application of the All-Japan approach in order to accommodate the 'wishes' of the superior and appeal to a general audience in Japan. This would have been a real concern for the All-Japan approach, if the security situation had not deteriorated in South Sudan in December 2013. Ironically, this set back, which forced Japanese aid workers to evacuate the area, saved the All-Japan approach from excessive enthusiasm in Tokyo. The security situation would not allow the SDF units in South Sudan to explore ways to collaborate with other Japanese actors on the ground.

Right now, UNMISS is the only UN PKO in which the SDF units are deployed. The Japanese government that advocates for "proactive contribution to international peace and security" will soon find another avenue for developing

---

57 UN Doc. S/RES/1996, 8 July 2011.

58 Honda, *Heiwa Kouchiku to Jieitai*, p. 185.

All-Japan projects. With the establishment of the National Security Council, which is expected to serve as a headquarters of the All-Japan approach and a mechanism for inter-ministerial coordination, and the National Security Strategy, which will navigate cooperation between different government agencies, Japan is now better equipped for pursuing the All-Japan approach. The recent discussion on the right to collective self-defense has generated a concern on Japan's policy and activities in IPC among the Japanese people and their neighbors. Under such a circumstance, it is well anticipated that the Japanese government would seek to accumulate more successful stories of the All-Japan approach in order to project a better image of the SDF in the eyes of the Japanese people. This constitutes an inherent danger of making the All-Japan approach an end itself rather than a means to address the challenges on the ground.

Conclusion

Integrated inter-agency/civil-military coordination can be an appropriate way to tackle various challenges in complex emergencies in which international peace operations are asked to deal with new challenges of state-building in a post-conflict society. The All-Japan approach, which is beginning to be recognized as a spearheaded of Japan's peace cooperation mode, can marshal limited resources for the maximum effect both in the domestic arena and in the area of deployment in terms of 'visibility' and 'accountability' of Japan's efforts. However, it must be underlined clearly that the All-Japan approach should not be pursued just for the sake of increasing Japan's footprint in the area of deployment and generating further public recognition/support at home for Japan's contribution to international peace operations. The priority should be placed on meeting the needs on the ground rather than as a priori advocacy of the All-Japan approach.

CHAPTER 8

Thailand's Participation in UN Peacekeeping Missions: The Reciprocal Transference of Expertise and Norms

Keokam Kraisoraphong and Brendan Howe

1 Introduction

As the demand for United Nations (UN) peacekeeping operations (PKOs) surged at the turn of the twenty-first century,[1] the need for more and better peacekeepers to undertake an expanded range of mandated tasks has become a key challenge for the UN.[2] The question as to "why UN member states do, or do not provide peacekeepers to UN-led missions" thus constitutes a vital part of this challenge – one which answers from a country perspective could likely provide significant insights.

Thailand is not currently a large contributor towards contemporary UN PKOs, ranking only 86 out of 123 contributors as of August 2014.[3] Thailand has, however, been identified as being among the emerging troop contributors with "the greatest untapped potential for UN peacekeeping".[4] Furthermore, as will be illustrated in this chapter, Thailand has a record of substantial contributions to the major, high profile, UN PKOs such as the United Nations Transnational Authority in Cambodia (UNTAC) from 1992–1993; the three missions in East Timor: International Forces in East Timor (INTERFET) from 1999–2000, United Nations Transitional Administration in East Timor (UNTAET) from 2000–2002, and United Nations Missions of Support in East Timor (UNMISET) from 2002–2005; and most recently, the African Union – United Nations Hybrid Operations in Darfur (UNAMID) from 2007–2010.

---

1 Bellamy, Alex J. and Williams, Paul D. *Understanding Peacekeeping, Second Edition* (Cambridge: Polity Press, 2010), p. 121.

2 Bellamy, Alex J. and Williams, Paul D. *Broadening the Base of United Nations Troop- and Police-Contributing Countries*. Providing for Peacekeeping No. 1 (New York: International Peace Institute, 2012), p. 1.

3 Ranking of Military and Police Contributions to UN Operations, http://www.un.org/en/peacekeeping/contributors/2014/aug14_2.pdf (accessed on 17 September 2014).

4 Bellamy and Williams, *Broadening the Base of United Nations Troop- and Police-Contributing Countries*, p. 12.

 | DOI 10.1163/9789004322059_009

Here, with the focus on high-profile and civil-military focused operations, we have perhaps the first indication of Thailand's particular motivations for participation in UN PKOs. These may differ from the norm among emerging contributors, but also point to the unique contributions Thailand can make in terms of state-building operations. Moving on from the reasons as to why and how Thailand provides peacekeepers to UN-led missions, this chapter examines the approach, unique perspectives, and expertise the Thai armed forces brought to PKOs. The chapter further addresses, however, the impact of the PKO experience upon the Thai military and wider society. In particular, this chapter explores the extent to which the UN's new approach to contemporary peace operations – particularly in terms of human security protection – has led to a diffusion of norms and functional competency among the Thai military and those who command them.

After this introduction the chapter begins with an overview of common rationales for supplying troops and police personnel to UN PKOs, and evaluates these motivations from the Thai perspective. The second substantive analytical section explores the development, current status, and experience of Thai peacekeeping, focusing on experience in UN peacekeeping missions, and highlighting the case of peace operations in East Timor; a watershed in Thailand's contributions to UN PKOs. The third part focuses on the Thai armed forces in their function as peacekeepers, the experience they have gained and the challenges they face in terms of norms and functional competencies for human security protection. Based on in-depth interviews, the chapter's analysis concludes in the fourth part, with some thoughts on whether there has been diffusion of such norms and functional competencies in the Thai armed forces.

II Rationales for Involvement in PKOs

Alex Bellamy and Paul Williams have identified five rationales for participation in peacekeeping operations: political, economic, security, institutional, and normative concerns.[5] These might all apply to all emerging contributors, but the hierarchical ranking of these motivations may vary among countries, and also within a country over time and through changing administrations. This has certainly been the case for Thailand. Political reasons may include "pressure or persuasion by allies, great powers, or the UN Secretary-General or Secretariat, and perceptions that peacekeeping contributions enhance the

5 Alex J. Bellamy and Paul D. Williams (eds.), *Providing Peacekeepers. The Politics, Challenges, and Future of United Nations Peacekeeping Contributions* (Oxford: OUP, 2013), pp. 17–21.

country's 'national prestige'".[6] Agents of governance in Thailand, including successive administrations, as well as the Thai military, have been keen to shore up international and domestic support for their governments, through repairing the damage done to the country's international reputation by internal governance failings. This remains a constant motivation for Thai participation in PKOs, and perhaps one explanation for heavy involvement in high-profile PKOs.

Economic rationales refer to economic incentives, whereas security rationales serve broader national security interests.[7] In Thailand's case both of these may perhaps differ from the norm among emerging contributors. Unlike some contributors, in particular developing countries and emerging contributors, Thailand does not use UN compensation payments to support its national budgets, but instead use it as direct payment in full to the deployed individuals.[8] In other words, the benefits of UN compensation payments fall with the individuals, not the national government or the armed forces as an institution. Thus economic motivations revolve around what benefits accrue individual members of society and, through the functioning of economic trickle-down effects, those that are dependent on these individuals, or who supply goods or services to them.

From the security perspective, due to the extensive involvement of the Thai military in internal governance in Thailand, UN PKOs can be seen as essential training opportunities for the security forces in the nuances of civil-military relations. The Thai military has traditionally prioritized, and continues to focus upon internal and external threats to national security. There has, however, been a transition in Thai military thinking from purely strategic security policy options such as defence and deterrence, to embracing the framework of a development-security nexus, better to engage directly with the people. This reflects closely the shift in international governance prescription from keeping parties with conflicting interests and agendas apart, to consideration of how to bring them actively together, as well as the shift from the prioritization of national rights (political sovereignty, territorial integrity, non-intervention) and security to human rights and security.

Institutional rationales may "stem from motives related to the country's armed forces, security sector, and bureaucratic dynamics".[9] Given the extensive role

6 *Ibid.*, p. 18.

7 *Ibid.*, p. 19.

8 Interview with Lt.General Sakda Sangsanit, first military officer to be appointed Military Advisor to the Permanent Mission of Thailand to the United Nations (2002). Interview date: November 1, 2013.

9 Bellamy and Williams (eds.), *Providing Peacekeepers* p. 20.

played by the military in Thai politics and governance, both historically and in contemporary terms, in Thailand's case consideration of elements related to the armed forces, security sector, and bureaucratic dynamics, amount to the same thing. Analysis of civil-military relations is key to the understanding of Thai motivations for involvement in PKOs. As will be explored below, the Thai military considers its extensive governance experience to be a major asset when engaging in UN missions, especially when restoring the rule of law to fragile states, or engaging in other state-building activities. On the other hand, experience gained by the Thai military on UN PKOs is applied back in domestic governance scenarios.

Normative considerations also play a major part in this analysis. It is important for Thailand to demonstrate leadership in its role as a "good Samaritan", and to show a principled commitment to the world organization as a "good international citizen".[10] This is particularly true when the Thai military is playing a role in domestic governance which is frowned upon by the international community. Thailand has long been perceived as a major promoter of human security-related concepts. Thailand championed the introduction of the paradigm into ASEAN in the late 1990s. In July 1998, then-Thai Foreign Minister Surin Pitsuwan proposed that ASEAN adopt a policy of flexible engagement, which involved discussions of fellow members' domestic policies. Although flexible engagement was rejected to become enhanced interaction, ultimately the new ASEAN political and security community came to the fore, which went much further in the direction of human security protection and promotion. On 6 May 2008, in a speech supportive of the concepts and critical of attachments to state sovereignty in the region, Pitsuwan (by this time ASEAN Secretary General) explicitly linked human security, the Responsibility to Protect and humanitarian intervention, emphasizing how the world has changed and that ASEAN and indeed the Asia-Pacific can do no less.[11] The May 2009 Europe-ASEAN Meeting (ASEM) in Hanoi, Vietnam was dominated by questions regarding an international response to the continued persecution of Burmese democracy leader, Aung San Suu Kyi, by the military junta. Thailand (at that time holding the chair of ASEAN) was accused of interfering in Myanmar's internal affairs by releasing the organization's critical message.[12]

Domestically, in 2002, Thailand also established a Ministry of Social Development and Human Security. This chapter further, however, examines

10 *Ibid.*, p. 20.

11 Surin Pitsuwan, ASEAN Secretary-General Keynote Address, RSIS Centre for Non-Traditional Security (NTS) Studies Launch, Traders Hotel, Singapore, 6 May 2008.

12 BBC 'Burma rejects EU, Asian pressure,' 25 May 2009, http://news.bbc.co.uk/2/hi/asia-pacific/8066513.stm. (Accessed on 18 September 2014).

the extent to which norm diffusion from the international community is channeled through experiences in UN PKOs to effect a transformative impact upon the culture and procedures of the Thai military itself. Thus not only have the motivations for Thailand's involvement in UN PKOs evolved over time, but so too have the agents of governance themselves, in particular the military. The next section considers the evolution of Thailand's involvement in UN PKOs.

III Thailand's Peace Operations: Development, Current Status and Experience in UN Peacekeeping Missions

Prior to the UN's first peacekeeping mission in the 1950s, the UN Emergency Force (1956–67) deployed to Egypt,[13] Thailand had had the experience of working under the UN framework via the UN Command in Korea (KOREA: UNC (1950–1955)). But it was not until over two decades later, after UN peace operations had undergone a period of "triple transformation" – quantitative, normative and qualitative[14] – that Thailand's participation in UN peacekeeping missions truly began. The UN Iraq-Kuwait Observation Mission (UNIKOM), launched in 1991, was the first mission to witness Thai participation, with the initial deployment of seven Thai military officers, followed by the further deployment of 50 officers to join the UN Guard Contingent in Iraq: (UNGCI: 1991–1994). In the following years, UN peace operations launched in countries such as Cambodia (in which Thai military personnel also played a substantial human security-related role clearing mines and reconstructing infrastructure) and Somalia during 1992–1993, were clearly qualitatively different compared to earlier missions as they merged peacekeeping with "delivery of humanitarian

13 The UN Emergency Force (1956–67), considered to be the UN's first peacekeeping mission, was the creation of a Canadian diplomat, Lester Pearson, in response to the Suez Crisis involving the invasion of Egypt by the UK, France and Israel.

14 A triple transformation – in quantity, norms, and quality – in peace operations, occurred as the Cold War came to an end between 1988 and 1993. See generally Bellamy and Williams *Understanding Peacekeeping, Second Edition* (2010) for a detailed overview. Quantitatively, UN peace operations increased in number to more than had been undertaken in the previous forty years combined. Normatively, there was a growing belief that peace operations should be broadened to involve the promotion of stable peace, which in turn resulted in the qualitative transformation – whereby the delivery of humanitarian aid, state-building programs, and local peacemaking and elements of peace enforcement were merged into peacekeeping.

aid, state-building programmes, local peacekeeping and elements of peace enforcement".[15]

Although a relatively small troop contributing country, Thailand became a member of the UN Standby Arrangement System for the provision of troops in 1998 – a year before renewed demand for peace operations began. As Bellamy and Williams point out, through the peacekeeping activities troop contributing countries earned "international prestige and moral weight at the UN and beyond".[16] International recognition of Thailand's contributions and the commensurate prestige came with its substantial role in the high-profile UN operations in East Timor during 1999–2005.[17] The recognition received made this mission a defining period for Thailand's standing and its policy as a troop contributing country to the peace operations which followed.

On the one hand, Thailand gained useful experience for its personnel through the UN peacekeeping activities while on the other hand, it brought to the missions the skills from the approach and perspectives deemed crucial and somewhat relevant to the then transformed peace operations. Such approach and perspectives were those which the Thai armed forces had accumulated over the decades from its own domestic experience with counter-insurgency, which involved strategic activities in line with its change in military thinking. On the other hand, however, through further experience with UN peacekeeping missions over the years, the Thai armed forces soon learned that the UN's new approach for contemporary peace operations comprised certain norms and functional competencies of which they must be aware and to which they must adhere. In order to do so this would require vital adjustments in the approach and perspectives they had domestically acquired and brought with them to the missions.

As a UN member country, and as member of the UN Standby Arrangement System since 1998, Thailand's policy towards UN peacekeeping has led it to establish a formal procedure for peace operations support – particularly to provide peacekeepers to UN-led missions. A number of key agencies in the Ministry of Foreign Affairs and the Ministry of Defence with related roles and responsibilities have been assigned to take part in this process.

15 Bellamy and Williams, *Understanding Peacekeeping, Second Edition*, p. 93.

16 *Ibid.* p. 58.

17 The UN missions in East Timor during 1999–2005 included the International Force in East Timor (INTERFET Peace Operations) 1999–2000, the UN Transnational Administration (UNTAET) 2000–2002, and the UN Mission of Support in East Timor (UNMISET) 2002–2005.

In December 2000 a permanent unit was transformed from the special warfare division of the Thai armed forces into the peace operations division by the Directorate of Joint Operations, the Supreme Command Headquarters – to undertake the tasks of the Thai armed forces headquarters in peace operations.

Since the triple transformation of UN peace operations during the period 1988–1993, Thailand, beginning with UNIKOM (the United Nations Iraq-Kuwait Observation Mission: 1991–2002) and UNGCI (UN Guard Contingent in Iraq: 1991–1994), has joined a number of UN peace operations over the last two decades. Important Thai contributions to UN missions during this period include *inter alia* UNTAC in Cambodia (1992–1993), UNAMSIL in Sierra Leon (1999–2005), INTERFET (International Forces), UNTAET (UN Transitional Administration), and UNMISET (UN Mission of Support) in East Timor (1999–2005), and most recently UNAMID in Darfur (2007–2010). Table 1 illustrates the nine UN peacekeeping missions in which the Thai armed forces have participated over the years and lists the number of men deployed as well as outlines the tasks they undertook during each mission. Among these missions, the UN operations in East Timor during the period 1999–2005 (INTERFET, UNTAET, and UNMISET) have somewhat benchmarked Thailand's peacekeeping, and will be explored in more detail below.

The Royal Thai armed forces participation in peace operations under UN framework and tasks in support of UN missions

Mission & period	Number of men dispatched	Tasks
United Nations Iraq-Kuwait Observation Mission: UNIKOM: 1991–2002	5–7	Undertake Duties in demilitarized zone along the Iraq-Kuwait borders.
United Nations Guard Contingent in Iraq: UNGCI: 1991–1994	50	Assist UN Sub-offices and Humanitarian Centre under the auspices of humanitarian assistance along the Iran-Iraq and Iraq- Turkey borders.
United Nations Transnational Authority in Cambodia: UNTAC: 1992–1993	705	Undertake Demining operations. Reconstruct infrastructure such as bridges and roads.

The Royal Thai armed forces participation in peace operations under UN framework and tasks in support of UN missions (cont.)

Mission & period	Number of men dispatched	Tasks
United Nations Mission in Sierra Leone: UNAMSIL: 1999–2005	5	Undertake Unarmed Patrol tasks to assess overall situation and civilian safety. Undertake Registrar tasks to collect weapons from groups involved in combat. Undertake UN Representative tasks to negotiate solutions to problems among various groups. Deliver paramilitary to training camps as part of the reintegration process.
International Forces in East Timor: INTERFET (Peace Operations): 1999–2000 United Nations Transitional Administration in East Timor: UNTAET: 2000–2002 United Nations Missions of Support in East Timor: UNMISET: 2002–2005	1,581	Restore peace, safety in life and property. Provide humanitarian assistance to the East Timor population. Provide assistance to the establishment of basic infrastructure to strengthen political, economic, military, social and bureaucratic capacity towards self- governance upon independence.
United Nations Operations in Burundi: ONUB: 2004–2006	177	Operationalize peacekeeping in cooperation with the UN under UN peacekeeping task force in order to support operations in accordance with the Arusha Agreement.
United Nations Mission in Sudan: UNMIS: 2006–2010	15	Undertake the tasks of Military observer to monitor human rights violations and operations during cease fire between rebel groups and government. Observe and support election process.

Mission & period	Number of men dispatched	Tasks
United Nations Political Mission in Nepal: UNMIN: 2007–2008	7	Assist the Nepalese government and the Maoist rebels in complying with the cease-fire agreement established by both parties.
African Union – United Nations Hybrid Operations in Darfur: UNAMID: 2007–2010	800	Check and verify hardware equipment. Undertake the tasks of military observer.

Compiled from: Peace Operations Centre (POC), Directorate of Military Operations, the Royal Thai Armed Forces Headquarters. *The Role of the Thai Armed Forces in Peace Operations (in Thai)*, 2013.

The UN peace operations in East Timor began with Indonesia's consent in 1999, after the wave of killing, ethnic cleansing and property destruction which followed the earlier UN-supervised referendum on independence (UN Assistance Mission in East Timor: UNAMET). As INTERFET was deployed to restore order during 1999–2000 the Thai armed forces participated in the mission with 1,581 military personnel – a Thai military officer was also then appointed Deputy Force Commander.[18] When INTERFET handed over to UNTAET in 2000, two Thai military officers were consecutively UN-appointed Force Commander.[19] UNTAET comprised forces from 36 nations with the mandate "to administer East Timor until it became independent and effectively constituted the territory's legal sovereign with international legal personality."[20] This involved assisting East Timor's transition to a democratic system through an election and the handover of power from the UN appointed ad-hoc government to the elected government, whereby ensuring that the election process supported national reconciliation and was supported by the international community.

18 Major General Songkitti Jakkabaht was appointed Deputy Force Commander of INTERFET.

19 Lt.General Boonsrang Niumpradit was Force Commander of UNTAET during July 2000-September 2001, and Lt.General Winai Phattiyakul was Force Commander during September 2001–May 2002.

20 Bellamy and Williams, *Understanding* Peacekeeping, 273. Under Security Council Resolution 1272.

After East Timor's declaration of independence on 20 May 2002, the Thai armed forces continued to provide peacekeepers to UNMISET, which was deployed to replace UNTAET, and tasked to operate for a period of two years. Thailand's provision of troop contingents to UNTAET and UNMISET were organized in nine shifts – each shift comprised a team of the infantry platoon, level 2 medical unit, and permanent operations command staff.[21] The East Timor mission was considered high-profile and exemplified the complete process of contemporary peace operations.[22] By extensive involvement throughout the duration of the mission the Thai armed forces undertook the many peacekeeping functions which have evolved as part of contemporary complex PKOs. In particular, the consecutive appointments of two Thai military officers as Force Commander by the UN is perceived to have helped enhance Thailand's role in prestigious diplomatic and peace making activities.[23] From a domestic perspective, particularly for the Thai armed forces at the time, contributing to peacekeeping operations provided invaluable overseas experience for its personnel.[24] As has been noted as being true for a variety of states – it provided a niche that brought to the Thai armed forces "greater respect and authority in the international institutions, especially the UN" which in turn domestically allowed them "more voice in international security issues than they otherwise would have".[25] As such, the Cabinet in September 2002 approved the Supreme Command Headquarters' proposal to establish the Office of the Military Advisor to the Permanent Mission of Thailand to the United Nations.[26]

By the time of the completion of UN peace operations in East Timor in June 2004, it was still generally believed that the Thai military had "returned to barracks" since 1992, as Thailand had been free from military coups for over a

21 Peace Operations Centre (POC), Directorate of Military Operations, the Royal Thai Armed Forces Headquarters. *The Role of the Thai Armed Forces in Peace Operations (in Thai)*, 2013.

22 Beginning with the use of *preventive diplomacy* and the *peace making* mission under UNAMET to provide supervised referendum on independence, followed by INTERFET to restore order which was then handed over to *peacekeeping operation* by UNTAET, to *peace building* by UNMISET – and finally to the stage of *peace making* by UNMIT (United Nations Integrated Mission in Timor Leste).

23 Interview with Lt.General Sakda Sangsanit, first military officer to be appointed Military Advisor to the Permanent Mission of Thailand to the United Nations (2002). Interview date: November 1, 2013.

24 Bellamy and Williams, *Broadening the Base of United Nations Troop- and Police-Contributing Countries*, p. 5.

25 *Ibid.* p. 4.

26 Col. Sakda Sangsanit was appointed as the first Military Advisor to the Permanent Mission of Thailand to the United Nations.

decade by this point, and appeared to have submitted to civilian control an non-interference in domestic governance in line with international norms. In fact, over the years which followed, as the UN peace operations increased in number and expanded in their tasks, so too did the UN's request for troop contributions from Thailand continue to increase. Under the circumstances, it was necessary for the Thai armed forces to develop its pool of relevant specialist capacities in order to sustain or expand its contribution to UN peacekeeping. Thus as instructed by the Commander in Chief, the Directorate of Joint Operations was directed to expand the structure of the peace operations division and to aim towards developing a regional peace operations centre.[27] On July 19th 2006, the Peace Operations Centre (POC) was thus established under the Directorate of Joint Operations, the Supreme Command Headquarters – exactly two months before the staging of Thailand's eighteenth coup on the night of September 19th 2006.[28]

IV The Royal Thai Armed Forces as Peacekeepers: Skill and Experiential Transference?

As much as the 2006 coup is deemed to demonstrate too well that "the claim that the military had 'returned to barracks' in 1992 was premature",[29] it also suggested that the institutional rationale that "participation in peacekeeping offers a way of keeping the armed forces occupied outside of the country rather than meddling in domestic affairs"[30] does not exactly apply to Thailand. For more than a decade Thailand has maintained a consistent level in its contribution of peacekeepers to UN peace operations, facilitated by the establishment of the Office of the Military Advisor to the Permanent Mission of Thailand to the UN and the Peace Operations Centre. A strategy for identifying prospective troop contributing countries lists Thailand among committed contributors having demonstrated a particular interest in UN peacekeeping – hence the aforementioned

27 Peace Operations Centre (POC), *The Role of the Thai Armed Forces in Peace Operations (in Thai)*, na.

28 This was the eighteenth coup since the overthrow of the absolute monarchy in 1932.

29 Beeson, Mark and Bellamy, Alex J. *Securing Southeast Asia, the Politics of Security Sector Reform*. Routledge Security in Asia Pacific series (London: Routledge, 2008), p. 101.

30 Bellamy and Williams, *Broadening the Base of United Nations Troop- and Police-Contributing Countries*, p. 5.

categorization of Thailand as being situated among countries with the greatest untapped potential for contributions to UN PKOs.[31] This does, however, raise the question as to whether Thailand is in fact becoming path dependent on its UN role and contributions.[32]

On the other hand, the Thai armed forces perceive their domestic experience gained through their role in national development during counter-insurgency efforts since mid-1960s to be a valuable asset in their role as peacekeepers.[33] Such actual domestic experience began when the continued failure of military suppression operations in the 1960s made it necessary for the Thai armed forces to rethink and review its military doctrine, strategy and tactics as it responded to the challenges of growing internal communist threats.[34] A basic assumption which partly underpinned this transformation in military thinking – from military means to political means – was that economic development and loyalty to the government were correlated. The problems were seen to stem from the lack of government presence in remote areas susceptible to communist infiltration, which, in turn, could become bases for anti-government operations. To negate this possibility it was deemed crucial to gain the people's allegiance through the promotion of their welfare whereby the military was entrusted with the task of securing the peripheral areas, and with concurrent responsibilities in rural development, crime suppression, and mass mobilization.[35]

Such was to be achieved through gearing government efforts toward rural development projects which would raise the people's living standards while providing a government presence and thus facilitating better communication

31 *Ibid.* p. 12.

32 *Ibid.* p. 6.

33 Interview with General Boonsrang Niupradit, Force Commander, UNTAET PKF (July 2000–September 2001). Interview date: January 10, 2014. Interview with Lt.General Sakda Sangsanit, first military officer to be appointed Military Advisor to the Permanent Mission of Thailand to the United Nations (2002). Interview date: November 1, 2013.

34 The failure of the initial counter-insurgency efforts, which stressed suppressive measures, were clearly reflected in the dramatic increase in the number of communist terrorists and their sympathizers.

35 Chai-Anan, Samudavanija, Kusuma, Snitwongse and Suchit, Bunbongkar. *From Armed Suppression to Political Offensive: Attitudinal Transformation of Thai Military Officers since 1976*, (Bangkok: Institute of Security and International Studies, Chulalongkorn University, 1990), pp. 9 and 72. The policy of political means, however, often had to start with military operations, especially in villages where the communist terrorists were well entrenched with established political infrastructure.

between the government and the people.[36] As such alternative required greater coordination of counter-insurgency efforts, steps were taken to issue Orders of the Office of the Prime Minister[37] and to set up organizations[38] in support of this change in strategy and establish a framework for a coordinated effort by civilian, police and military services. These organizations then functioned with intelligence and psychological warfare centres and with Joint Security Centres (JSC)[39] attached. In this regard, the most significant lesson the Thai armed forces learned in embracing the framework of development security nexus was "the need to end their isolation from the people, and for this, primarily political measures were required".[40] This basically meant military actions must aim to support political actions and objectives.

Over time, this line of thinking further evolved into an added dimension – the use of democracy to fight communism. This involved the promotion of political participation as well as supporting all existing democratic movements, the treatment of communist insurgents, defectors or prisoners as fellow countrymen, dissemination of information, and particularly psychological measures. Programs such as the Volunteer Development and Self-Defence program were a significant part of the political means designed with the basic concept to encourage the people to run their own villages under the guidance of the Internal Security Operations Command (ISOC). Such programs have become known as the integrated rural development to promote national security.[41] The practical mechanisms of the process have been outlined by Chai-Anan, Samudavanija, et al. as follows:

36 Chai-Anan, Samudavanija, et al., *From Armed Suppression to Political Offensive*, pp. 51–52. The stipulation of the armed forces role in national development in 1976 specified the objectives of the Army's assistance program which involved providing support to the government in community development and supplementing the development work of other government agencies. The aim was also to ensure the people's positive attitude and support for the army's operation. This was to be done through the monitoring of intelligence needed for military operations and promotion of national security. Ultimately, the goal of the programs was to support the army's plan for armed suppression of communist insurgency.

37 The series of Orders issued include Order No.219/2508 (issued 1965), Order No.110/2512 (issued 1969), Order No.298/2519 (issued 1976), Order No.66/2523 (issued 1980), Order No.66/2525 (issued 1982).

38 The first organizational response to overt armed insurgency was to set up the Communist Suppression Operation Command (CSOC) in 1985. To alleviate the severe criticisms of CSOC.

39 The JSC were established to combine the input of the various intelligence services working in the affected areas.

40 Chai-Anan, Samudavanija, et al., *From Armed Suppression to Political Offensive*, pp. 68–69.

41 *Ibid.* p. 106.

> With the help of military and government officers, the villagers were trained in self-defence and various subjects relevant to rural development such as management, agriculture, public health, and village industry. Courses in government administration and politics are also taught. The people's participation in the management of the village's activities were emphasized. Committees on administration, education, public health, development, finance, social welfare and village security were set up under the supervision of the military to facilitate villagers' participation.

The experience gained from these activities – referred to as "civil affairs", came to characterize the institutional knowledge of the Thai armed forces on civil-military relations. The skills which have been honed in the domestic setting have come to be perceived as increasingly relevant and suited for the tasks that have come to be required of contemporary peacekeeping agenda.[42] The "thinking and practice on matters such as the protection of civilians, use of force, human rights, and the acquisition and management of consent"[43] are some of the human security related tasks among "some 300 individual functions that fall under twenty-one broad categories"[44] which the Thai military have undertaken during UN peacekeeping missions. Clearly then, it seems that, despite their controversial involvement in domestic political processes, the Thai military have something to offer contemporary peacekeeping operations in terms of the experience they have gained and skills they have honed as a result of these operations. It remains to be discussed, however, the extent to which experience of UN PKOs have transformed the Thai military as it operated in the domestic arena. This is the subject taken up in the following and final analytical section.

V Norm Diffusion as a Result of International Engagement

Thailand's decision to participate in peace operations is made on a case-by-case basis, depending on the size and type of troops requested and the status of the

42 Interview with General Boonsrang Niupradit, Force Commander, UNTAET PKF (July 2000–September 2001). Interview date: January 10, 2014.

43 Bellamy and Williams, *Broadening the Base of United Nations Troop- and Police-Contributing Countries*, p. 7.

44 Bellamy, Alex J. and Williams, Paul D. *Providing Peacekeepers: The Politics, Challenges, and Future of United Nations Peacekeeping Contributions* (Oxford: Oxford University Press, 2013), p. 40.

operations, as well as whether budget commitment is required. In principle, the most important determinant is political oversight, as the authority to approve troop contribution to peace operations rests with the Cabinet. On the other hand, the Prime Minister may have the case brought to the National Security Council for approval prior to the Cabinet's consideration. At the level of the Ministry of Defence deployment of troops for peace operations is based on the Defence Council's approval, which in principle would be in accord with the Cabinet's resolution. But in practice, because the assessment of the armed force's capacity to participate rests with the armed forces, the military's view on the matter serves as a powerful determinant to the decisions of the political and civilian authorities.

On the one hand, participation in UN peacekeeping operations has benefited the Thai armed forces in several ways. To individual officers, the UN's compensation payments have been economically beneficial as they provide a considerable added amount to their domestic salary.[45] This, together with the perception, recognition, and sense of prestige identified with the status of those recruited to join UN peacekeeping missions has significantly contributed to the increasing number of applicants registered in the Peace Operation Centre (POC)'s recruitment process.[46] The international exposure through UN peacekeeping missions has also provided invaluable overseas experience for those deployed. In fact, UN peacekeeping missions are among the strongest, most direct links to the international community that the armed forces are able to provide for their personnel.

UN minimum standards of training and capability set for the fulfilment of individual functions necessary to implement the multifaceted tasks have also been a significant source of knowledge and experience for the military. This is particularly true with regard to human security related issues in contemporary peace operations. In this respect, through the UN's principles of humanity, neutrality, and impartiality,[47] the Thai military has been directed to carry out their functions in adherence to the principle of consent among the local parties with whom the peacekeepers must operate, and to not provide tacit support to one of the parties to a conflict. For this reason, the Thai military has been cautioned against the use of military psychological operations, and to instead resort to neutral and impartial methods such as to act as an objective

---

45 In the case of Thailand, UN compensation payments are not used to support the national budget nor to augment the security sector's budget in any way – instead the total amount is passed on only as compensation payments to individual officers.

46 Interview: General Boonsrang Niumpradit, January 10, 2014.

47 POC, *The Role of the Thai Armed Forces in Peace Operations*, p. 41.

source of public information, and provide humanitarian assistance in civil-military co-ordination activities through civil society coordinator working groups.[48]

On the other hand, in the case of Thailand, the benefits from UN peacekeeping deployments have fundamentally been the gains for individuals – be it prestige, experience and knowledge, or financial reward. This leads to two further observations. First, as mentioned previously, the benefits of UN compensation payments fall with the individuals, not the armed forces as an institution. Secondly, it is more likely that the experience and knowledge gained, in terms of norms and functional competencies, stand a better chance of being diffused and institutionalised when those who have had the experience with UN peacekeeping missions come to assume a position at the decision-making level. This was clearly the case during the period between the late 1990s up to 2008 when General Boonsrang Niumpradit, Force Commander, UNTAET PKF (July 2000–September 2001), became the Commander of the Royal Thai Armed Forces Headquarters in 2006, and in that same year General Winai Phattiyakul, the consecutive Force Commander (September 2001–May 2002) became Permanent Secretary for Defence and Secretary-General of the National Security Council (NSC). Otherwise, however, benefits from experience and knowledge remain within the limited circle of each of the individuals rather than diffusing throughout the institutional framework.

Given Thailand's decision-making structures with regard to peacekeeping operations, troop contributions have been the results of formal procedures of civilian-military and bureaucratic considerations – the military being the key determinant since assessment as to whether it is within Thailand's deployable capacity to accept the expressed mission requests ultimately rests with the armed forces. But while the military has always been a willing party in support of Thailand's participation in UN peace operations the prospect that it would increase its troop deployment capacity for this purpose has been limited. Such limitations stem partly from the attitude within the armed forces that were the military to direct their efforts toward more significant contributions – beyond token contributions[49]– the military would be tacitly assuming the role of mercenaries. Therefore, despite the military's existing "size, quality, and posture"[50] for greater troop contribution potential, and despite the supporting foundation

48 *Ibid.* p. 43.

49 Bellamy and Williams, *Providing Peacekeeping*, p. 9: defines token contributions as "contributions of fewer than forty uniformed personnel to a mission, where these personnel do not make up a specialized unit".

50 Bellamy and Williams, *Providing Peacekeeping*, p. 15.

established during the past decade,[51] such an attitude has made gaining high-level support difficult for those working to maintain or even more so to continue improving with the activities required for forming troop contingents that would advance further future contributions.

In sum, the prestige associated with UN peacekeeping notwithstanding, the fact that training soldiers to be peacekeepers is of secondary importance to internal security concerns together with the perception that Thai soldiers are not mercenaries, has made it that much more difficult to diffuse the norms and functional competencies achieved by the Thai armed forces' participation in UN peacekeeping operations.

VI Conclusions

UN peacekeeping missions which have increasingly been "in the midst of or in the aftermath of internal conflict between sub-groups"[52] have come to define contemporary peacekeeping agenda, the nature of which is now known to be multidimensional, more multifaceted and complex. Military forces utilised as peacekeepers are now tasked to engage in individual functions shared with civilian personnel. These tasks range from restoration of basic services for the population to promoting human rights and fostering political dialogue and national reconciliation. Most of these objectives and foci are in line with the Thai armed forces' cumulative experience in "civil affairs" over the years of counter-insurgency since the 1960s. Such experience have provided the skills which underpinned a significant part of the Thai armed forces performance in UN peacekeeping missions.

All of the motivations listed in the first analytical section have played a part in stimulating the participation of Thailand in UN PKOs. Most important among them in the Thai case, however, are the institutional and normative drivers. This is perhaps not surprising when taken in the wider context of the role of the Thai military in domestic governance, but also, and somewhat paradoxically, the assertive normative international role assumed by successive Thai government administrations. The state-building and civil-military cooperation experience and expertise has come in useful in various UN peacekeeping missions. That being said, the organizational and operational culture of the Thai military has come under scrutiny when they have looked to transfer

51 Such as the Office of the Military Advisor to the Permanent Mission of Thailand to the UN and the POC.

52 Bellamy and Williams, *Providing Peacekeeping*, p. 39.

certain methods and experience to peacekeeping operations. Foremost among the fundamental principle of UN peacekeeping is the injunction to obtain "consent of local parties amongst which the peacekeepers must operate".[53] The Thai military have, however, been cautioned under the UN minimum standards and capability regulations to abstain from the use of military psychological operations which had been a main feature of the Thai military's approach to counter-insurgency – the reason being that they must not function in tacit support to one of the parties to a conflict.

The prestige, economic reward, and invaluable learning experience from participating in UN peacekeeping operations notwithstanding, the attitude towards future troop contribution among the military decision-makers suggests that the norms and functional competencies human security protection acquired through past operations under UN peacekeeping missions have remained within the circles of those deployed and has yet to be effectively diffused. Likewise the security drivers tend to mitigate against increased involvement from the Thai military in international PKOs, as the focus remains on national security.

Nevertheless, as the UN seeks to expand its pool of peacekeeping capabilities and given the identification of Thailand as an emerging troop contributor with "great untapped potential" it seems the UN could well encourage the diffusion of relevant norms and functional competencies in the Thai armed forces through lessons learned and synthesized from the operational level. Self-imaging as good international citizens would likely be a normative rationale that could compel the armed forces to take a posture of strengthening contributions to UN peacekeeping. Under such circumstances further systematic and in-depth studies are needed to understand and explain the issue of norm diffusion and the necessity of continued functional competency development – whether and to what extent courses, training curriculum or handbooks have systematically synthesized the skills, knowledge, and expertise – in the Thai case as well as on comparative cases of other countries.

53 *Ibid.* p. 40.

CHAPTER 9

Why Contribute? Understanding Asian Motivations for Troop Contribution to Peace Operations

Xenia Avezov

1 Introduction

South Asia contributes thirty percent of all military and police personnel for United Nations peace operations. Over the past nine years, India, Pakistan and Bangladesh ranked in the top three troop-contributing countries (TCCs), reaching the peak of their contributions between 2006 and 2011. Nepal and Sri Lanka have steadily increased their contributions over the past decade.[1] Northeast Asia contributes another four percent of all UN uniformed personnel. While their contributions are smaller and more recent, TCCs in this region and China and Mongolia in particular have also increased participation in recent years.

Military and Police Personnel 2005-2014

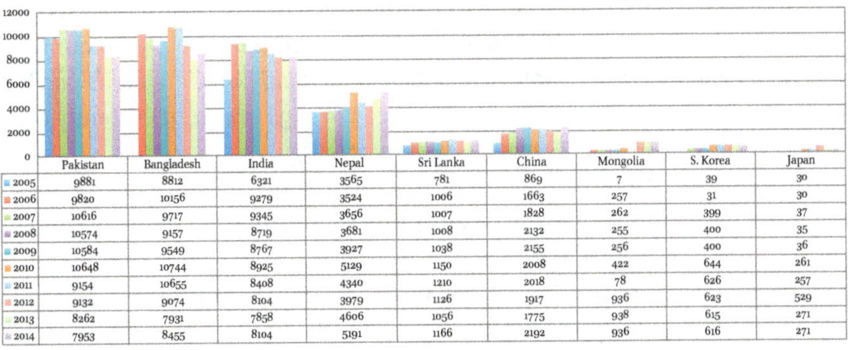

	Pakistan	Bangladesh	India	Nepal	Sri Lanka	China	Mongolia	S. Korea	Japan
2005	9881	8812	6321	3565	781	869	7	39	30
2006	9820	10156	9279	3524	1006	1663	257	31	30
2007	10616	9717	9345	3656	1007	1828	262	399	37
2008	10574	9157	8719	3681	1008	2132	255	400	35
2009	10584	9549	8767	3927	1038	2155	256	400	36
2010	10648	10744	8925	5129	1150	2008	422	644	261
2011	9154	10655	8408	4340	1210	2018	78	626	257
2012	9132	9074	8104	3979	1126	1917	936	623	529
2013	8262	7931	7858	4606	1056	1775	938	615	271
2014	7953	8455	8104	5191	1166	2192	936	616	271

The participation of Mongolia, Bangladesh and Nepal is most prominent when considering contribution relative to military strength.[2] Given Mongolia's

1 Contribution to United Nations Peacekeeping Operations as of August 31st, 2005-2014, United Nations Peacekeeping Statistics, http://www.un.org/en/peacekeeping/resources/statistics/.

2 Data for military and police personnel contributions is as of August 14 and is taken from United Nations Peacekeeping Military and Police Contributors, http://www.un.org/en/peacekeeping/contributors/2014/aug14_1.pdf.
Data for military strength is taken from: (2014) Chapter Six: Asia, The Military Balance, 114:1, 201–296, DOI: 10.1080/04597222.2014.871879.

 | DOI 10.1163/9789004322059_010

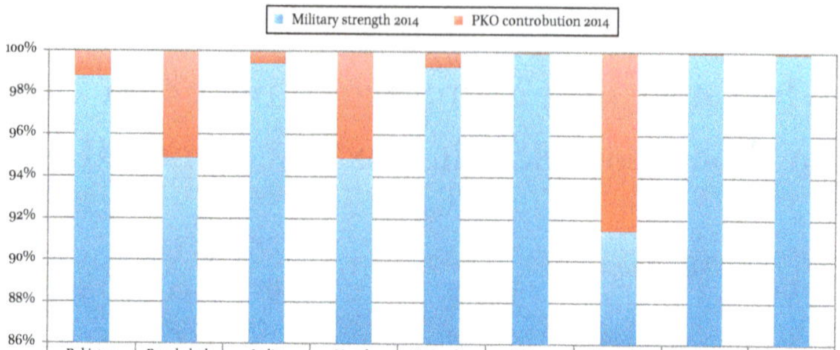

	Pakistan	Bangladesh	India	Nepal	Sri Lanka	China	Mongolia	S. Korea	Japan
PKO as % of military strength	1.23%	5.38%	0.61%	5.42%	0.72%	0.09%	9.36%	0.09%	0.10%
PKO controbution 2014	7953	8455	8104	5191	1166	2192	936	616	271
Military strength 2014	643800	157050	1325000	95750	160900	2333000	10000	655000	247150

relatively modest military strength, its contribution of ten percent of its military personnel to UN peace operations is striking. The rule of thirds in military planning requires any military activity to maintain three different sets of troops per operation—one third that is currently deployed, one third that is training to replace the force currently deployed and an additional third that is recuperating after deployment.[3] Therefore, the Mongolian commitment can be alternatively viewed as nearly thirty percent of its military strength. Countries like Pakistan and India contribute much more personnel but significantly smaller share of their overall military strength compared with countries like Nepal and Mongolia. While China has significantly accelerated its participation from 869 uniformed personnel in 2005 to 2,192 in 2014, it currently contributes only 0.09% from its overall military strength.

This chapter attempts to identify the drivers of contributions in these regions as well as the underlying factors that shape the size, type of personnel deployed, and level of commitment to contribution. Findings are also intended to inform policy conversations on the future of UN peace operations by creating an in-depth analysis of Asian TCCs, their motivations for participation, and how such motivations inform the level of contribution.

Section 2 of this chapter presents the methodology: existing literature is distilled into several groups of common motivations for participation. This theoretical frameworkwill be applied to the nine selected countries. Since this study focuses on motivations, it will not offer a comprehensive analysis of the inhibitors or barriers for contribution. However, section 2.2 provides a short overview of common barriers or inhibitors for contribution that were

3 Jair van der Lijn, 'Grenzen aan de Nederlandse Capaciteit voordeel Name aan Vredesoperaties', *Internationale Spectator*, vol. 61, issue 1, 2008.

considered. Section 3 provides an overview of the nine TCCs motivations for participation, using multiple sources for verifying each country's motivations and dividing them into five distinct clusters. Section 4 presents key findings that emerge from the clusters in section 4 and suggests possible implications.

2 Methodology and Definitions

This chapter is based in part on the New Geopolitics of Peace Operations Initiative at the Stockholm International Peace Research Institute (SIPRI). The initiative investigates the perspectives, motivations, and underlying normative calculations of emerging global powers and large troop-contributing regions on the future of peace operations. Regional dialogues with participants from the policy, military, and academic sectors have been conducted in Northeast and South Asia, among other regions. During meetings, participants are asked to discuss their perspectives on four general themes covered in every meeting: (1) The changing world order including common threat perceptions, (2) Norms and concepts in peace operations, (3) National motivations for contribution to peace operations, and (4) perceptions about the future of peace operations. Regional dialogues in Northeast[4] and South[5] Asia have provided the context and initial identification of the common motivations outlined in section 2.1. Several sources were used to verify and deepen the theoretical framework for this chapter and to identify the main motivation for personnel contribution to peace operations.[6]

4 Xenia Avezov, *The New Geopolitics of Peace Operations: A Dialogue with Emerging Powers. North East Asia Regional Dialogue*, (Stockholm: Stockholm International Peace Research Institute SIPRI Workshop Report, 2013) http://www.sipri.org/research/conflict/pko/other_publ/ngp-workshop-report-april-2013.

5 Xenia Avezov, 'The New Geopolitics of Peace Operations: A Dialogue with Emerging Powers. South Asia Regional Dialogue', *Journal of International Peacekeeping*, vol. 17, May 2013, pp. 149–161.

6 Main literature that was used to identify motivations for contribution includes: *Asia profiles, providing for peacekeeping*, http://www.providingforpeacekeeping.org/profiles/asia/, 29 August 2013; Alex J. Bellamy and Paul D. Williams, *Broadening the Base of United Nations Troop- and Police- Contributing countries: Providing for Peacekeeping No.1* (New York: International Peace Institute, 2012); Donald C.F. Daniel and Leigh C. Caraher, 'Characteristics of Troop Contributors to Peace Operations and Implications for Global Capacity,' *International Peacekeeping*, vol. 13 no. 3, Nov 2006, pp. 297–315; Trevor Findlay, *Challenges for the New Peacekeepers* (Stockholm: Stockholm International Peace Research Institute, 1996).

2.1 *Motivations for Contribution*

The motivations for participation identified in this chapter are grouped into six distinct categories: (1) national economic motivations where participation is driven by benefit to the national economy (2) military motivations in cases where participation benefits the military on an institutional, financial or political level (3) domestic-political motivations where participation is driven by domestic considerations such as public opinion or civil military relations (4) international-political motivations where participation improves the TCC's standing and influence in the international architecture or is driven by strategic foreign affairs considerations such as image or geostrategic status, (5) security motivation where TCCs are willing to contribute to missions that would improve their regional or domestic security and (6) normative motivations based on good will, belief in international humanitarian norms, or a desire to contribute to global peace and security.

National Economic

The national economic category contains motivations for participation that are based on actual or perceived benefits to the national economy of TCCs. Shimizu and Sandler found that TCCs are more likely to contribute to countries where they have an economic investment or connection.[7] Contribution can be a way to safeguard destabilization that might affect the regional economy or investment in the host country. During the workshop held in South Asia, participants noted that individual troops and at times even governments benefit from UN compensation, although participants from Pakistan and India noted that such compensation no longer provides a substantial incentive.[8] Indeed, some low-income countries view participation as a source of national income.[9] Finally, in instances where a low-income country may be dependent on foreign aid, participation is sometimes perceived as establishing goodwill and attracting foreign investment.[10]

Military

The military category contains institutional, financial or political military incentives for participation. According to Bellamy and Williams, "security

7 Hirofumi Shimizu and Todd Sandler, 'Peacekeeping and burden-Sharing, 1994–2000,' *Journal of Peace Research*, vol. 39, no. 6, pp. 651–668, p. 656.

8 Avezov, 'The New Geopolitics of Peace Operations: A Dialogue with Emerging Powers. South Asia Regional Dialogue,' p. 4.

9 See section 3.1.

10 Rashed Uz Zaman and Niloy R. Biswas, 'Bangladesh', in Alex J. Bellamy and Paul D. Williams (eds.), *Providing Peacekeepers: The Politics, Challenges, and Future of United Nations Peacekeeping* (Oxford: Oxford University Press, 2013), pp. 184–203, p. 194.

sectors might utilize UN compensation payments to augment their budgets."[11] Troop reimbursements largely cover costs of salaries and military equipment, so they can be used to maintain military strength and troop surplus through participation. Participants in both workshops have cited training and field experience in multidimensional peace operations as a motivation.[12] Participation could also preserve the institutional legitimacy or influence of the military by contributing to national and international interests.[13] In some cases, participation is also driven by institutional habits that have solidified peacekeeping through past political and material investments in contribution.[14]

Domestic Political

The domestic-political category contains motivations where participation is driven by domestic considerations such as public opinion or civil military relations. Contribution may improve civil-military relations domestically by socializing the army to international norms such as human rights and civil liberties, preventing a military from interfering in domestic affairs, and promoting a positive domestic image.[15] Public opinion can be an additional domestic factor that drives contribution. According to Trevor Findlay, public opinion can at times "steel the altruism of governments and cause them to act, particularly in humanitarian crisis."[16]

International Political

The international-political category contains motivations where participation improves national standing or benefits the TCC's overall geostrategic goals. According to Bellamy and Williams, "established and rising powers may see UN peacekeeping as a useful foreign policy tool, especially when it helps support

11 Bellamy and Williams (2012), *Broadening the Base of United Nations Troop- and Police-Contributing Countries: Providing for Peacekeeping Nò. 1*, p. 5.

12 Avezov, *The New Geopolitics of Peace Operations: A Dialogue with Emerging Powers. North East Asia Regional Dialogue*, p. 6; Avezov, 'The New Geopolitics of Peace Operations: A Dialogue with Emerging Powers. South Asia Regional Dialogue,' p. 155.

13 Jose Martin Roodettes, *Peacekeeping and the Armed Forces of the Southern Cone: Current trends and Future Prospects* (Naval Postgraduate School Masters Thesis, March 2002), p. 6. www.dtic.mil/cgi-bin/GetTRDoc?AD=ADA403556.

14 Dipankar Banerjee in Alex J. Bellamy and Paul D. Williams (eds.), *Providing Peacekeepers: The Politics, Challenges, and Future of United Nations Peacekeeping* (Oxford: Oxford University Press, 2013), pp. 226–243, p. 227.

15 See Wendy Hunter, State and Soldier in Latin America: Redefining the military's role in Argentina, Brazil and Chile (Washington, D.C.: U.S. Institute of Peace, 1996).

16 Trevor Findlay, *Challenges for the New Peacekeepers*, p. 8.

regional order or prestigious diplomatic and peacemaking activities."[17] More specifically, participation in peace operations can provide greater influence over the direction of mandates as well as location and outcome of a peace operation. During both workshops, participants from smaller countries such as Mongolia[18] noted that participation allows its voice to be heard internationally, where bigger contributors such as India are given not only recognition but also more decision-making power in the international architecture.[19] In some cases, TCCs also hope to leverage their participation in order to justify a bid for a permanent or nonpermanent membership at the UN Security Council.[20]

Participation can strengthen bilateral relations with fellow TCCs or with the host country. South Africa, for example, has significantly improved its relationship with Nigeria, arguably the country's most important ally in Africa, through cooperation on peace operations in the region.[21] In some cases, participation assists with geostrategic foreign affairs goals by leveraging relationships and power in the international and regional theaters. For example, Pakistan's contribution to UN peacekeeping is at least partly driven by regional and global competition with India.[22] International pressure to contribute, either from the UN or strong allies can also drive TCCs to participate. While South Korea's

17 Alex J. Bellamy and Paul D. Williams, *Broadening the Base of United Nations Troop- and Police- Contributing countries: Providing for Peacekeeping No. 1*, p. 4.

18 Avezov, *The New Geopolitics of Peace Operations: A Dialogue with Emerging Powers. North East Asia Regional Dialogue*,for Mongolia, p. 5–6. Avezov, 'The New Geopolitics of Peace Operations: A Dialogue with Emerging Powers. South Asia Regional Dialogue', pp. 156–157.

19 Kabilan Krishnasamy, 'Recognition' for Third World peacekeepers: India and Pakistan,' *International Peacekeeping*, vol. 8, no. 4, 2001, pp. 56–76, p. 58.

20 See UN announcement for elected non-permanent Security Council members for the 2013–2014 where peacekeeping was mentioned as an important factor for the election of Rwanda, Argentina, Australia: Five New Non-Permanent Security Council Members for 2013–2014, http://www.unelections.org/?q=node/2393, 20 January 2014. See Rohan Mukherjee and David M. Malone's article about India's approach of using its peacekeeping capabilities and contribution as a basis for contending for a permanent sit at the Security Council: Rohan Mukherjee and David M. Malone, 'India and the UN Security Council: An Ambiguous Tale,' *Economic and Political Weekly*, Princeton University, vol. xlviii, no. 29, 2013.

21 Adekeye Adebajo, 'The Bicycle Strategy of South Africa's Bilateral Relations in Africa, *South African Journal of International Affairs*, vol. 15, no. 2, pp. 121–136, p. 126.

22 Kabilan Krishnasamy, 'Pakistan's Peacekeeping Experiences', *International Peacekeeping*, vol. 9, no. 3, 2002, pp. 103–120, p. 112.

reasons for participation in peace operations vary, its military alliance with the United States also influences its participation; the United States expects South Korea to contribute to global security.[23] Finally, participation in operations can also help a TCC to promote or shape its international image by signaling political-military intentions, demonstrating international responsibility, or projecting military capabilities in a nonthreatening way.[24]

Security

The security category contains common motivations where contribution may improve or safeguard regional or domestic security. According to Bellamy and Williams, national and by extension regional security are major motivating factors for participation in peacekeeping.[25] In this sense, the proximity and level of threat will influence the readiness of the TCC to contribute. Countries like China that have great numbers of national civilians working abroad have a direct interest in fostering stability in unstable regions or countries. Furthermore, participation may facilitate better access for protection of its own civilians in case of an emergency.[26]

Normative

Normative considerations for participation, such as promoting global peace and stability through international cooperation and contributing to the international humanitarian and development agenda, are common factors for contribution. In some cases, normative motivations for participation are also rooted in previous experience with instability or war as in the case of South Korea.[27] While normative considerations are common, according to Findlay, "altruism is today more likely to be outweighed by other factors."[28]

---

23 Bruce Klingner, *Transforming the US-South Korean Alliance* (The Heritage Foundation Backgrounder #2155 on South Korea, 2008).

24 On China's image shaping through peacekeeping: Chin-Hao Huang, 'PLA Engagement with International Partners: PLA Involvement in International Peacekeeping and Humanitarian Assistance and Disaster Relief', in Roy Kamphausen, David Lai and Travis Tanner (eds.), *Learning by Doing: The PLA Trains at Home and Abroad* (Strategic Studies Institute of the US Army War College (SSI), Carlisle, United States, 2012), pp. 259–295.

25 Bellamy and Williams (2012), *Broadening the Base of United Nations Troop- and Police-Contributing countries: Providing for Peacekeeping No. 1*, p. 5.

26 Avezov, *The New Geopolitics of Peace Operations: A Dialogue with Emerging Powers. North East Asia Regional Dialogue*, p. 5.

27 See section 3.3.

28 Trevor Findlay, *Challenges for the New Peacekeepers*, p. 8.

2.2 *Barriers for Contribution*

Although this chapter focuses on motivations, a brief examination of some of the common inhibitors or barriers for contribution provides a more complete picture of the variety of factors that constitute a TCC's decision-making process. Sometimes the barrier to participation is simply the absence of one or more of the key motivators described above. Lack of interest from domestic constituencies in peace operations or lack of international pressure to contribute can impede participation. China's growing participation is the case in point as it is partly motivated by domestic and international pressure to demonstrate its intentions as a harmonious and responsible power.[29] Often countries are motivated to participate by a combination of military and political interests but have a lesser incentive when they can achieve national or institutional goals through other diplomatic, political or financial means.[30] Lack of financial gain from reimbursement or in some cases the financial burden from participation is an additional barrier. This is particularly relevant to middle income countries like India and Brazil that are developing rapidly while UN reimbursements continue to stagnate.[31]

Aside from the absence of incentives for contributions, some countries do not contribute or limit their contribution based on actual or perceived barriers. For some TCCs like Japan, the constitutional or legal framework limits the type of activities that the army can engage in during an operation which can impede contributions to certain types of missions or greatly limit the amount of personnel sent to a given mission.[32] The presence of more urgent regional or domestic priorities might also impede contribution. In terms of international projection of image, some countries view contribution as lacking prestige and as a task for less developed states. Others are concerned that the increasing emphasis on conduct issues and the possibility of a failed mission or escalating

29 Lei Zang, 'Two Pillars of China's Global Peace Engagement Strategy: UN Peacekeeping and International Peacebuilding,' *International Peacekeeping*, vol. 18, no. 3, 2011, pp. 344–362, pp. 346–347.

30 Alex J. Bellamy and Paul D. Williams, 'Explaining the National Politics of Peace Keeping Contribution', in Alex J. Bellamy and Paul D. Williams (eds.), *Providing Peacekeepers: The Politics, Challenges, and Future of United Nations Peacekeeping Contributions*, 2013, pp. 418–436, p. 419.

31 Alex J. Bellamy and Paul D. Williams, 'Explaining the National Politics of Peace Keeping Contribution', pp. 421–422.

32 Mayumi Itoh, 'Expanding Japan's Role in the United Nations', *The Pacific Review*, vol. 8, issue 2, 1995, pp. 283–301, p. 285.

conflict would damage their reputation.[33] Some countries, especially small and low-income countries, simply lack the military experience or capacity to participate.[34] In addition, some countries and military forces take issue with the complexity of the command and control framework of UN peace operations.[35] Increases in robust peacekeeping mandates and growing emphasis on protection of civilians is a disincentive for countries that view modern peacekeeping trends as a challenge to national sovereignty and traditional principles of peacekeeping. Lastly, many countries fear that peacekeeping casualties, particularly in difficult missions, would be unacceptable to domestic constituencies.[36]

3 Country Clusters

The nine countries examined in this chapter are divided into five clusters in this section: (1) Bangladesh, Nepal and Sri Lanka; (2) India and China; (3) Japan and South Korea; and two individual cases: (4) Pakistan and (5) Mongolia. Countries are clustered according to similarity between their motivations for participation as well as other similar behavior in the area of peace operations. Five distinct contributor type profiles emerge through the analysis in this section.

3.1 *Bangladesh, Nepal & Sri Lanka*

Bangladesh, Nepal and Sri Lanka have much in common: all three countries are developing, have a military surplus, have recent experience with civil and regional conflict, and are working towards economic stability and democratization. All three countries are generous TCCs, and Bangladesh regularly ranks in the top four of UN contributors.[37] Although Sri Lanka has not been a

33 Alex J. Bellamy and Paul D. Williams, 'Explaining the National Politics of Peace Keeping Contribution', p. 420.

34 Xenia Avezov, *The New Geopolitics of Peace Operations: A Dialogue with Emerging Powers. Central Asia Regional Dialogue*, (Stockholm: Stockholm International Peace Research Institute SIPRI Workshop Report, 2013) http://www.sipri.org/research/conflict/pko/other_publ/ngp-workshop-report-november-2013, p. 5.

35 Trevor Findlay, *Challenges for the New Peacekeepers*, p. 14.

36 Avezov, *The New Geopolitics of Peace Operations: A Dialogue with Emerging Powers. North East Asia Regional Dialogue*, p. 4.

37 'Ranking of Military and Police Contribution,' Troop and Police Contributors Archive (1990–2013), United Nations, http://www.un.org/en/peacekeeping/resources/statistics/contributors_archive.

consistent contributor over the past four decades, it has increased its contribution since 2005.[38] Countries in this cluster are largely motivated by economic and military considerations, with domestic and international political motivations as important secondary factors.

Troop reimbursements provide a strong incentive for participation in all three cases as they allow these TCCs to maintain a troop surplus, subsidize their armed forces and even benefit the national economy. Sri Lanka has received $142 million in UN remunerations since 2004 but only $95 million was used for individual troop reimbursement. The remaining funds went towards purchasing military equipment, maintaining the next round of trained troops, and to the country's economy as a whole.[39] Troop reimbursement provides an individual incentive for Bangladeshi peacekeepers but also helps the military maintain its troop surplus, modernize its equipment and provide welfare programs to veterans.[40] In addition to the $1.28 billion that Bangladesh earned from its participation in peace operations between 2001 and 2010,[41] UN remittances also generate revenue through foreign exchange. Bangladesh has significant external debt of $28 billion and still relies on foreign aid.[42] Participation is therefore also seen as a way to attract foreign investment by creating good will with foreign governments and improving the image of the country in the business world.[43] In Nepal, where per capita income is $742, troop reimbursement provides both an individual as well as an institutional motivation for participation.[44] Therefore, troops earn about four to ten times more then they

---

38 See section 1.

39 See 'Sri Lanka Earns Over 18 Billion Rupees from UN Peacekeeping,' Government of Sri Lanka, News Line, 29 July 2012; Also Dinouk Colombage, *Sri Lanka Earns in Excess of Rs. 18.4 Million From Peace-keeping, The Sunday Leader*, http://www.thesundayleader.lk/2012/07/08/sri-lanka-earns-in-excess-of-rs-18-4-billion-from-peace-keeping/, accessed on 8 Oct, 2013; Nathaniel Camelia, 'Sri Lankan Peacekeepers have made us proud', Ministry of Defense and Urban Development, 13 July, 2012.

40 Dipankar Banerjee, 'South Asia: Contributors of Global Significance' in Donald C.F Daniel, Patricia Taft, Sharon Wiharta (eds.), *Peace Operations: Trends, Progress, and Prospects* (Washington DC, USA: Georgetown University Press, 2008), pp. 187–201, p. 195 ; Shekh Mohammad AltafurRahman, 'Democratization in Bangladesh: An Analysis of Bangladesh Armed Forces' Non-intervention in Politics Influenced by the Participation in United Nations Peace Keeping Operation', *Nepalese Journal of Public Policy and Governance*, vol. xxx, no. 1. June 2012, pp. 47–58, p. 52.

41 RashedUzZamanand Niloy R. Biswas, 'Bangladesh,' p. 194.

42 *Bangladesh- The World Fact Book*, https://www.cia.gov/library/publications/the-world-factbook/geos/bg.html, accessed on 8 Oct 2013.

43 Rashed Uz Zaman and Niloy R. Biswas, 'Bangladesh,' p. 194.

44 Rajan Bhattarai, *Contributor Profile: Nepal* (New York: International Peace Institute, 2013).

would as civilians. The army also uses the UN allowance to help maintain its troop surplus, fund its defense budget and provide welfare services for its troops.[45]

Aside from the financial benefits for the armed forces, institutional military motivations also factor strongly into the participation of all three countries and are often interconnected with national and international political motivations. The convergence of military motivations and national and international political motivation in this cluster can be explained by the primacy of military institutions. Sri Lanka views participation as an opportunity to train and socialize its military on international humanitarian law, which it hopes will improve the country's civil-military relations over the long term.[46] The military is also eager to apply "counter-terrorism" skills it gained during the war.[47] On 31 March 2011, the UN published an investigation of alleged human rights violations and war crimes committed by both the Sri Lanka government and the Liberation Tigers of Tamil Eelam (LTTE).[48] In response to the report result, which found that both parties had indeed violated international law during the last stages of the conflict, Sri Lanka reinforced its commitment to increase its contribution to peacekeeping at the UN.[49] Promoting a positive international image of its military and of the country as a whole has become an important motivation for Sri Lankan contribution.

According to Kabilan Krishnasamy, an important factor motivating Bangladesh to contribute is that "it keeps the military from meddling in domestic affairs and reduces the chances of a military coup."[50] Participation also

45 Surendra Singh Rawal, United Nations Peacekeeping Participation and Civil-Military Relations in Troop Contributing Countries (Monterey: CA: Naval Post Graduate School, Master of Arts in Security Studies, March 2010), p. 72; for more information on Nepalese economic motivations for participation see Sotomayor, 'Nepal' in Bellamy, Alex J. and Paul D. Williams, *Providing Peacekeepers: The Politics, Challenges, and Future of United Nations Peacekeeping* (Oxford: Oxford University Press, 2013), pp. 304–305.

46 Pradeep Seneviratne, *Sri Lanka army making a difference as UN peacekeepers*, Khabar, 16 July, 2012, http://khabarsouthasia.com/en_GB/articles/apwi/articles/features/2012/07/16/feature-06, accessed on 10 Aug, 2013.

47 Nathaniel Camelia, 'Sri Lankan Peacekeepers have made us proud', 13 July, 2012.

48 See 'Report of the Secretary General's Panel of Experts on Accountability in Sri Lanka,' United Nations, 31 March 2011, http://www.un.org/News/dh/infocus/Sri_Lanka/POE_Report_Full.pdf.

49 Colum Lynch, 'The UN Accused Sri Lanka of Killing Civilians at Home; Will it now Seek its Helps Saving Lives Abroad', *Foreign Policy*, 15 June, 2011.

50 Kabilan Krishnasamy, 'Bangladesh and UN Peacekeeping: The Participation of a 'Small' State', *Common Wealth and Comparative Politics*, vol. 41, no. 1, Sep 2010, pp. 24–47, p. 39.

provides training and professional opportunities for the troops, modernizes the army, and facilitates interaction with other militaries.[51] Bangladesh is aware of the politicized nature of its army as a result of the partition of 1971 and is therefore also motivated to improve the international image of the military.[52] The Nepalese military also views participation as an opportunity to train its military in a variety of environments and contexts, which enables it to "excel in missions of the 21st century."[53] Similarly to Bangladesh and Sri Lanka, there is a dichotomy in Nepalese military motivations, on the one hand seeking to improve civil-military relations while on the other hand attempting to preserve the institutional primacy of the military.[54] In Nepal, "the unstable nature of domestic politics in fact enables the army to formulate defense and military policies with relative autonomy."[55] As a small country located in a sensitive geopolitical region, Nepal also views participation as a way to project its neutrality and prove its commitment to multilateralism. Nepal hopes that increasing its visibility and activism at the UN will help to protect its sovereignty and territorial integrity in the long term.[56]

Although it is difficult to estimate the role that normative considerations play in the decision-making process of any TCC in terms of participation, it is important to note that all three TCCs in this cluster explicitly recognize their commitment to international peace and security as a key part of their foreign policy values.[57] In 2008 while Sri Lanka was still in the grips of a civil war, the country committed to share the efforts of the UN in the area of peacekeeping as a "manifestation of Sri Lanka's solidarity with the international community

51 Rashed Uz Zamanand Niloy R. Biswas, *Contributor Profile: Bangladesh* (New York: International Peace Institute, 2013).

52 Rashed Uz Zaman and Niloy R. Biswas, *Contributor Profile: Bangladesh* (New York: International Peace Institute, 2013).

53 Abhay Chhetri, Harbingers of Peace: Nepali Peacekeeping Tradition, Republica, 4 August, 2013.

54 Rawal, United Nations Peacekeeping Participation and Civil-Military Relations in Troop Contributing Countries, p. 63.

55 Arturo C. Sotomayor, 'Nepal', in Alex J. Bellamy and Paul D. Williams (eds.), *Providing Peacekeepers: The Politics, Challenges, and Future of United Nations Peacekeeping Contributions*, 2013, pp. 292–310, p. 301.

56 Rajan Bhattarai, *Contributor Profile: Nepal, 2013*.

57 See: 'Sixty years of peacekeeping: Sri Lankan peacekeeper honored,' Ministry of External Affairs Sri Lanka, media release, 30 May 2008; 'Nepal's Role in UN Peacekeeping,' Government of Nepal Ministry of Foreign Affairs, headlines, November 2012; Press Release, People Republic of Bangladesh Ministry of Foreign Affairs, 8 June 2011, http://www.mofa.gov.bd/PressRelease/PrintPRDetails.php?txtUserId=&PRid=432.

and determination to shoulder international responsibilities."[58] Bangladesh's commitment to maintaining global peace is delineated in its constitution: "The State shall base its international relations on...peaceful settlement of international disputes, and respect for international law and the principles enunciated in the United Nations Charter."[59] It is also possible that for low-income countries, troop contribution to peace operations is the most viable way to realize a commitment to international peace.[60] Nepal's foreign affairs policy is "guided by the international law and other universally recognized norms governing international relations. The value of world peace also constitutes a significant element guiding the foreign policy of the country."[61] While normative considerations do play a role in contribution among these countries, a "diffusion wave" in South Asian policies on peacekeeping may be driven by competition between Pakistan and India in the area of troop contribution.[62]

Economic and military considerations seem to be the strongest motivating factors for Sri Lanka, Bangladesh and Nepal, with domestic and international political motivations as secondary. Financial gains from UN troop reimbursements for national economies and the armed forces are key factors for contribution in this cluster. Institutionally, the armed forces benefit through financial gain, training opportunities, and reinforcement of the role and primacy of the military within and outside the country. Political factors for participation are secondary but also crucial for participation, in particular improving civil military relations and international image shaping. Security and normative motivations are generally outweighed by other considerations.

3.2 *Pakistan*

Pakistan has much in common with countries in the previous cluster: it is still a developing country despite its lower middle-income status, it has a military surplus, it has recent experience with regional conflict, and it too is working towards development and stability.[63] Pakistan is also a major troop contributor

---

58 'Sixty years of peacekeeping: Sri Lankan peacekeeper honored,' Ministry of External Affairs Sri Lanka, media release, 30 May 2008.

59 The Constitution of the People's Republic of Bangladesh, Fundamental Principles of State Policy, 2010, Part II Section 25.

60 Banerjee, 'South Asia: Contributors of Global Significance,' p. 195.

61 'Nepal's Foreign Policy,' Government of Nepal Ministry of Foreign Affairs, http://www.mofa.gov.np/en/nepals-foreign-policy-24.html, accessed on 26 Feb, 2014.

62 Sotomayor, 'Nepal', p. 298.

63 Pakistan, http://data.worldbank.org/country/pakistan#cp_gep, accessed 26 Feb 2014.

to UN peace operations and has regularly ranked in the top two in the past decade.[64] Yet Pakistan's motivations for contribution are slightly different from the previous cluster: international-political issues are primary and military and domestic-political motivations are also important.

Pakistan views its contribution as a political tool that allows it to demonstrate its "good international citizenship...[and] unwavering support for an active role by the UN for the preservation of international peace and security."[65] Participation also sheds a positive light on the country that it can leverage in international circles such as the UN to further geostrategic priorities like the outstanding Kashmir dispute with India.[66]According to Inam-ur-Rahman Malik, Pakistan regards participation as a "counterweight to Indian regional as well as global ambitions," including India's bid for a permanent membership at the UN Security Council.[67] The country has also cited its contribution as grounds for serving as a non-permanent member of the Security Council in 2012–2013.[68] The impressive level of troop contribution is also driven by competition with India.[69] Lastly, Pakistan wishes to raise its status in the Muslim world by participating in missions such as the United Nations Protection Force in Bosnia and Herzegovina where Pakistani peacekeeping served alongside other peacekeepers from Muslim countries.[70]

While national economic benefits from troop reimbursements are likely negligible, reimbursements improve Pakistan's ability to maintain its military surplus and still provides a tangible economic benefit to individual peacekeepers.[71] On 26 August 2011, acting Permanent Representative of Pakistan to the UN, Mr. Raza Bashir Tarar, commented on the need for reevaluating the sustainability of current troop remittances in the Security Council's open debate

64 'Ranking of Military and Police Contribution,'accessed 24 Feb 2014.

65 C.S.R Murthy, 'Unintended Consequences of Peacekeeping Operations for Troop Contributing Countries from South Asia', in Chiyuki Aoi, Cedric De Coning, Ramesh Chandra Thakur (eds.), *Unintended Consequences of Peacekeeping Operations*, 2007, pp. 156–170, p. 158.

66 Kaliban Krishnasamy, 'Pakistan's Peacekeeping Experiences,' *International Peacekeeping*, vol. 9, no. 3, 2002, pp. 103–120, p. 112.

67 Inam-ur-Rahman Malik, 'Pakistan', in Alex J. Bellamy and Paul D. Williams (eds.), *Providing Peacekeepers: The Politics, Challenges, and Future of United Nations Peacekeeping Contributions*, 2013, pp. 204–224, p. 212.

68 Pakistan at the Security Council, Pakistan Mission to United Nations, http://www.pakun.org/PakistanSC/, accessed 26 Feb 2014.

69 Krishnasamy, 'Pakistan's Peacekeeping Experiences,' p. 113.

70 Krishnasamy, 'Pakistan's Peacekeeping Experiences,' p. 114.

71 *Why South Asia Loves Peacekeeping*, accessed 9 Sep 2013.

where he argued that reimbursement must be adjusted for modern cost of living and inflation to ensure the sustainability of contribution.[72] Nevertheless, there are other military and institutional benefits of Pakistani participation beyond reimbursement. For the military, which already holds significant weight in international and domestic politics in Pakistan, participation further solidifies such influence through a prestigious cause while providing training opportunities in a variety of skills and facilitating interaction and training with other forces.[73] On a national-political front, participation improves military-civilian relations domestically by keeping the military engaged on external issues and reduces meddling in domestic politics.[74]

The distinction between Pakistan and the Bangladesh-Sri Lanka-Nepal cluster is that while Pakistan is still a developing country, it is not as motivated by national economic considerations and has a stronger emphasis on political and foreign affairs motivations, appropriate for a middle power that seeks to establish and project its growing influence. On the other hand, Pakistan is still very much aligned with these countries because its armed forces benefit from participation in peace operations which provides practical training opportunities and a way to maintain the country's military surplus. Participation is also a way to keep the dominant military engaged in external matters and thus improve civil-military relations. Security and normative considerations are in this case outweighed by the factors noted above.

3.3 *India & China*

India and China share many economic and political characteristics. While China's economy is considered to be upper middle income, it is still a developing country and about 98.99 million people were living under the national poverty line at the end of 2012, which is the highest number of people living under the poverty line following India.[75] India is still considered a lower middle-income country but has made tremendous progress in its economy and social welfare over the past decade.[76] Both countries have significant international

72 Statement by Mr. Raza Bashir Tarar, Acting Permanent Representative of Pakistan to the UN, in the Security Council's Open Debate on "Peacekeeping: taking stock and prepare for the future," Pakistan Misssion to the United Nations, http://www.pakun.org/statements/Security_Council/2011/08262011-01.php, accessed 26 Feb 2014.

73 Malik, 'Pakistan', p. 215.

74 Krishnasamy, 'Pakistan's Peacekeeping Experiences', p. 114.

75 China Overview, The World Bank, http://www.worldbank.org/en/country/china/overview, accessed 26 Feb 2014.

76 India: Development Policy Review, http://web.worldbank.org/WBSITE/EXTERNAL/COUNTRIES/SOUTHASIAEXT/0,,contentMDK:20980493~pagePK:146736~piPK:146830~theSitePK:223547,00.html, accessed 26 Feb 2014.

and regional influence and play an important role in UN peace operations. Aside from its role as a Security Council member, China significantly increased its participation in recent years, reaching 2,186 military and police personnel as of January 2014.[77] A veteran contributor, India has participated in 43 UN peacekeeping missions and has contributed over 100,000 military and police personnel.[78] Political motivations seem to be the primary contribution drivers, with military and normative considerations as imperative but secondary.

China hopes to assuage regional and global concerns about the so-called "China threat," through its participation. The country also hopes that participation will help reduce tensions about PLA capabilities and intentions in the region and beyond.[79] Chinese policy makers "see engagement in peacekeeping, and in conflict resolution, as a way for China to project a more benign and 'harmonious' image beyond its borders, to reassure neighbors about its peaceful intentions, and to softly balance US and other Western influence while gradually but more firmly establishing China's status as a great power."[80] On a national level, China's domestic constituencies also prefer a foreign policy that is aligned with the image of a responsible power.[81]

Literature and data reflect that India's contribution is driven by political and normative considerations, with the desire to be seen as a major global player being the primary consideration.[82] India often refers to its contributions as a justification for its bid for a permanent seat on the United Nations Security Council.[83] Improving bilateral relations in host countries, particularly in resource-rich countries such as the Congo, and competing with Pakistan for contributions and influence also represent important goals.[84] There is a

77 'Contribution by Country', Troop and Police Contributions, United Nations, http://www.un.org/en/peacekeeping/resources/statistics/contributors.shtml.

78 http://www.un.int/india/india%20&%20un/peacekeeping.pdf.

79 Chin-Hao Huang, 'PLA Engagement with International Partners: PLA Involvement in International Peacekeeping and Humanitarian Assistance and Disaster Relief', p. 261.

80 Gill Bates and Huang Chin-hao, *China's Expanding Role in Peacekeeping: Prospects and Policy Implications* (Stockholm: Stockholm International Peace Research Institute SIPRI Policy Paper no. 25, 2009), p. 12.

81 Zhao Lei, 'Two Pillars of China's Global Peace Engagement Strategy: UN Peacekeeping and International Peacebuilding,' *International Peacekeeping*, vol. 18, no. 3, 2011, pp. 344–361, p. 346.

82 Banerjee, 'South Asia: Contributors of Global Significance', p. 191.

83 Kaliban Krishnasamy and Auriol Weigold, 'The Paradox of Indiaapos;s Peacekeeping', *Contemporary South Asia*, vol. 12, no. 2, 2003, pp. 263–280, p. 273.

84 Krishnasamy and Weigold, 'The Paradox of Indiaapos;s Peacekeeping', p. 275; and David Axe, *Why South Asia Loves Peacekeeping, The Diplomat*, http://thediplomat.com/2010/12/20/why-south-asia-loves-peacekeeping/, accessed 9 Sep 2013.

minority group of Indian policy makers who raise questions on the purpose of Indian contributions. They argue Delhi should focus more on domestic and regional challenges.[85] Furthermore, they argue that as major troop contributors to peace operations are often developing countries, a big contribution is tainting India's international prestige.[86]

Aside from political motivations, India's contribution is also driven by normative considerations and its legacy as a peacekeeper. India "strongly supports the purposes and principles of the UN [and] ...views its membership at the United Nations as an important guarantee for maintaining international peace and security."[87] According to Raja C. Mohan,[88] "the initial impulse for South Asian peacekeeping came from Jawaharlal Nehru, India's first prime minister (1947–64), who had a strong commitment to liberal internationalism and a desire to strengthen the UN...Nehru envisaged an active international role for India." A relatively recent contributor, China has been gradually more accepting of peacekeeping and the international global norms that underlie it. At the same time, the country hopes that its contribution will ultimately grant it greater legitimacy to influence the direction of peace operations and prevent unwanted robust or interventionist mandates.[89]

Both countries value the benefits of participation to their militaries, whether financial, institutional or tactical. The training that peacekeeping provides to the PLA allows it to be better prepared to carry out Military Operations Other Than War (MOOTW) and "to strengthen the PLA's emergency response system and enhance its capacity for rapid deployment both inside and outside China."[90] Participation also trains troops in a variety of environments and allows the PLA to test new capabilities.[91] Unlike China, India shares similar considerations of other developing countries in South Asia, namely that contribution to peace operations

85 Avezov, 'The New Geopolitics of Peace Operations: A Dialogue with Emerging Powers. South Asia Regional Dialogue,' p. 158.

86 Banerjee, 'India', p. 243.

87 'India and the United Nations,' Ministry of External Affairs Government of India, http://www.mea.gov.in/india-and-the-united-nations.htm, accessed on 26 Feb 2014.

88 Raja C. Mohan, *India and International Peace Operations* (Stockholm: Stockholm International Peace Research Institute SIPRI Insights on Peace and Security, no. 3, 2013), p. 2.

89 C. Huang, 'Principles and Praxis of China's Peacekeeping', *International Peacekeeping*, vol. 18, issues 3, 2011.

90 Bates and Chin-hao, *China's Expanding Role in Peacekeeping: Prospects and Policy Implications*, p. 15.

91 *China's Growing Role in UN Peacekeeping* (Beijing/New York/Brussels: International Crisis Group (ICG) Crisis Group Asia Report No. 166, 17 April 2009), p. 15.

is still a relatively affordable way to maintain its military surplus.[92] However, since the "Indian government does not deduct any amount for maintenance or miscellaneous from the UN allowances and pays its soldiers the amount in full when received from the UN," participation does not benefit the overall economy.[93]

For China and India, economic considerations do not play a significant role. Some commentators claim that China's peacekeeping activities in Africa are driven by the country's desire to improve its 'strategic presence on the continent', but the link between participation in peacekeeping and better access to natural resources has not been proven.[94] It is more likely that China's interest to protect its investments abroad by promoting stability drives its participation: "with the growing globalization of its interests, public and private, China needs stable overseas markets to secure its sustainable economic development. Instability in energy-producing parts of Africa and the Middle East is clearly not in China's interest."[95] Furthermore, given that there are many Chinese enterprises around the world and many Chinese nationals working in unstable regions, China is also somewhat motivated by protecting its civilians.[96] India has also promoted goodwill and improved diplomatic relationships through its contributions in East Africa, from which it imports approximately a fifth of its oil.[97] According to Mohan,[98] "India is dependent on imports of natural resources and export markets to sustain its recent high economic growth rates and improve the living standard of its populations." Still, contribution to peacekeeping is only one of many tools that both China and India utilize to maintain and improve their presence in Africa. The significant development assistance that both countries provide to continent is likely more effective.[99]

While the contribution profiles of China and India are by no means identical, the countries share some motivations for contribution. Both emerging

92 *Why South Asia Loves Peacekeeping*, accessed 9 Sep 2013.

93 Banerjee, 'India,' p. 242.

94 Huang Chin-hao, *Contributor Profile: China* (New York: International Peace Institute, 2013).

95 Lei, 'Two Pillars of China's Global Peace Engagement Strategy: UN Peacekeeping and International Peacebuilding', p. 348.

96 Avezov, *The New Geopolitics of Peace Operations: A Dialogue with Emerging Powers. North East Asia Regional Dialogue*, p. 4.

97 ViraVarun, 'India and Un Peacekeeping: Declining Interest with Grave Implications,' Small Wars Journal, 13 July 2012, http://smallwarsjournal.com/node/12949#_ftn9, accessed 26 Feb 2014.

98 Mohan, *India and International Peace Operations*, p. 5.

99 See 'China Commits Billions in Aid to Africa as Part of Charm Offensive', *The Guardian*, 29 April 2013; 'A Global Shift in Foreign Aid, Starting With India,' *New York Times*, 15 Nov 2012.

global powers use their contributions primarily to project their international image and influence and to balance their complex global and regional roles and aspirations. Military and normative considerations play a secondary role in their contribution. National economic motivations such as fostering diplomatic relationships with resource-rich countries and protecting international investments are less prominent drivers for these countries. Finally, China and India have distinct motivations for participation: China's participation is also driven by public opinion and a security concern for national civilians abroad, while India seeks to increase its influence at the UN and, like countries in previous clusters, its armed forces still benefit financially from UN remittances.

3.4 *Japan & South Korea*

Although Japan and South Korea have gradually increased their participation over the past 10 years,[100] their contribution is still modest. South Korea ranks 35th and Japan ranks 49th as of January 2014.[101] Both contributions also represent a relatively negligible part of their overall military strength, with Japan contributing 0.1% of its overall military strength and South Korea 0.09% of its military strength.[102] The two high-income countries also contribute to UN activities in other ways; for example, Japan provides the second highest financial contribution to UN peacekeeping, roughly 10.83% of the overall budget.[103] Among South Korea's many different contributions to the UN, the country served as a non-permanent member of the Security Council twice and the current Secretary General Ban Ki-moon is a former ROK foreign minister.[104] For Japan and South Korea, international-political and security considerations are primary motivations for participation. Normative and national political considerations are imperative but secondary.

International-political and security considerations are in many ways the primary motivations for South Korean and Japanese participation in peace

100 See graph A for breakdown of contributions between 2005–2014. Japan's contributions have decreased between 2012 and 2013 due to the draw down of the Japanese engineering unit from MINUSTAH.

101 'Ranking of Military and Police Contributions,' United Nations, http://www.un.org/en/peacekeeping/contributors/2014/jan14_2.pdf, accessed 26 Feb 2014.

102 See Graph B.

103 *Financing Peacekeeping*, http://www.un.org/en/peacekeeping/operations/financing.shtml, accessed 26 Feb 2014.

104 Terence Roehrig, 'South Korea, Foreign Aid, and UN Peacekeeping: Contributing to International Peace and Security as a Middle Power', *Korea Observer*, vol. 44, no. 4, 2013, pp. 623–645, p. 634.

operations. Japan's participation in peacekeeping fits with its overall foreign policy and security priorities such as prevention of arms buildup and escalation of conflicts in its region and beyond. Japan recognizes that global security challenges require multilateral cooperation and views its participation as show casing its commitment to global peace and security and pursuing its own national and strategic interests. Japan also views participation as potentially encouraging regional confidence building and reducing tensions in Northeast Asia.[105] According to Katsumi Ishizuka, "Japan sees peacekeeping as a way of enhancing its international prestige, identifying itself as a benign civilian power, and supporting its diplomacy—especially in relations to the promotion of human security."[106] Japan's bid for a permanent seat at the UN Security Council and its will to balance its close relationship with the United States have also driven the country to increase its overall activism and its contribution to the UN.[107]

Fluctuations in contributions under the past three South Korean administrations demonstrate the primacy of political and foreign affairs considerations.[108] Korean president (2008–2013), Lee Myung-Bak, a former CEO in a large corporation, was dedicated to strengthening Korean contributions under his 'global Korea' diplomacy. The policy sought to establish the national brand as a responsible middle power, improve the country's image, and promote overall favorable global conditions for economic growth. Finally, South Korea depends on the US and the international community in the event of an escalation in the Korean peninsula. Participation in peacekeeping is viewed as one of the "counter measures in the potential of regime collapse in North Korea."[109] In other words, the South Korean military can gain helpful experience through participation and more importantly maintain key relationships with allies in the West and at the UN that would be more willing to act decisively in the case of an escalation.

105 Avezov, *The New Geopolitics of Peace Operations: A Dialogue with Emerging Powers. North East Asia Regional Dialogue.*

106 Katsumi Ishizuka, 'Japan' in Bellamy, Alex J. and Paul D. Williams (eds.), *Providing Peacekeepers: The Politics, Challenges, and Future of United Nations Peacekeeping*, 2013, pp. 396–414, p. 404.

107 Ishizuka, 'Japan', p. 405.

108 Avezov, *The New Geopolitics of Peace Operations: A Dialogue with Emerging Powers. North East Asia Regional Dialogue.*

109 Sangto ko, 'Korea's Middle Power Activism and Peacekeeping Operations', *Eurasia Journal*, vol. 10, pp. 287–299, p. 293.

National politics, particularly public opinion, and normative considerations play a key secondary role in the participation of Japan and South Korea. The legacy of World War II has created a culture of pacifism in Japan. The United Nations is therefore viewed as an organization through which Japan could make its contribution to global peace and security.[110] Public opinion polls indicate that about 80% of citizens in Japan support participation in peacekeeping and roughly 30% would support an increase in troop contributions.[111] The South Korean Ministry of Foreign Affairs website states: "UN Peacekeeping Operations are integral to maintaining international peace and security," and that therefore the government of ROK is working towards expanding its engagement in peace operations in a variety of ways, including troop contribution.[112] The support of the South Korean public also plays a role, especially because of the public memory of the UN brokering the cease-fire agreement between North and South Korea during the Korean War.[113]

Lastly, domestic laws limit the nature and length of participation in both countries: South Korea's "Law on Participation in the United Nations Peacekeeping Operations" stipulates that the country can only participate in non-military operations that have the consent of the host state. In addition, the law requires a one-year limit for participation and parliamentary approval for each additional year. The law also does not allow the country to participate in hybrid or non-UN missions.[114] The Japanese International Peace Cooperation Law (PKO law) is almost identical to the Korean law with an additional caveat-that limits use of force to self-defense.[115]

Japan and South Korea share almost identical motivations for participation. Both countries are primarily motivated by international-political and security considerations such as safeguarding regional security, balancing relationships with strong allies, and promoting their international standing and image. Their secondary motivations are domestic-political and normative: domestic laws limit participation and public opinion is largely positive about contribution. Aside from the legal limitations, these countries' modest contributions can be

110 Katsumi Ishizuka, *Contributor Profile: Japan* (New York: International Peace Institute, 2013).

111 'Greater Peacekeeping Role OK, Not Truce Enforcement,' *Japan Times*, 23 Mar 2010.

112 'UN Peacekeeping Operations,' Ministry of Foreign Affairs Republic of Korea, http://www.mofat.go.kr/ENG/policy/pko/overview/index.jsp?menu=m_20_50_10, accessed 26 Feb 2014.

113 Ko, 'Korea's Middle Power Activism and Peacekeeping Operations,' p. 293.

114 Chung Eun-sook, 'Korea's Law on UNPKO and Participation in International Peacekeeping Missions', *Korea Focus*, vol.18, no. 2, 2010.

115 Ishizuka, *Contributor Profile: Japan*.

partly explained by a lack of significant military or economic motivation for participation and by their ability to pursue national interests through other diplomatic and political means.

3.5 *Mongolia*

Mongolia is a small lower-middle-income country with a population of roughly 2.5 million.[116] Despite the country's size, it has significantly increased its contributions to peace operations in the past 10 years, from 7 troops in 2005 to 936 in 2014.[117] In 2014, it deployed nearly 10% of its overall military force in UN peace operations.[118] Mongolia's primary consideration for is international-political motivations and its regional and domestic security, followed by military considerations as secondary.

As a small democratic country that is located between two nuclear powers, namely China and Russia, Mongolia is attempting to strike a delicate balance in cooperating with, but remaining independent from, its two large neighbors. Mongolia views participation in peacekeeping as a part of its "third neighbor-policy" that builds on its diplomatic ties with large states and organizations within and beyond its immediate region.[119] Peacekeeping is particularly attractive because it increases the country's visibility and improves its international standing and military prestige without creating tensions with its neighbors. This is particularly important as the country seeks to maintain diplomatic ties in Pacific Asia and the former Soviet Union and subscribes to a non-aligned foreign policy.[120] Mongolia's increased activism at the UN can also be seen in the context of the shifting geopolitical dynamics in the region. Since the end of the Cold War, the country has made strides towards improving its bilateral relationship with Russia. However, its increasing economic dependency on China has created a strong incentive to actively participate in peacekeeping and pursue stronger diplomatic ties with the international community and the US.[121]

In addition to political motivations, Mongolia's contribution is driven by the opportunity to modernize, finance and train its army while "rebranding" it for

116 'Mongolia,' http://data.worldbank.org/country/mongolia, accessed 26 Feb 2014.

117 See graph A.

118 See graph B.

119 Avezov, 'The New Geopolitics of Peace Operations: A Dialogue with Emerging Powers. South Asia Regional Dialogue,' p. 158.

120 'Mongolia's Foreign Policy in the Political Field,' Ministry of Foreign Affairs Mongolia, http://www.mfa.gov.mn/index.php?option=com_content&view=article&id=80%3Aii-&catid=36%3A2009-12-20-21-52-14&Itemid=55&lang=en, accessed 18 Sep 2013.

121 Jeffrey Reeves, 'Mongolia's Evolving Security Strategy: omni- enmeshment and balance of influence', *The Pacific Review*, vol. 25, no. 5, 2012, pp. 589–612, p. 600.

international service.[122] Troop reimbursements do indeed provide individual and institutional incentive for the armed forces; however, the national economy does not significantly benefit from contribution to peace operations since 70% of UN remittances is used to pay individual troops and 30% is used to “finance military and institutional reform and improve its personnel social welfare and life conditions.”[123]

Mongolia views participation in peacekeeping as a way to foster international engagement and visibility by facilitating diplomatic ties with the international community.[124] The country considers engagement in peace operations as a way to maintain its national security and territorial integrity. Military motivations such as UN troop reimbursements and the opportunity to modernize and train its armed forces are also significant. While the country subscribes to the UN charter and mission, its political and geostrategic priorities override normative considerations. National-economic and domestic politics are not important incentives for contribution in this case.

4 Conclusion

The size of the economy, level of development, and the nature and role of the military determines to a large extent the motivating factors behind contribution. While the nine TCCs examined in this study share some motivations for participation, the size of contribution can be explained by the prominence of economic, military and political factors in the country's decision to participate. In the case of developing countries like Bangladesh, Sri Lanka and Nepal, economic benefits for participation might appear to be the primary drivers of a relatively large contribution. However, when also considering other South Asian TCCs such as India and Pakistan, military and either political or economic considerations emerge as most prominent for a higher level of contribution. In all four cases, military factors are the most important driver for large

122 Jargalsaikhan Mendee and David Last, ‘Whole of Government Responses in Mongolia: From Domestic Response to International Implications’, in Ann Livingstone (ed.), *Opportunities for Enhancing Cooperation and Coordination in Peace Operations*, The Pearson Papers, vol. 11, issue 2, Fall 2008.

123 Ariunbold Dashjivaa, Why Mongolia Choses to Participate in Peace Operations: An Analysis of Current Trends and Future Opportunities (Naval Postgraduate School Masters Thesis, June 2012).

124 Jargalsaikhan Mendee, *Mongolia's Peacekeeping Commitment: Training, Deployment, and Evolution of Field Information Capabilities* (Washington, DC: National Defense Intelligence College Discussion Paper No. 15, 2007).

contributions. When countries have a military surplus and when the military enjoys a prominent role in decision making, a combination of financial, institutional, or tactical military motivations for participation seem to be strongest factors. In particular, Pakistan and India have very little national economic motivations while their militaries benefit institutionally and financially. While providing its military with training opportunities and experience in MOOTW does factor into China's increasing participation, the country is far more motivated by political rather than military considerations.

In general, political motivations for participation increase in prominence as the level of development increases. Bangladesh, Nepal and Sri Lanka all wish to improve internal civil-military relations and their international standing, but economic and military motivations override political considerations. Pakistan is motivated by its international competition with India while India wishes to improve its international standing at the UN and beyond through its participation. However, in both cases, military considerations explain the extent of contribution despite being secondary. For China, which is more developed and influential than India but still has some domestic challenges, projecting a positive international image and satisfying public opinion at home are the primary factors for participation, while military considerations play a secondary role. On the other side of the spectrum, developed countries like South Korea and Japan view participation as one of many tools to achieve their political interests. These countries are similar to Western countries that have dramatically reduced their participation in UN peace operations since the Cold War. The absence of military or economic incentive for participation limits the size of contribution in both cases.

Mongolia is an exception. The small country contributes a significant amount of its military strength to peace operations. While Mongolia has some military motivations for participation, it is largely motivated by security and political considerations that center on maintaining its territorial integrity and sovereignty by increasing international visibility and cooperation through peacekeeping. This could indicate that in cases where contribution is driven mainly by security considerations, a TCC will be more willing to contribute regardless of its military size or other benefits.

Normative considerations are relevant in every case although they are seldom primary and are likely insufficient to guarantee contribution. In all cases, countries have both normative and international image considerations that blur the lines between normative intention and public relations. Nevertheless, the fact that normative considerations do indeed play a role in all the TCCs examined indicates that participation is not only determined by material or political interests but also by a country's will to contribute to international peace and security.

Index

www.ingramcontent.com/pod-product-compliance
Lightning Source LLC
Chambersburg PA
CBHW071449230926
51846CB00001B/384
9789004322042